the EFFECTIVE
BOARD

the EFFECTIVE
BOARD

Building individual and board success

WRITTEN BY
NEVILLE BAIN
AND ROGER BARKER

RECOMMENDED BY
INSTITUTE OF DIRECTORS

KoganPage

LONDON PHILADELPHIA NEW DELHI

This book has been published by the Institute of Directors in association with Kogan Page.

The views expressed in this book are those of the authors and are not necessarily the same as those of the Institute of Directors.

Publisher's note

First published in Great Britain in 2010 by the Institute of Directors.

Reprinted 2013 (twice), 2014 (twice), 2015

2nd Floor, 45 Gee Street
London EC1V 3RS
United Kingdom
www.koganpage.com

ISBN 978 0 7494 6249 9
E-ISBN 978 0 7494 6289 5

British Library Cataloguing-in-Publication Data

A CIP record for this book is available from the British Library.

Typeset by Jean Cussons Typesetting Ltd, Diss, Norfolk
Production managed by Jellyfish
Printed and bound by CPI Group (UK) Ltd, Croydon, CR0 4YY

Contents

Foreword

How can the board do better?

All organisations want to succeed. Companies strive for long-term profitability and growth for the benefit of shareholders and stakeholders.
Public sector bodies have an obligation, on behalf of taxpayers, to be as
effective with public funds as possible. Charities need to secure the
resources to continue their work – and to do it well.

An organisation is often a complex network of people, scattered across
departments and locations. However, any organisation is ultimately only
as good as those who lead it. It is those on the boards who define the
vision, decide the strategy and goals, manage the risks, set the tone and
create the culture of every organisation. This makes the question 'How
can the board do better?' crucially important.

This book is written for all practising directors, and explains how the
collective and individual performance of members of the board can be
improved and what being an effective director actually means. Benefiting
from the extensive know-how of the authors and the longstanding experience of the Institute of Directors in developing the next generation of
board leaders, it is based on proven best practice. It shows how directors
(or those in equivalent roles) can add real value to their boards and, in
the process, gain a strong sense of satisfaction from their contribution to
the long-term success of their organisations and the economy and society
as a whole.

Miles Templeman
Director General, Institute of Directors

Foreword

Raising professional standards

As a Chartered Director, and the chairman of the IoD's Chartered Director Committee (CDC), I welcome and commend this book.

The CDC's main objectives are to raise the professional standards of directors and persuade organisations and individuals (across all sectors) that properly functioning and balanced boards are the key to added value.

Directorship brings with it significant responsibilities. It requires special attributes and abilities, knowledge of legal duties and statutory and regulatory codes, and it requires a willingness to learn. Directors have a duty to update their knowledge and skills; to be equipped for the challenge of today and tomorrow.

The Effective Board provides a core text that highlights what individuals need to do to be better informed and fulfil their duties. It is an excellent grounding for the IoD's Certificate and Diploma in Company Direction, which leads to Chartered Director (C.Dir.) and supports continuing professional development.

Peter Hammonds
Chairman, Chartered Director Committee, Institute of Directors

Acknowledgements

This book has been written with the help and advice of Dr Roger Barker, head of corporate governance at the IoD. He has revised Chapters 2 and 3, written Chapter 11 (to which I have added the Sharon Jones diaries) and provided material for other chapters, which I have greatly appreciated.

In writing this book I've been very fortunate in being able to draw upon the experience and expertise of the directors and staff of the Institute of Directors. They have provided material, suggestions and helpful comments as this work has progressed. However, responsibility for the work remains mine alone. The personal views expressed throughout this text are also my responsibility and may not always reflect the views of the Institute.

I also wish to acknowledge the important contribution of Tom Nash, freelance publisher and formerly a colleague at the IoD. He is a significant supporter of this book. He has added value through his guidance and professional input. Contributions were also made by the Institute's Chartered Director Committee (CDC) and by Janet Gardner, head of professional standards at the IoD. This work has also been supported by Peter Hammonds, chairman of the CDC and his successor, Ian Dormer.

Malcolm Small of the IoD has reviewed the material on pensions, which has been very helpful.

Philippa Foster Back provided material from the Institute of Business Ethics, which helped me with Chapter 12, and additionally provided advice and insights for this chapter.

I was privileged to have the very talented Caroline Proud sub-editing this book. She has challenged, corrected and improved the original text, for which I am extremely grateful.

About the Authors

Neville Bain, current chairman of the Institute of Directors (IoD), was born and educated in New Zealand. He has a double bachelor degree in accounting and economics and a master of commerce with honours, and has been awarded a doctor of laws by Otago University. He is a fellow of the IoD, a fellow of the Institute of Accountants and a fellow of the Royal Society of Medicine.

He started his career as a chartered accountant in New Zealand and then spent 27 years with Cadbury Schweppes, working first as finance and export director in NZ, then moving to general management in South Africa. In 1980 he was appointed to the main board in London as group strategy director and went on to run the worldwide confectionery business. His last appointment with Cadbury Schweppes was as deputy group chief executive and finance director. In 1990, he was headhunted to become chief executive of the textile, clothing and fashion business, Coats Viyella.

Since 1996, he has held a number of non-executive roles with high-profile British businesses and invested in and acted as an adviser to small and medium-sized companies. He has been chairman of The Royal Mail (1997 to 2001), SHL Group (1998 to 2003) and Hogg Robinson (1997 to July 2006). Until May 2007, he chaired the audit committee of Scottish & Newcastle.

He currently sits on the board of Biocon, the Indian biotechnology company, and is chairman of Scottish & Newcastle Pension Trustees Ltd and of the Hogg Robinson Pension Fund. His consultancy work is focused on board effectiveness in the commercial, not-for-profit and pension trustee sectors. He undertakes this work mainly in the UK, India and Russia. He became chairman of the IoD in April 2006.

Dr Bain has published numerous papers on the effective management of people, on governance, on the audit committee and risk assessment and control. He has also written three previous books, all published by Macmillan: *Successful Management*, 1995; *Winning Ways through Corporate Governance*, 1998, with David Band; *The People Advantage*, 2000, with Bill Mabey.

The Effective Board, published first as *The Effective Director* in 2008, includes material from Roger Barker, head of corporate governance at the IoD.

Dr Barker initially trained as an economist and went on to hold several senior investment banking roles in both the UK and Switzerland. He has a doctorate in corporate governance from Oxford University and was formerly stipendiary lecturer at Merton College, Oxford. He has also acted as an adviser on corporate governance to the EU Economic and Social Committee in Brussels.

He currently sits on the corporate governance advisory boards of the European Confederation of Directors' Associations (ecoDa), the Institute of Chartered Accountants in England and Wales (ICAEW) and RiskMetrics European Governance Exchange. He is also a visiting lecturer at the Said Business School (University of Oxford) and the Ministry of Defence.

Dr Barker's latest book – *Corporate Governance, Competition, and Political Parties: Explaining corporate governance change in Europe* – was published by Oxford University Press in January 2010.

About this Book

The Effective Board follows on from *The Effective Director*, first published in January 2008. It updates the original book to reflect changes in the business environment over the past two years, including amendments to the UK Corporate Governance Code (formerly the Combined Code).

The format that was successfully used in *The Effective Director* has been maintained, but there is considerable additional material. The original chapters have been rewritten and revised and three new ones have been added: Chapter 11 looks at the work of NHS Foundation Trusts and the challenges they present for directors; Chapter 13 focuses on lessons to be learnt from the 2008 credit crunch and the subsequent economic crisis; Chapter 14 provides a reference point for the issues no board today can ignore – the pensions crisis, sustainability and CSR, and risk management and assessment.

This book is written in an easy-to-read style, with an emphasis on practical insights from real experience. It is neither dogmatic nor prescriptive; the aim, rather, is to share experiences and knowledge for the benefit of anyone who wants to improve the effectiveness of their organisation, be it an NPO, a family business, a private company, or a larger FTSE corporate. In essence, it's an *insight* into the workings of the board, how its performance can be improved and the benefits to be derived from good governance. Case studies, based on real companies, real events and real people, supplement and amplify the key points.

Much of the content applies internationally, and this will be reflected in the readership of the book. *The Effective Board* will be provided to all candidates for the diploma stage of the chartered director programme, including those from overseas. But it is not for them exclusively. It is for those committed to the principle of continuous professional development – whether or not they are IoD members, whether they are new or experienced directors.

The importance of director development has been highlighted in the UK Corporate Governance Code, which encourages the chairman to discuss individual training and development plans with each director, and recommends that the annual board evaluation exercise is externally reviewed at least every three years. A practical approach to improving board performance through an evaluation review is included in Chapter 4.

The Effective Board is the sister publication to *The Director's Handbook*, a guide to the rules that govern the board. First published in 2005 and updated in 2007, the Handbook has also been re-launched for 2010, looking in detail at changes to the legal and regulatory framework for directors. It is an excellent reference book; and *The Effective Board* is meant to complement it.

One of the book's starting points is that there are certain 'universal truths' about good governance. Effective companies have a clear sense of strategy, supported by a well-promulgated understanding of vision, mission and values. They have the right people in the right roles, and this focus continues through to the board. The tone and performance of the board is, to a large extent, a reflection of the performance of the chairman. This is supplemented by having the right mix of skills and experience on the board and by having the counterbalance of independent non-executive directors who are both knowledgeable and challenging.

Effective directors are well informed and know the legal framework in which they operate. They appoint the right people for the right roles, motivating them to succeed and developing them for the future; they understand that talent is a precious resource that must not be wasted. They want employees to be a credit to the organisation – but, just as important, they want the organisation to be a credit to employees.

The Effective Board begins with a series of core or general chapters, covering the role of the board, the duties and liabilities of directors, the role of the chairman and non-executive directors, governance and the key board committees. Subsequent chapters cover the softer, but equally vital, area of building effectiveness and value through leadership and people. Later chapters discuss more specific topics, including small and medium-sized companies, so important in economies around the world, NHS Foundation Trusts, and charities, the not-for-profit sector and ethics.

The book concludes with an examination of corporate governance in turbulent times and of some current important issues. The final chapter summarises the book's key messages, and will provide the reader with the basis for a review of their own performance and the governance challenges in the organisations they represent.

The Role of the Board: An overview

Introduction

A company is a separate legal entity from those who manage it and those who have put up the capital. The key parties are the shareholders, the management and the directors. The directors must act in the best interests of the company at all times and not represent any special group of shareholders.

Increasingly, companies recognise that their success depends on those employed in the business and on being 'good citizens' in the communities in which they operate. Boards are aware that stakeholders' interests need to be reflected in decision-making if they are to act in the best interests of the company. Stakeholders typically include creditors, employees, customers, suppliers and communities. Consequently, responsible operating will include making concern for people and the environment a key part of policy and practice. Many companies will, for example, report annually on their compliance with environmental policy, often retaining an objective third party for this purpose.

At the same time, the directors are looking to add long-term value through the execution of a well-thought-through strategy in a competitive and changing world.

Are we getting the most from our boards?

Many corporations are failing to obtain full value from their boards, say Chris Thomas, David Kidd and Claudio Fernandez-Araoz in the 2007 winter issue of the *MIT Sloan Management Review*. This lost opportunity not only applies to dysfunctional boards but also to successful companies. The authors say their research highlights five key problems:

1. *Inadequate competencies.* While most directors are capable, they lack the competence to deal with difficult, sensitive issues. Only 60 per cent of the directors in the research sample believe that all board members understand the key operating issues or the main sources of risk. (This is borne out by my own experience, and is a compelling argument for making risk assessment and control a key issue for directors.) The MIT Sloan research also finds that 70 per cent of directors believe that their colleagues are inadequately prepared for meetings, and just 60 per cent feel all directors participate effectively.

2. *Lack of diversity.* Appointments tend to follow a common mould so that richness of debate is lost. It is important to get the right balance on the board – see 'Board composition' on the following page.

3. *'Under-utilisation' of skills.* Only 60 per cent of directors believed that the company was getting the best from them. It should be possible to engage non-executive directors more without having them encroach on management territory.

4. *Dereliction of duties.* Only 45 per cent of the sample felt that the company was seizing strategic opportunities and, in many cases, directors felt that there was insufficient attention to strategic debate. The effort spent on short-term issues was seen as disproportionate.

5. *Poor selection and assessment.* Less than 60 per cent of the sample felt that there was an appropriate system for board selection, and many criticised assessment methods. This is a powerful reason to focus on selecting the right people for the right roles and to ensure the process of reviewing the board and appraising individual directors is robust.

The recent credit crunch and recession demonstrated that the track record of boards has been mixed at best. In the financial sector, boards of directors either did not fully understand the risks they took in pursuit of profits or failed to monitor the risk profile effectively. (This was one of the key criticisms made by Sir David Walker in his 2009 review of the banking sector.) The commercial sector generally was remiss in its stewardship. Evidence suggests that:

- boards spent too little time on examining the worsening economic conditions and their implications for the business and its strategy;

- cash management was not always receiving the attention that was needed, and balance sheets had been weakened by gearing up and share buy-backs;

- many managements and boards had little or no experience of managing in a severe downturn, with the result that actions were suboptimal or late;

- board agendas allowed too little time for the big decisions and too much for the minutiae of governance compliance, driven by a box-ticking mentality.

While any organisation will benefit from incremental improvement, the experience to date is that boards of directors can and must do better.

In response to the Walker Report, published in November 2009, Sir Christopher Hogg, then chairman of the Financial Reporting Council, said:

> Boards must think deeply about their individual and collective roles and responsibilities. The chairman has a vital role to play in ensuring the executives have appropriate freedom to manage the business but also accept the importance of opening themselves to challenge and earning the trust of the whole board. For their part, the non-executives must have the skills, experience and courage to provide such challenge.

In an endeavour to raise standards and improve board effectiveness, the UK Corporate Governance Code, revised in light of the Walker Report, emphasises the importance of board evaluations and a greater focus on risk management.

Board composition

The company's articles of association will prescribe the way directors are to be appointed, and often a minimum and maximum number of directors. For companies with a Premium Listing on the London Stock Exchange, there will be further requirements under the UK Corporate Governance Code, formerly known as the Combined Code on Corporate Governance. (Note that the Code does not apply to AIM-listed companies and includes some concessions for smaller companies; see Chapter 9 for information specific to SMEs.)

Key to a successful, productive board is a good balance. There should be a mix of independent non-executive directors and executive directors and, importantly, of skills and experience. The non-executive directors must be able to devote the time to understand the business and to contribute to its development fully.

The UK Corporate Governance Code says that at least 50 per cent of the members of the board should be independent directors and that the roles of chairman and chief executive should be separated. Further, it says that the chairman should not be a former chief executive. When companies believe they have good reason to go against these recommendations, they need to state their case in their annual reports. (The Code's regime continues to be one of 'comply or explain' – see the Appendix at the end of the book.)

The board will work best if non-executives have a variety of experiences, skills and backgrounds: diversity will add the most value to debate and decisions. Non-executive directors are appointed through the nomination committee after a rigorous process that starts with a definition of the role and a description of the competencies and experience sought. The nomination committee makes its recommendations to the members of the board, who make the final decision on appointments.

Typically, board composition and effectiveness are examined annually by the chairman. A longer-term view of the board is taken as part of the succession planning process. Box 1.1 shows an action list for deciding who sits on the board.

Box 1.1
Action list for deciding board composition

■ Consider the ratio of non-executive to executive directors.

■ Think of the future needs of the business; consider the energy, experience, knowledge, skills and personal attributes of current and prospective directors; ensure there's a proper process for appointing directors.

■ Consider the cohesion of the board and the chemistry between the directors when making new appointments.

■ Make succession plans for members of the board and senior executives and update them regularly.

■ Agree the procedures for appointing the chairman and the chief executive.

■ Appoint a nomination committee whose terms of reference ensure that the range of potential candidates is wide; recommendations are made to the board only after a rigorous selection process.

■ Assess the contribution of each director in an annual review. (The chairman should lead the review and arrange individual development programmes where necessary or, in cases of persistent unsatisfactory performance, ask the director to leave the board.)

■ Provide new members with a comprehensive induction programme.

In recent times, especially in the banking sector, there has been pressure from oversight bodies for more non-executive directors with specialist knowledge and experience. This is helpful – to the extent that it will aid the understanding of the board of the risks and detail of strategy. However, the appointment of experts should not be at the expense of the wider experience that non-executives bring. As with any team, total contribution and effectiveness is enhanced by the diverse skills and personalities brought to it.

This view is not novel. Dr Mike Rugg-Gunn, director of the leadership consultancy at executive search company, Norman Broadbent, observed in a 2009 paper:

> There is considerable research to support the view that groups composed of individuals with diverse backgrounds make different and better decisions than those with homogeneous backgrounds. For example, diverse groups deliberate longer, raise more facts about the issues under review, and conduct more wide-ranging deliberations, making fewer factual errors. When errors do occur, these are more likely to be rectified during the deliberations. This is less an issue of colour or creed but more that different perspectives, hewed from differing backgrounds and experiences, will enrich the quality of debate around the board table.

As we will see later in the book, the performance of the best-constituted board will be enhanced or negated by the leadership of the chairman.

Four key tasks of the board

In the IoD publication, *Standards for the Board*, four key tasks of the board are identified. These can be summarised as:

1. establish and maintain vision, mission and values;

2. decide the strategy and the structure;

3. delegate the authority to management and monitor and evaluate the implementation of policies, strategies and business plans;

4. communicate with senior management.

These key tasks are further expanded in the Appendix at the end of this chapter. However, it is helpful to briefly define some of the terms used here:

Vision is a view of the future state of the company. The best visions give a picture of the potential of the company and therefore inspire people; a leader uses a 'vision' to describe to colleagues what the company can be and to urge them to achieve.

Mission is a statement of what needs to be done to achieve the envisaged state.

Values are a set of principles, standards of conduct and deeply held beliefs; a leadership style that drives the decision-making of the company.

The values of an organisation are increasingly important. They inform standards of expected behaviour within the organisation and 'advertise' the organisation to new recruits: no one wants to work for an employer they can't be proud of. The directors, once staff are on board, have the challenge of ensuring through their own scrutiny that the values are being applied in practice.

Matters reserved to the board

One of the board's earliest tasks is to decide the way it will work and to identify and agree the things that cannot be delegated. Following on from that, and cascading through the organisation, will be a delegation of powers – to the executive committee, the subsidiary boards where applicable, and the senior management.

Matters reserved to the board should be reviewed annually to ensure currency and relevance. They will include not only those powers that no board should surrender, but also items that relate to the *particular* needs of the organisation.

Box 1.2 is an example of a statement of reserved matters in a fairly generic form. Box 1.3 is a list of items reserved for the board of the Institute of Directors; this also refers to delegated powers.

Box 1.2
Example of statement of reserved matters

1. Statutory obligations

1.1 Approval of:

▦ the interim report and dividend;

▦ the annual report and accounts;

▦ the final dividend;

▦ circulars to shareholders, including those convening meetings.

1.2 Consideration of returns to overseas stock exchanges where applicable.

1.3 Recommending to shareholders:

▦ changes to the Articles of Association;

▦ proposals relating to the appointment and removal of auditors and the approval of their fee (although this is often delegated to the audit committee).

2. Strategic and financial matters

2.1 Consideration of:

▦ the company vision, mission and values, and any changes to them;

▦ the strategy and the annual review of it;

▦ budgets, and regular review of progress against them, and the delivery of strategic milestones.

2.2 Approval of:

▦ treasury, risk management and capital policies, including funding and the issue of new shares of any class and of loan capital in excess of a prescribed value;

▦ capital expenditure in excess of agreed levels, acquisitions, joint ventures and disposals;

▦ significant changes in accounting policy (these would usually be first approved by the audit committee and noted by the board).

3. Human resource matters

Approval of:

■ the appointment or removal of the managing director, other executive directors or the company secretary;

■ the appointment or removal of other directors recommended by the nomination committee;

■ the roles and duties of the chairman and managing director and their discretionary powers;

■ the arrangement of directors' and officers' liability insurance.

4. Other matters

4.1 Approval of:

■ any matter that would have a material impact on the company's financial position, liabilities, future strategy or reputation;

■ significant contracts not in the ordinary course of the business;

■ health and safety policy (this should be reviewed across the business to reflect changes such as new risks and new regulations);

■ values statements and systems to monitor how the organisation's values apply in practice.

4.2 Delegation of:

■ the board's powers and authority to sub-committees that will regularly report to the board and make minutes of their meetings available to the board.

Box 1.3
Institute of Directors – levels of authority and authorisation procedures

Matters reserved to the board

(Please note that the IoD policy is to go beyond statutory obligations and observe best practice principles, as laid down by the UK Corporate Governance Code.)

Companies Act requirements

■ Approval of annual report and accounts.

■ Approval of any significant change in accounting policy.

■ Appointment or removal of the institute secretary.

■ Remuneration of auditors, and recommendations for appointment or removal of auditors.

Stock Exchange requirements

■ Approval of press releases concerning significant matters described by the board.

Management

■ Approval of the institute's principal commercial and policy strategies.

■ Approval of the institute's annual operating budget.

■ Approval of the institute's annual capital expenditure budget.

■ Terms and conditions of employment of directors or other staff and their service contracts if the salary exceeds £100k pa or the term of office exceeds six months (except to the extent that such matters are referred by the board to the remuneration committee).

■ Major changes to the institute's management and control structure.

Board membership and board committees

■ Board appointments and removals.

■ Terms of reference of chairman, deputy chairmen, director general, chief operating officer and other executive directors.

■ Terms of reference and membership of board committees.

Significant decisions for the board

▦ Major capital projects (above £300k in budget or £150k unbudgeted).

▦ Major long-term arrangements, for example: contract or lease where the institute's obligations last for three years or more (unless the total payment/cost to the institute is less than £150k); material contract or lease lasting for one year or more that grants another party sole rights in relation to the institute or that restricts the institute from carrying on any particular activity.

▦ Material contracts of the institute or any subsidiary in the course of ordinary business, eg loans and repayments above £300k.

▦ Investments or disposals above £300k.

▦ Risk management strategy – any material changes.

▦ Health and safety policy – any material changes.

▦ Treasury policies and strategy amounting to a significant change.

Miscellaneous

▦ Trustees or rules of the institute's pension schemes – any significant changes.

▦ Benefits under any pension scheme or other employee benefit arrangement – any significant changes.

▦ Prosecution, defence or settlement of litigation involving sums above £250k, or being otherwise material to the interests of the institute.

▦ Environment policy – any significant changes.

▦ Ethics policy and social responsibility policy – any significant changes.

▦ Published policies – significant change in the institute's stance on public (external) policy issues or the adoption and/or publication of a stance on a significant public issue.

- Donations policy – significant changes (on the understanding that donations to political parties should never be made because of the institute's apolitical platform).

- Directors' and officers' liability insurance – any material changes.

- Executive directors' external interests and any external interests of non-executive directors that may conflict with the activities of the IoD.

- Common seal and deeds – policy on use of common seal and the execution of deeds.

- Internal control arrangements – any significant changes.

- Closure, creation or merger of branch, division or region.

- Procedures for conduct of business and activities of regions and branches – any significant changes.

- Professional qualifications offered by the institute – any significant change in nature.

Committees of the board

The board delegates powers to its main committees and lays out formal terms and conditions for them, which it reviews annually. The UK Corporate Governance Code and the Stock Exchange Listing Rules oblige a company to have three committees of the board – the audit, remuneration and nomination committees. Chapter 5 looks at these committees in detail, particularly the audit committee, which has a pivotal role in ensuring effective governance.

Other committees

Depending on the size and nature of the organisation, other committees may be necessary.

In businesses with significant borrowings in multiple currencies there may be a case for a *treasury committee*. This consists of the finance director and a specialist group of non-executive directors who, together, review treasury policy, taking into account the company's exposure to fluctuations in foreign exchange rates and interest rates and its need to protect overseas assets and manage foreign currency borrowings. Where there are banking covenants or agency credit assessments to rate the company debt, the treasury committee will monitor these at quarterly meetings. The committee will recommend to the board changes in policy, having diligently reviewed proposals and alternatives. The board takes a good deal of comfort in the fact that this complex area receives the detailed scrutiny of non-executives with experience in accountancy and finance.

In some companies, there will be a separate *health and safety committee*. Obvious examples include airlines, railways and petrochemical businesses, where health and safety risks and hazards are potentially high. The committee will monitor compliance with health and safety guidelines throughout the business and put right any discovered breaches.

In a number of cases, *risk assessment and control* is taken away from the audit committee, which many observers feel is overloaded, and handed to a separate group. Given the increasing recognition of the role of the board in the management of risk, there may be a case for this, especially in larger companies. The Walker review strongly endorsed the idea of a separate committee in large financial institutions.

It should be noted that the risk assessment process is an integral part of the audit process for both internal and external audit. Therefore, where the risk and audit committee roles are separate, there is a need for excellent communication and information sharing between both bodies.

Improving the board's performance

The board is always capable of improving its performance. No board has reached a state of absolute perfection. Even a state of near-perfection can never be taken for granted! The board constantly needs to fine-tune its performance if it's to be sure of being able to respond quickly and appropriately to changes in the wider environment.

The UK Corporate Governance Code recommends that the effectiveness of the board is reviewed annually, and that the senior non-executive, after discussion with directors, assesses the chairman's performance annually. The wise chairman will, at least once a year, hold one-to-one meetings with the non-executives to discover what each sees as his or her strengths and weaknesses and where his or her contribution could be improved.

Some boards ask an independent third party such as the Institute of Directors to carry out the appraisal. This can be a way of maximising objectivity and credibility. However, the boards of smaller companies may be unable to justify the cost of an external board evaluation and may therefore decide to undertake the exercise in-house. The in-house approach often takes the form of a questionnaire, with the results collated by a trusted person such as the company secretary. Some companies use the questionnaire as the basis for discussion and then have the company secretary and the head of internal audit conduct interviews and compile a report. Whatever the approach, the performance review, if sufficiently robust, can be an enlightening and value-adding exercise.

Sir Christopher Hogg, who is a widely experienced company director, has observed that there are three principal questions to ask when judging a board's effectiveness:

1. Is the entire board fully engaged in and contributing to the strategy?

2. Does the board effectively review its own performance?

3. Does it give sufficient time to succession planning?

Box 1.4 contains the questionnaire used by the IoD for its latest board evaluation. (Chapter 4 includes a template for a board effectiveness review at a FTSE 100 company; see page 65.)

Box 1.4
Institute of Directors board effectiveness review

A. Leadership

1. Does the board provide sufficient leadership to the institute?

2. Does the board clearly set the institute's strategic aims?

3. Does the board ensure that the necessary financial and human resources are in place for the institute to meet its objectives?

4. Does the board review management performance appropriately?

5. Is there an appropriate management development and succession planning process?

6. Does the board set and support the company's mission, vision, strategic objectives and values?

7. Does the board take the time to ensure that the values are maintained across the institute?

8. Are the processes for discussing and setting strategy, the strategic plan and the annual budget appropriate?

B. Board composition

1. Is the board of the right size?

2. Does the board have the right balance of: skills and experience; executive and non-executive directors?

3. Is the division of responsibilities between the chairman and director general clear and appropriate?

4. Are there constructive relations between executive and non-executive directors?

C. Board meetings

1. Does the board meet sufficiently regularly to discharge its duties effectively?

2. Is sufficient time allowed for debate?

3. Is the formal schedule of matters specifically referred for the board's decision appropriate?

4. Looking at the agendas over the past 12 months, does the time allocated to items reflect their importance? Are there any significant gaps that need to be addressed?

5. Does the chairman hold annual meetings with non-executive directors without the executives present?

6. Do the non-executives add value by providing good challenge and judgment but stop short of interfering with the detailed management?

7. Are board and committee papers clear, of the right level of detail and supplied in a timely manner?

8. Do the board minutes properly record discussion and, where appropriate, individual or collective reservations or concerns?

9. Are board dinners and interfaces with senior management effective?

10. Do all board directors make an effective contribution at meetings?

11. Is the quality of debate open and robust?

12. Do board discussions reach satisfactory closure?

13. Does the secretariat provide the right level of service?

D. Appointments to the board

1   Is the procedure for appointment of new directors to the board sufficiently formal, rigorous and transparent?

2. Are appointments to the board made on merit and against objective criteria?

3. Are plans in place for an orderly succession for appointments to the board and to senior management?

4. Is the membership of the nomination committee appropriate?

5. Are the terms of reference of the nomination committee clear and appropriate?

6. Is committee membership regularly refreshed?

E. Information and professional development

1. Is the board supplied in a timely manner with information in a form and of a quality that enable it to discharge its duties?

2. Do directors receive an appropriate induction on joining the board?

3. Do directors regularly update and refresh their skills and knowledge?

4. Should there be a formal recording of director hours on training and continuous professional development?

5. Is the information flow between the board and its committees and between senior management and non-executive directors of sufficient frequency and quality?

6. Are committees provided with sufficient resources to undertake their duties?

F. Performance evaluation

1. Is the annual performance evaluation for the board, committees and individual directors sufficiently formal and rigorous?

2. Does the institute act on the results of the performance evaluation appropriately?

G. Remuneration

1. Are levels of remuneration in the institute sufficient to attract, retain and motivate senior management and executive directors without the institute paying more than is necessary for this purpose?

2. Is the remuneration committee sensitive to pay and employment conditions in arenas competing for our senior staff?

3. Does the remuneration committee receive up-to-date advice on developments in remuneration elsewhere?

4. Do the performance-related elements of remuneration form an appropriate proportion of the total remuneration package of executive directors and senior managers?

5. Is the make-up of the remuneration committee appropriate?

6. Are the terms of reference of the remuneration committee clear and appropriate? Is the procedure for developing policy on executive remuneration and for fixing the remuneration packages of individual directors sufficiently formal and transparent?

H. Internal control

1. Is the system of internal control sufficiently sound to safeguard institute investments and assets?

2. Are the arrangements for identifying, evaluating, monitoring and mitigating risks appropriate?

3. Are we satisfied that management has embedded risk assessment and control in the decision-making of the institute?

4. Is the make-up of the audit committee appropriate?

5. Does at least one member of the audit committee have recent and relevant financial experience?

6. Are the terms of reference of the audit committee clear and appropriate?

7. Are the arrangements by which institute staff may, in confidence, raise concerns about possible improprieties in financial reporting or other matters appropriate?

8. Where auditors provide non-audit services, are appropriate arrangements in place to ensure that auditor objectivity and independence are safeguarded?

I. Membership

1. Does the institute maintain an appropriate dialogue with its members?

2. Do we communicate effectively with the membership?

3. Is the board seen to be acting in the best interests of members in general?

4. Is the board confident that it robustly puts forward policies to opinion-formers that are credible and in the best interests of the membership?

K. Generally

1. In what areas in your view has the board performed most effectively?

2. In what areas in your view is the board least effective?

Is there anything that you feel we need to spend more time addressing?

Information for the board

Newly appointed directors must have an induction programme that will help them get up to speed as quickly as possible. The precise content of this programme will vary from director to director; however, there are some core elements. Discussions with the key executives are one; the provision of information is another. The list of information for new directors will include:

■ the company's memorandum and articles of association, which outline key aspects of the company's governance framework;

■ the latest strategy document, showing the key milestones and progress to date;

■ the budget for the current year and the company's progress against it;

■ minutes of the past year's meetings and a list of any significant developments that are being considered in the current year;

■ details of any significant legal actions or major disputes;

■ a review (where relevant) of the latest analysts' notes, including the broker's note;

■ complete documentation of the most recent board meeting.

Thereafter, directors should receive the information they need to monitor the business. This will include regular, up-to-date financial statements and information on everything that materially affects the business or could do so.

Many medium and larger companies use a form of 'balanced scorecard', so that dimensions beyond finance are included in the regular reports. Scope typically includes the marketplace and customers, human resources and, perhaps, the supplier or cost base. The reports will start with a review of the wider environment, including government regulations and competitors, and then move on to the specific areas.

Each director will also, of course, receive minutes of meetings. These should be agreed and circulated quickly – if possible, within seven days. Many companies give non-executives access to the top level of their databases and allow them to request permission to 'interrogate' the lower levels.

Special attention needs to be given to the strategy discussion, which is often reserved for dedicated 'away days'. Knowledge of macro market trends, competitor analysis and assessment of the success of the current strategy make for a better, more informed debate. While presentations from executives are an inevitable feature of these meetings, sufficient time must be allowed for the input of the non-executives.

The preparation and agreement of the budget is a very important item on the agenda and should not be rushed. The assumptions will need to be tested, and the expected results measured against the relevant year of the strategy and, in the case of a listed company, the expectations of the City.

Other periodic exercises that require information to be supplied to the board include:

■ management development and succession plans;

■ health and safety reviews;

■ risk assessment and control, and the identification of the high-level risks;

■ comparison of share price trends with index and peer group (for listed companies);

■ a review of significant shareholdings.

Testing the statement of values

The statement of values is one of the key board statements but it means little without the behaviours that support it. Assessing the extent to which values are embedded in the organisation – in the way it works, the way it is managed – is a vital exercise. But too few boards approach it in a formal or systematic way.

To build and maintain the company's reputation, boards should look once a year at the way the statement of values applies in practice. Directors may get a sense of the importance of values in the decision-making process in the way that projects or proposals are put to the board. It can, for example, be relatively easy to spot the senior manager whose commitment to ethics and corporate social responsibility does not extend beyond complying with the letter of the law. International companies often operate in countries where bribes are routinely offered to secure contracts, and directors will need to be vigilant if they're to ensure that the company's values are applied universally. As we see in Chapter 12, the new UK Bribery Act 2010 creates a legal requirement to ensure a bribe free environment.

Breaching standards or rules and taking inducements to secure contracts can result in heavy fines from statutory authorities in the UK, Europe and the United States. Individual directors should spend time talking to key people in their own environments and getting more insights into the values of the company.

Some approaches review the way that customers and suppliers are treated or the way that employees are encouraged and rewarded. Surveys of employees, customers and suppliers can help test the statement of values against the reality of what's going on. Such surveys are best carried out by professional third parties.

Appointing a new chief executive

The appointment of a new chief executive is one of the most critical decisions a board can face. It is vitally important to get the right leadership to release the talent from the team, and to have the right experience to move the organisation forward. There may well be executives within the organisation who would lay claim to the role, and succession planning may have included the development of those considered contenders.

(Much will depend on the extent to which the departure of the current chief executive was planned.) The lead internal candidate will have been identified before the incumbent leaves.

The nomination committee will typically require an external search. The case for an external appointment is compelling where significant change is needed. At former monopoly Royal Mail, for example, the board judged that only someone from outside the organisation could lead it into the new commercial realities of full competition. Adam Crozier, former head of the advertising agency Saatchi and Saatchi and the Football Association, was brought in. He has since become CEO of ITV, where his experience seems a more perfect fit. The Royal Mail has once again appointed from outside the organisation for this important role.

What are the rules for appointing a chief executive? Good practice suggests the following:

■ understand the strengths and personality styles of the current top team;

■ clarify from the strategy the key drivers of value for the next five years;

■ understand the implications of the two points above for the experience and competencies required for a new chief executive;

■ prepare a job description and a profile of the ideal candidate, clearly identifying the business needs;

■ take stock of the lead internal candidate and establish how closely the fit of skills is to the business needs;

■ brief a search consultant, preferably one that has previous knowledge of the organisation;

■ shortlist external candidates;

■ ask the consultant to interview and evaluate the internal candidate;

■ involve non-executives outside the nomination committee in the selection process – their input can be invaluable.

The nomination committee will receive written reports on candidates (which may include the results of psychometric tests) and will interview those on the shortlist. When a preferred candidate emerges, references should be taken and any concerns followed up before making an offer and agreeing terms. The potential consequences of mishandling the selection of the new chief executive are set out in the case study on pages 22–23.

What if things go wrong?

Adherence to legal requirements and knowledge of the principles and provisions of the UK Corporate Governance Code (accepted by a wide variety of organisations as the blueprint for best practice) are essential: they form the framework for good governance. They do not, however, guarantee that things will not go wrong.

The list of problems that could have a significant impact on the organisation and require immediate action is long. It includes:

- strategic mishaps resulting in a significant loss of value;

- disagreements that render the board dysfunctional (serious conflict between the CEO and the chairman is the most damaging);

- appointment of a chief executive who's unsuited to the strategic direction of the organisation, or is not compatible with its culture and has to be replaced;

- a failure in the control environment resulting in mis-statement of earnings or fraud;

- a breakdown in the values of the organisation resulting in a serious complaint, eg discrimination (this may well come to the board's attention as a result of a complaint under the organisation's 'whistle-blowing' policy);

- a major health and safety failure resulting in serious injury or death;

- inability to recruit, retain and motivate people with the required skills to deliver the strategy;

- a serious product recall or service failure resulting in reputational damage.

There is always the prospect that the board will need to face up to issues like these during a director's term of office. The board's response to the crisis very much determines the extent of the potential damage or that already caused.

The first observation is that prevention is better than cure. The approach to governance must be robust; in other words, the theory (the understanding of governance structures) must be matched by what happens in practice.

Ensuring that there is a tight control environment will help to limit the probability of unwelcome events. The application of risk assessment and control, discussed in Chapter 5, is an excellent starting point. Small companies can follow the essence of the approach without too much of the process detail. A strong, independent audit committee is integral to the control environment.

There must be clear policies on areas such as health and safety; and processes to ensure that disagreements at board level can be tackled quickly and resolved effectively. The board effectiveness review and the appraisals of individual directors are a key element in keeping the board in good 'working order'. They are discussed further in Chapter 4.

There have been further lessons to take on board as a result of the credit crisis and its impact on economies around the world. The chairman must use their leadership skills to ensure full understanding of such substantial changes in the operating environment and ensure that the board agenda and timings are adjusted to reflect the new reality. The topic of corporate governance in difficult times is dealt with in more detail in Chapter 13, and examples given there reflect companies' experiences both in the UK and internationally.

Case study: Cosgrove Manufacturing plc

Cosgrove was a FTSE 350 conglomerate operating in a number of traditional sectors and with a significant manufacturing base in the UK. It made ingredients for food products, a selection of condiments under a retail brand marketed solely in the UK and also 'own label' products for the big retailers. Another division produced enzymes for use in textiles, among other industries, and for bio fuel, and included a specialist engineering company.

The company had grown over 50 years from small beginnings. It owed much to the entrepreneurial zeal of the founder, a strong individual who had floated the company in 1987 to free up some personal capital and to provide equity for an acquisition. Ten years on, he remained both chairman and chief executive, with a stake of 25 per cent in his and his family's name.

Increased competition meant that earnings were static, to the displeasure of the City, which was already uncomfortable with the founder's lack of communication and his autocratic style.

The board decided that the roles of chairman and chief executive needed to be split. There were three internal candidates for CEO but none was seen to have the skills to lead the group or to bring about change – or to counter the founder, who, as executive chairman, watched every move. Two candidates for CEO were put forward by a search agent. The founder insisted on doing several one-to-one interviews with both of them. The candidates were concerned by his style and approach.

The chosen chief executive, Stephen Oakes, came from the branded food industry and agreed to an initial-term appointment of three years. During that time, the group was restructured, skills across the company were raised and new people introduced. The company made financial and strategic progress.

In 2000, there was one internal candidate capable of taking over from Oakes, but the chairman did not feel the chemistry was right and he vetoed the appointment. Oakes agreed to stay for up to another year while they sought a chief executive from outside.

The selection process, however, was flawed: the board had become fixated on the need to hire someone capable of working with the chairman. No job specification was prepared, and no thought given to the qualities needed to take the company to the next stage of its development. There was no nomination committee, and the chairman started to interview people he knew and people suggested by a 'friendly' head hunter. After about six months, feeling that change needed to be made soon, the board endorsed Mervyn Frost.

Recently made redundant from a FTSE 250 engineering company, Frost was well known to the chairman. He seemed from the start not to engage with the team or to put in the hours that had come to be expected in the role. He played golf every Wednesday and was seen not to add value or to be active in the future plans of the group. The chairman enjoyed the relationship at first – and the opportunity to get deeper into the business. But Frost was disheartened from very early on. The job was not as described to him during the interview and he was exasperated by and opposed to the board's decision to dispose of the engineering division, the area he felt most at home in and hoped to improve. The cosy relationship with the chairman disintegrated, and there were loud public rows.

Despite the obvious signs of problems, the board took no action in the first year. It felt it would lose face if a new appointee was dismissed with a pay-out of two years' salary, as required by his contract. The business deteriorated over 2000–2002, and Frost signed an agreement to go, with two years' pay. Two years later, the company was taken back into private ownership, for 10 per cent of the share price pertaining in 1997 and 40 per cent of the share price when Frost was appointed.

The names of the company and the individuals involved are fictitious.

Summary

The role of the board is contained in a set of important principles that directors need to understand. The early part of this chapter reminds the reader of the environment in which the company, a separate legal entity, operates. Directors need to act in the best interests of the company at all times – and this increasingly means having regard to wider issues of good citizenship such as the environment and the interests of stakeholders.

The chapter refers to the recommendations of the UK Corporate Governance Code as well as to legal requirements, and much of it strictly applies only to larger, listed companies. However, the principles discussed are good for companies and organisations of all sizes. Getting the right balance on the board makes decision-making more robust: even smaller companies benefit from non-executive input to the deliberations of the board. (The governance of small and medium-sized companies is discussed separately, and in more detail, in Chapter 9.)

Directors need to be clear about what is expected of them, and careful consideration needs to be given to the matters reserved for the board. The statement of matters reserved for the board can be usefully supplemented by a statement of delegated powers to committees of the board or to individuals. The main committees of the board are those set out in the UK Corporate Governance Code – the audit and risk committee, the remuneration committee and the nomination committee. There may also be a case for other special committees such as a treasury and a health and safety committee. Many boards insist that health and safety is of such paramount importance that it needs to appear on the board agenda at least twice a year.

Board performance is improved by:

▓ annual appraisals for directors;

▓ feedback from the senior non-executive to the chairman; and

▓ a formal review of the board's own effectiveness (ideally conducted by an external assessor).

Early on, the board needs to decide when and how frequently meetings will be held and the information that should be provided to directors. Most companies recognise that financial information alone is not adequate to monitor the health of the business and have adopted a form of balanced scorecard.

Even when all the set pieces are in place, there remains the prospect of things going wrong. A swift but informed response is critical in stemming losses or protecting reputation. The same approach is equally valid in dealing with systemic shocks or major changes in the operating environment. Here the board must be flexible enough to focus on the really important, often strategic, issues at the expense of time on those things that are more process led.

One of the most significant decisions a board must make is the selection of the person who will take the company to the next stage of development and address the main strategic challenges.

Appendix: Four key tasks of the board

(Summarised from *Standards for the Board*, IoD July 2006)

A. Establish and maintain vision, mission and values

▪ Determine/maintain the company's vision and mission to guide and set the pace for its current operations.

▪ Determine/maintain the values to be promoted throughout the company.

▪ Determine/maintain and review company goals.

▪ Determine/maintain company policies.

B. Decide strategy and structure

▪ Review and evaluate present and future opportunities, threats and risks in the external environment, and current and future strengths, weaknesses and risks relating to the company.

▪ Determine strategic options, select those to be pursued, and decide the means to implement and support them.

▪ Determine the business strategies and plans that underpin the corporate strategy.

▪ Ensure that the company's organisational structure and capability are appropriate for implementing the chosen strategies.

C. Delegate to management

▪ Delegate authority to management, and evaluate the implementation of policies, strategies and business plans.

▪ Determine the monitoring criteria to be used by the board.

■ Ensure the internal controls are effective.

■ Communicate with senior management.

D. Account to shareholders and be responsible to stakeholders

■ Ensure that communications both to and from shareholders and relevant stakeholders are effective.

■ Understand and take into account the interests of shareholders and relevant stakeholders.

■ Monitor relations with shareholders and relevant stakeholders by gathering and evaluation of appropriate information.

■ Promote the goodwill and support of shareholders and relevant stakeholders.

The Company and Legal Duties and Liabilities of Directors

Introduction

This chapter focuses on some of the main obligations of boards under UK law. For directors of public companies, there may be additional requirements under the Stock Exchange's Listing Rules and the UK Corporate Governance Code (formerly the Combined Code on Corporate Governance).

It should be noted that the law does not differentiate between non-executive and executive directors: many of their legal duties (and therefore their liabilities) will be the same.

A more detailed examination of the Companies Act 2006 and directors' responsibilities is given in *The Director's Handbook*, the sister publication to this book.

The company

As we've seen in the first chapter, a company, as far as the law is concerned, exists in its own right: it is a separate entity from its management and shareholders. There are two very important consequences for directors or those performing the role of director. First, they are not liable for the company's debts and cannot, as a general rule, be forced to pay them (unless creditors have separately required them to guarantee loans with their personal assets). Second, they can be convicted of stealing from their company (even if they own all the shares).

In some companies, liability for debts will be *limited by guarantee*. Instead of shareholders, there will be guarantors – people who agree to pay a limited sum towards the settlement of debts if the company is wound up. Many charities are limited by guarantee. By far the most common form of company, however, is one where liability is *limited to share capital*, where the shareholders' responsibility for debt cannot exceed the sum they have invested.

There are two important groups with direct financial involvement in the company. First are the shareholders who have put up the risk capital and who have rights that flow from this. In the case of a public company, the shares will be listed on the stock market and will be traded at prices that reflect its current and expected performance. Second are the creditors who lend money or provide goods and services on credit, and therefore are at risk if the company fails.

In the event of a winding up, assets must, by law, be distributed in a 'pecking order'. First in line are creditors who have some security attached to particular assets of the company, next are preferential creditors as prescribed by law, then ordinary creditors. Shareholders are last in line and therefore expect a premium to reflect that risk.

Private equity holders

Companies come in a number of forms and are funded in a number of ways. There are small private companies that have a limited number of shareholders; there are family-owned companies; there are quoted companies with shares traded on a public market such as the AIM or the London Stock Exchange; and there are companies financed partly by high-net-worth individuals or the specialist private equity funds.

Private equity is a common source of capital for small businesses that are starting to expand. It is medium- to long-term finance provided in return for an equity stake in potentially high-growth unquoted companies. It can be used for:

■ business development plans;

■ buy-outs of existing shareholders by existing management;

■ buy-ins – whereby existing shareholders are bought out and some key managers come into the business.

Private equity is very different from debt finance. Whereas banks and other lenders look for security and have the right to payment of interest and capital ahead of shareholders, private equity holders are investors whose returns are dependent on the success of the business.

The focus of private equity providers is businesses with good prospects of appreciable growth in sales and in profits. They put money on the future performance of a business, and they expect a significant reward for the risk they take. They typically look for an exit route after five years and have in the past expected returns of 25 to 35 per cent, based on a tax paid internal rate of return (IRR). They have often achieved this through gearing up the company significantly with debt and quasi debt instruments as well, of course, by focusing on strategic transformation and ruthless operational efficiency.

In recent years, activity in the private equity sector has been relatively subdued. There has been less use of debt in the financing of transactions (ie, less gearing). Furthermore, the credit crunch has led to a reduction in the overall number of companies benefiting from private equity investment. Private equity providers' fees are high as there is usually considerable due diligence before an investment.

The factors that will persuade private equity professionals to put in money include:

■ a credible business plan that sets out clear actions and milestones;

■ a clear, competitive product or service advantage or unique selling proposition (USP);

■ a top-class management team with the right balance of skills and, crucially, the right leader;

■ a hunger for growth;

■ internal controls that are robust in a growth phase.

Crucially, as far as this book is concerned, *private equity often results in significant change to the way the company is governed.* Private equity providers will usually insist on one or two seats on the board, depending on their level of interest. Where they provide the majority of capital, they may insist on appointing their own nominee as chairman. There will be greater emphasis on change, cash generation and extracting optimum value from the business. The profit and loss account will be examined each month, and the private equity nominee directors will drill down to quite a detailed level to ensure the extraction of value. Pressure will be brought to bear to replace those people who are not performing to the standards required. Unlike owner-managers or founders, private equity professionals will be emotionally detached from the company and will therefore be likely to take a more clinical, pragmatic approach.

Shareholders and stakeholders

Directors are fiduciaries, acting on behalf of shareholders, and a company's purpose is to continue to perform satisfactorily and provide adequate returns for shareholders. (The interests of creditors only take precedence in the event of an insolvency; see page 33.)

However, the concept of what the Labour government termed 'enlightened shareholder value' means that the interests of shareholders are increasingly seen as linked to those of other groups. These are often called 'stakeholders' and include customers, suppliers, employees, government and the community at large.

It is clear that a company is an *economic organisation* and a major contributor to the wealth of the countries in which it operates. But it is also clear it is a *social organisation*, which means that decisions may be more complex than first envisaged because non-economic factors need to be taken to account.

The UK Companies Act, supported by case law, makes it clear that directors are to run the company in its best interests and to the benefit of shareholders. But revisions to the Act made in 2006 require directors to take into account specified corporate social responsibility factors when making their decisions, enshrining the concepts of the stakeholder and enlightened shareholder value in UK law.

Directors' duties

For over 250 years, common law has said that directors need to act in good faith and with honesty, and exercise due care and skill in carrying out their duties. Sections 171–177 of the Companies Act 2006 'codify' those duties in a statutory statement. There are seven key legal duties owed by directors; these are summarised in Box 2.1.

Box 2.1
Seven general duties of directors

1. To act within the powers of the company.

2. To promote the success of the company for the benefit of its members as a whole, paying due regard in decision-making to: likely long-term consequences; employees' interests; the need to foster relationships with suppliers, customers and others; the impact of operations on the community and the environment; the need to maintain high standards of business conduct and to act fairly between members of the company.

3. To exercise independent judgment.

4. To exercise reasonable care, skill and diligence.

5. To avoid conflicts of interest.

6. Not to accept benefits from third parties.

7. To declare, where applicable, any interest in a transaction or arrangement with the company.

The general duties will be owed to the company and apply to all directors and shadow directors (those other than professional advisers who exert a material, long-term influence on the board). The powers and rules of the company are set out in the articles of association, which place limits on what the company can do.

Directors have a complex role. They are, as Box 2.1 suggests, required to balance often competing or conflicting demands. Think of these potentially paradoxical statements:

▪ The board must be entrepreneurial and drive the business forward while keeping it under control.

▪ The board needs to have a clear risk assessment and control process to manage agreed risk, but, at the same time, must be prepared to take calculated risks (profits are, in some part, the rewards of risk-taking).

▪ The board needs to be informed about the workings of the company but not interfere in the day-to-day management.

▪ The board must be sensitive to short-term issues but remember that its overriding goal is the creation of long-term value.

■ The board must be sensitive to local issues but be aware of non-local influences such as macro-market trends, the actions of competitors and supplier opportunities. (Increasingly, trade unions take an international view in their negotiations with companies.)

Record-keeping and other duties

Directors are legally bound to keep proper accounting records and accurate minutes of meetings and to file the required information with Companies House. Although administrative duties are delegated to the company secretary, the ultimate responsibility remains with the board.

There is a plethora of other regulations that affects the company and therefore the directors. Relevant areas of the law include employment, health and safety, the environment, data protection, labelling and consumer rights, taxation and market abuse. In some of these areas, for example health and safety, breaches may create personal liability for directors. While almost all companies provide directors' and officers' liability insurance, any serious breach will be a significant cost in terms of reputation – for both the organisation and director involved.

If a company involved in the provision of financial services is regulated under the Financial Services and Markets Act 2000 (FSMA), there will be specific additional rules. Directors in breach of FSMA will be pursued by the Financial Services Authority (FSA) and can face criminal prosecution and hefty fines. (Note that insurance policies won't cover fines imposed by either the criminal courts or the FSA.)

Preparation of accounts

Directors must approve both the annual report and accounts and press releases that accompany publicly released information.

The form of the annual report and accounts is prescribed, and copies must be sent to all shareholders and to the registrar of companies. With the permission of individual shareholders, an abbreviated report and accounts can be sent out.

Publication of the report and accounts can be by e-mail or via the company website, provided that intended recipients are informed. A company is legally required to send unabridged hard-copy versions of the annual report and accounts to shareholders who request them. The period allowed for delivering the report and accounts is within nine months from the end of the relevant accounting year for a private company and six months for a public one.

Small and medium companies have some leeway: they can elect by resolution to dispense with the laying of the report and accounts before the shareholders in general meeting. This is also true for subsidiary companies.

Insolvency

In normal circumstances, the accounts are signed off on a 'going concern' basis. This means that the directors and the auditor declare they are satisfied that there is sufficient cash resource or facilities to meet the cash requirements of the company for 12 months from the date of signing. Directors will expect to see the evidence of this in the form of forward cash projections, and any assumptions that are made in this projection (such as the renewal of banking covenants) should be carefully looked at.

Where a company is currently unable to meet its liabilities as they fall due or if the liabilities exceed the assets, the company is deemed insolvent. *Directors may be held personally liable if they continue to trade while the company is insolvent.*

In cases of insolvency, the focus of directors' attention changes. Instead of acting in the best interests of the shareholders in general, they must put the interests of creditors first. This means taking all steps possible to avoid loss to creditors. Directors must not act for personal gain or in a way that gives preference to any creditor, save for those that are properly designated as a preferred creditor in the event of liquidation. If the company becomes insolvent, the Insolvency Act imposes duties and responsibilities on the directors to protect creditors. The effect of these duties is that:

> the directors may be liable for *unlawful trading* unless they have taken all proper steps to minimise the creditors' losses, once they were aware, or reasonably should have been aware, that there was no reasonable prospect that insolvency could have been avoided.

Breach of this provision may result in directors being ordered by the court to contribute to the assets of the company and/or their disqualification. In addition, there is the possibility of civil action against them.

All this means that it is essential that directors act with extreme care if their company gets into financial difficulties. They must act objectively rather than recklessly, and they will need to be able to demonstrate that they sincerely believed there was a reasonable prospect that the company could have avoided insolvent liquidation. Insolvency and its implications for directors are covered in Chapter 10 of the 2010 edition of *The Director's Handbook*, but in circumstances where there is the prospect of insolvency it is prudent to take professional legal advice.

In some cases, one option might be the 'pre-pack', which has become more common in recent years. This is an insolvency procedure in which the sale of a company's assets is arranged before the appointment of the administrator. The administrator executes the sale immediately after the company enters administration.

Pre-packs have proved controversial, as the buyers of the assets are often the directors or management of the insolvent company. Critics claim that the procedure allows management to set up a new company with the same assets and employees, but freed of previous obligations to creditors. Understandably, this can cause significant disquiet among creditors who are not repaid. On the other hand, the goodwill and continuity of the business are preserved, and this may allow the administrator to realise a greater amount for creditors than would otherwise be the case. The prospects for employees may also be better than with a conventional administration.

While pre-packs may in certain circumstances be viable, directors should be aware of the sensitivities involved. Pre-packs should always be undertaken in accordance with regulatory guidelines that seek to maximise the fairness and transparency of the process.

Disqualification

In addition to civil and criminal liabilities, errant directors can face disqualification for between 2 and 15 years. As well as wrongful trading, a director can be disqualified for:

■ serious or persistent offences in connection with the direction and/or management of the company;

■ fraud and tax evasion;

■ failure to file documents with Companies House;

■ unfit conduct at a company that has, at any time, become insolvent.

Shareholders as well as others, such as creditors, may apply to the court for a disqualification order. If the disqualified director continues to act, he or she can be imprisoned for up to two years, fined or made personally liable for the debts of the company.

Expectations of directors

We've already seen that directors must operate within the articles of their company and not exceed the powers or constraints set out there.

Directors must use reasonable skill, care and diligence in carrying out their duties if they are to avoid liability for negligence. Directors are also held to a higher standard by the law if they possess specific knowledge or skills. For example, if a director is a chartered accountant, he or she will be held to a higher standard in respect of financial matters than a director without such knowledge and training. Similarly, a higher level of technical or scientific judgment would be expected of a professional scientist or chartered engineer.

Directors need to be present at meetings. Indeed, it is now highly unusual for a director to miss a scheduled board meeting.

There is a requirement for directors to act in good faith and in the best interests of the company, and not place themselves (knowingly or unknowingly) in a position of conflict. These obligations arise from the director's position as a fiduciary – someone who looks after assets on behalf of others.

The word 'probity' probably best sums up the qualities required. The key imperatives are listed in the IoD publication *Standards for the Board*; see Box 2.2.

Box 2.2
Examples of the probity required of directors

■ Boards must comply with all relevant laws and regulations.

■ Directors must act with integrity.

■ Company assets and resources must be applied for proper purposes.

■ Directors must exercise their powers in the interests of the company as a whole, not any particular group or individual.

■ There should be no conflicts of interest; if they arise, they must be openly reported to the board; no director should be involved in decisions about transactions in which they have a personal interest.

■ A director must not seek or obtain gain from their role.

■ Inside information must not be used or passed on to others.

■ A director must not trade their shares in closed periods or during any time inside information is held.

Source: *Standards for the Board*, 2006 edition.

Summary

Directors have legal responsibilities to shareholders, creditors and to others affected by their activities. This applies irrespective of the size or type of company.

The company will have a written constitution, the articles of association, which lays out what it can and can't do. But it's just part of a vast rulebook; the Companies Act 2006 is reputedly the longest piece of legislation ever to have been passed by the UK parliament, although much of it is a collation of previous company acts and case law.

Directors do not need to be legal experts to be effective, but they do need to have a working knowledge of the laws that relate to them and their organisations. Those who break the rules face censure, fines and, in certain circumstances, disqualification and imprisonment.

The role of director is challenging, the expected standards increasingly high. But for those who bring the weight of their experience and good judgment to add real value to the company, it is also immensely rewarding.

Directors must act in the best interest of the company at all times. In the case of insolvency, the directors must act in the interests of creditors, protecting as far as possible their position. Directors' personal reputation and effectiveness depend on their personal standards, as delivered through the consistency of their actions.

Governance

Introduction

Governance is now widely seen as a central, if not *the* central, role of the board. As such, it's a theme that runs throughout this book. But what exactly is governance? And what distinguishes good governance from bad?

This chapter offers some answers. Much of it is relevant to any organisation, of any size.

Some first thoughts

Although the term 'corporate governance' has only been in widespread use since the 1980s, the concept is nothing new: private-sector companies have implemented various kinds of governance frameworks since the emergence of the first joint stock companies in the middle of the 19th century. Governance itself pre-dates commercial organisations. Ever since we started living in groups, we've needed to develop formal and informal organisational frameworks for resolving disputes and achieving agreed goals.

The need for a governance framework becomes apparent when the owners or creators of an organisation are not involved in its day-to-day management. In such circumstances, the owners must delegate a significant amount of decision-making to professional managers. This gives rise to a fundamental problem: how can the owners ensure that the organisation will be effectively managed? This is an issue that must be addressed by all but the smallest owner-managed enterprises.

The legal and regulatory framework

The idea of a company is inherently a legal construct. Consequently, it's unsurprising that the initial 'ground-rules' for corporate governance in the UK were provided by company law. The Companies Acts (culminating in the Companies Act 2006) established the board as the firm's main governing body and thereby made sure directors were legally accountable.

Today, there's a vast rulebook with which the board must comply. Successive governments (both in the UK and in other jurisdictions) have enacted rules and regulations to:

■ ensure competitive markets, based on the principles of fair trade;

■ regulate markets that are natural monopolies or imperfectly competitive;

■ maintain a balance between capital and labour, and protect the rights of workers;

■ sustain investor and public confidence in the capital markets;

■ protect consumers from unsafe products and from fraud;

■ promote equality of opportunity irrespective of race, religion, sex, disability or sexual orientation;

■ protect the environment.

In addition, corporate governance codes have exerted increasing influence over the ways boards are run. In particular, the UK Corporate Governance Code has played a major role in shaping the governance of the UK's listed companies over the past two decades.

The Code's provisions are not compulsory, but are applied on the basis of 'comply or explain': enterprises can deviate from them – as long as they explain why in their annual reports. Such flexibility permits UK companies to tailor their governance frameworks more closely to their specific needs, albeit within the broad parameters of widely accepted 'best practice'. Importantly, it allows them to avoid the kind of regulatory costs faced by US companies in the wake of the Sarbanes-Oxley Act 2002.

The effectiveness of the UK Corporate Governance Code depends on the willingness of shareholders to monitor the application of the Code, and maintain an active dialogue with boards on corporate governance. This can present a logistical challenge to institutional shareholders (eg pension funds, insurance companies, mutual funds), whose investment portfolios are typically diversified across ownership stakes in hundreds of individual companies.

The UK Stewardship Code, published in July 2010, aims to encourage closer relationships between institutional investors and companies. The new Code outlines a series of best practice principles in respect of company-shareholder engagement. Analogous to the UK Corporate Governance Code, it is applied by institutional shareholders on the basis of 'comply or explain.' It is hoped that this new initiative will further strengthen the important role of shareholders at the heart of the UK corporate governance system.

The UK approach to corporate governance has been widely emulated. By the end of 2009, 26 EU countries had corporate governance codes that were applied on the basis of 'comply or explain' rather than involuntarily imposed. A September 2009 study from the European Commission, 'Monitoring and Enforcement Practices in Corporate Governance in the Member States', found 'an overwhelming support' for the comply or explain regime among European regulators, companies and shareholders.

Other influences on corporate governance

External stakeholders or interest groups may seek to reshape an organisation's decision-making framework via changes to government policy. In recent times, policy makers have sought to respond to public concerns about the power of modern corporations; much of the legislation referred to above can be described as an attempt to prevent abuses of corporate power.

The growth of the trade union movement, with centralised bargaining for workers, was a major development and an important consideration in much of corporate decision-making. While trade union membership has declined in Britain steadily over the past 30 or so years, it has increased in some other EU member states and is expected to grow in the developing world. The right of workers to free association is, of course, a fundamental tenet of the International Labour Organization and it needs to be respected by any company that 'offshores' operations.

The internal framework

Company law only prescribes a basic framework for the operation of the board and other aspects of governance. Many boardroom processes and procedures are defined by the board itself in response to the demands of the business environment. So what does governance mean for the practicalities of running an organisation?

At its broadest level, it is about the exercise of power. In both commercial and non-commercial settings, it is invariably necessary to grant particular individuals the authority to take decisions on the organisation's behalf. However, how do we identify the right individuals for this task? Furthermore, how do we establish their objectives and hold them accountable? These questions can only be resolved through the establishment of an effective internal governance framework, normally co-ordinated by a governing body of some kind.

The nature of governance can be further clarified by distinguishing it from the activity of management. Management is the daily process of running an organisation. In contrast, governance refers to the system through which management decision-making takes place.

Governance is hence less concerned with the operational activity of the company. Rather, it is about giving overall direction to the enterprise, and overseeing the executive actions of management. It's also about ensuring that there is appropriate accountability between the organisation and its legitimate stakeholders.

Defining 'good' governance

The imperative for good governance applies across the differing organisational forms, from companies to charities and NPOs. However, it is interesting to note that no single approach has proved right for all organisations. For example, in the private sector, commercial success has been achieved by companies around the world employing a variety of corporate governance frameworks, with significant differences in the structure and composition of their boards, and in the relative power of shareholders or employees over corporate behaviour.

Nonetheless, good governance has a number of common features. A key principle is that there is more to governance than box ticking, compliance, or simply following the rules of whatever jurisdiction you're operating in. Governance is also fundamentally concerned with the enhancement of corporate performance. It means adopting a *modus operandi* or a *modus vivendi* that will add value to your organisation. In other words, it's a state of mind.

Some of the main 'windows' on governance are board structure; risk oversight and internal control; internal information; external information and disclosure; performance evaluation and monitoring; succession planning; compensation levels; the treatment of shareholders. These are discussed below.

Board structure and independence

As we have seen in Chapter 1, the UK Corporate Governance Code is clear on what is required for UK listed companies. While it strictly applies only to those companies with a Premium Listing on the London Stock Exchange, it is widely accepted as a blueprint for best boardroom practice.

The main principles of the Code are reproduced in Appendix 1 of this book. What follows is a summary of some of the main principles for board composition:

■ The board should have a balance of skills and experiences, and in the case of larger companies, at least half of its members should be independent non-executive directors. (See Chapter 4 for the Code's definition of 'independence'.)

■ The role of chairman and chief executive should ideally be separated, with the former running the board, the latter the company. No one person should have unfettered powers of decision-making. (This means that smaller and family-owned companies, where the roles of chairman and CEO are usually combined, should have the counsel of a non-executive director who will bring independence and balance to the board.)

■ There should be a rigorous process for selecting directors, and each director should have a letter of appointment (usually broadened to a contract for the executive directors and, perhaps, the chairman).

■ All directors should be subject to re-election; the membership of the board should be refreshed to reflect the company's changing needs and to preserve objectivity and independence.

Risk oversight and internal control

Recent amendments to the UK Corporate Governance Code have emphasised the importance of establishing robust systems of risk management and internal control. The practice of providing assurance of this differs from organisation to organisation. At the most basic level, a company will have an accountant draw up the annual accounts that need to be filed with Companies House. At more sophisticated levels, there will be an audit – an inspection of accounts and accounting procedures.

Some larger companies will have an *internal audit function* where the control environment is reviewed as part of an integrated programme relied upon by the external auditor. These companies will also have a competent *audit committee* that will, on behalf of the board, review and form an opinion about the control environment. (See Chapter 5 for further information.)

Where an audit does take place, the auditor will testify that the client's financial statement is accurate. Where it doesn't, they will want to preclude their opinions being relied on by creditors, etc. Even if there isn't a need for audited accounts, the auditing firm should be encouraged to review the controls in the business and report to the directors on its findings. The directors will then decide whether or not any action is needed. It's important to stress that risk assessment and control, the foundation of a healthy control environment, cannot be 'outsourced': it remains the ultimate responsibility of the board – which is also responsible for defining the risk tolerance of the organisation – and demands regular attention from both directors and managers. The best leaders in business and in other organisations recognise it as an integral part of effective management.

A 2007 survey of Asian financial services by the Economist Intelligence Unit for PricewaterhouseCoopers concluded that 'firms will not reap maximum value from risk management unless their culture, organisation, processes and data are all properly aligned'. The same observation applies to other sectors, too.

It's important to remember that the system for internal control should be comprehensive. The 1998 Turnbull Report, annexed to the UK Corporate Governance Code, emphasised the need to think not only of 'narrow financial risks' but also those relating to business reputation and the environment. (For some companies, climate change presents a significant business risk.)

Information for the board

As discussed in Chapters 1 and 4, the board needs the right information at the right time if it's to do its job properly. The timely flow of clear, useful and accurate information is a governance tool. It enables the board to understand and monitor progress towards strategic objectives and to assess, identify and anticipate risks. The IoD's *Standards for the Board*, which has been followed by and endorsed by chartered directors (those who hold the institute's professional qualification), emphasises the need for information to support internal control, for information that is:

■ timely enough for directors to prepare themselves;

■ informed by recent activities;

■ sufficient to judge the likelihood of relevant risks;

■ sufficient to improve the company's ability to reduce the incidence of and impact of risks.

External information disclosure

Governance is an increasingly important criterion in investment decisions. Fund managers do think about the perceived level of governance in the organisation, as we see in the next chapter. Low standards of governance relative to the peer group mean a lower rating and, therefore, a lower market capitalisation.

Since soft measures are thought of as unreliable, some analysts will rely solely on financial performance when rating a company, taking the view that performing as or better than the market expected is a sign of good governance. Other investors will undertake a more informed assessment and will take account of published and other publicly available information. This means that annual reports and presentations to analysts and key shareholders need to find a credible way to reflect the state of governance in their company.

The problem is that published information is often sanitised by compliance-driven, risk-averse lawyers, and the essence of the message is lost. There can be great similarity between published governance statements – most of the FTSE 100 statements included in annual reports have the same structure and headings. A summary of their main content is included in Box 3.1.

Box 3.1
Main content of the corporate governance statement in annual report and accounts

■ The extent to which the company has followed the UK Corporate Governance Code – and the reasons for any non-compliance.

■ The role of the board and how it is governed; changes in board membership during the year; matters reserved for the board and its main committees; the name and duties of the senior independent director.

- The way the chairman and chief executive operate; their main responsibilities.

- The work of the board during the year; a list of board meetings and sub-committee meetings and the attendance of directors at each.

- Induction for new directors; training and development for all directors.

- How the company communicates with its shareholders; how companies can use the senior independent director if the occasion demands; procedures for informing shareholders of annual meetings or of extraordinary meetings.

- Notifiable interests of shareholdings in excess of 3 per cent.

- A statement about performance evaluations of the board, its committees, the chairman and each director.

- Individual reports from the chairmen of the main committees.

- Directors' interests if any. (*Details of any director who has a trading relationship with the company are particularly important.*)

- Internal control and audit; an outline of the responsibilities of the board; the process of identifying and managing significant risks.

- A statement on internal audit; how the internal audit function operates and the assurance it gives the board.

- A statement of 'going concern'; a declaration that the directors believe that there are sufficient cash resources or facilities to allow the company to operate for the foreseeable future.

Many organisations will publish supporting or additional information on their websites. This will give an excellent insight into the principles by which a company is run. Cadbury, recently taken over by the Kraft Corporation, was one of the earliest companies to provide information on governance and the company values that inform the business. (Its former chairman, Sir Adrian Cadbury, led the first inquiry into corporate governance in the 1990s and his subsequent report formed the basis of the UK Corporate Governance Code.)

Monitoring the business

This does not begin and end with financial reporting. In many organisations, monthly reports go beyond the numbers to include all the measures the board has agreed for assessing the health of the business. The concept of the balanced scorecard is now well understood. It rates performance against strategy and vision, and typically has four dimensions:

1. *Financial* – measures that show what the organisation needs to do to provide the right returns to shareholders.

2. *The customer* – measures of success with customers. (Of course, these are also indicators of financial performance and long-term health.)

3. *Knowledge, or learning and growth in the organisation* – what changes do we need to make to the organisation as it moves along its strategic path towards its vision? (Again, this dimension is related to the financials and the long-term health of the business.)

4. *Internal business processes* – those processes a company must excel at if it is to make real progress towards its vision.

Some companies add a further dimension – monitoring the supply base – where this is critical to the delivery of the business plan. Subsets of the four core dimensions include:

■ financial results compared with the plan, with a description of reasons for variances;

■ progress of the business against predetermined strategic milestones;

■ health and safety issues and standards;

■ progress of significant projects against agreed milestones;

■ evaluation of significant completed capital projects to understand and disseminate lessons learnt;

■ debt levels against facilities and banking covenants;

■ audit committee reports, with special reference to reported weaknesses, breaches of standards, or frauds;

■ occasional employee surveys to understand the messages being fed back and how the company needs to respond to be a 'best in class' employer;

- monitoring compliance with the values and ethical leadership set by the board (while it's difficult to get hard metrics for this, feedback from employees, customers and suppliers will add to the observations directors will make from their site visits);

- finally, and worthy of a separate discussion, is succession planning.

Succession planning

One of the most important tasks of a board is to ensure that the people in the organisation are in the right jobs, are properly trained and are motivated to perform. Without appropriate management development and succession plans, the structure of governance is doomed to collapse.

Succession planning is as least as important as the strategic planning exercise but it does not always get the same attention. It must be brought to the board; the board must seek assurance it's being handled properly.

The succession of the chief executive is, of course, particularly important. The board must identify the key skills and competencies that are needed for the delivery of the next stage of the organisation's plan. Where the date of the departure of the chief executive is known, there should be an appropriate period of transition. This is discussed in more detail in Chapter 1.

Compensation levels

Institutional investor bodies such as the Association of British Insurers (ABI) and the National Association of Pension Funds (NAPF) see the approach to compensation as an important element of governance. The report by the remuneration committee in the annual report will give a good insight into how pay is decided. Investors will look for a balanced package that includes performance-related elements. An executive's total ability to earn from salary, annual bonus and long-term incentives will be carefully monitored.

Where shareholder total returns have fallen, especially in relation to the company's peer group, investors find it difficult to understand why top executive directors should be rewarded beyond their salary. Payments into 'top-hat' pension schemes now also come under scrutiny. This is not just because such payments are effectively deferred income: many final salary schemes in the UK have significant deficits when measured against the accounting standard IAS 19.

Compensation should be competitive, aligned with shareholders' interests and not out of line with the peer group. (Benchmarking exercises form an important part of the work of the remuneration committee.)

The typical remuneration report in the annual report and accounts includes the content listed in Box 3.2.

Box 3.2
Form for a typical remuneration report in the annual report

■ The members of the committee (the names of all the non-executive independent directors who comprise the committee and the executives who regularly attend meetings).

■ The role of the committee; its terms of reference (which will usually be published on the company's website).

■ The names of advisers to the committee.

■ Remuneration policy.

■ Details of incentives and performance criteria, including annual bonus arrangements and long-term incentives.

■ In the case of long-term incentives dependent on how the company performs relative to its peer group, details of the comparator group and its performance.

■ Individual executive directors' interests in bonus shares and options.

■ Pension and life assurance arrangements.

■ Full details of all directors' salaries, bonuses and other remuneration, including benefits and increases in pension benefits for the year.

■ Directors' shareholdings.

■ A statement of how non-executive directors' fees are decided.

Shareholder treatment

Investors need to be satisfied that all classes of shareholders are treated equally. The interests of one group should not come before those of another. *Minority shareholders must be seen as part of the total group in whose interests the directors act.*

Some companies have differing classes of shares where one class may have a share of the voting that's disproportionate to its economic interests; promoters of the business may hold such rights as a way of controlling the company. This, however, is unacceptable to most institutional investors and is becoming increasingly uncommon in the UK.

Nuts and bolts

There are procedural, everyday elements to organisational good governance. These should be obvious to anyone who's ever been involved in the management of an organisation, at whatever level, but, for the sake of completeness, they're listed here.

■ The board must be properly constituted and have sufficient resources – both in terms of board members and support staff – to undertake its duties. Non-executive directors should be able to dedicate sufficient time to their roles.

■ The number of meetings should be sufficient to allow the board to discharge its duties; and meetings must be planned well in advance to ensure that all directors are able to attend.

■ Agendas should be planned annually so that all important topics are included.

■ The specific agenda for a meeting should be given out seven days in advance and be properly supported with papers that are clear and concise.

■ There should be enough time to devote to the items on the agenda; and the time spent on each item should be commensurate with its importance.

■ Minutes should be complete and accurate and available within seven days of the meeting.

Governance in times of change

One of the key challenges for the board will be making sure the business does not outgrow its governance structures. During times of change and development, cracks can start to appear.

A private company that's expanding or wants to raise new capital may decide to 'go public'. In the UK, small and medium-sized companies may choose to float on the AIM, the junior market that's relatively light touch in terms of regulation; larger ones may head for the London Stock Exchange, where they'll be bound by the Listing Rules and, in the case of a Premium Listing, the UK Corporate Governance Code.

A company that wants to come to market needs to take time to prepare itself for an Initial Public Offering (IPO), and this could well take the best part of a year. The groundwork needs to be thorough, and in many cases the existing owner-manager will need to be prepared to change the way they've managed the business. *In other words, the governance of the company will enter a new phase.* This can be seen in the case study of a real company, called, for the purposes of this book, Holden Services plc.

Case study: Holden Services plc

The background

Holden Services (not its real name) was a business services company in the private sector with a controlling shareholder owning 60 per cent. The balance of the shareholding was owned by staff members and other family members.

The company relied upon excellent contacts across the UK, and leveraged these to provide computer-based 'processing' solutions to the public sector, mostly at local authority level, and also to the private sector. In addition, it had a sprinkling of business with large charities.

Its services included payroll, inclusive of pensioner payroll, pension services, human resource back-office systems, Council Tax demands and collections, and a number of bespoke systems for special clients. The company was an approved implementer of SAP systems and would quote for this business, often winning – in part because of its low overheads and reputation for delivery.

It had annual turnover of £42 million and had been expanding at 15 per cent compound annual growth rate over the past three years. It had a pre-tax margin of 17 per cent, and its advisers put its value at around £85 million to £100 million.

However, for five years, the profit record had been variable with quite large margin swings. The chief executive, John Holden, attributed this to the costs of winning and implementing new contracts. (His approach was to define strictly what was included in the quote and pitch at low margins, knowing that incremental work nearly always followed, and at very attractive margins. Anything outside the initial contract was charged at the normal rates.)

Holden had founded the business 15 years previously when he'd resigned from a senior position in a large plc. Aged 58, he was a strong manager with firm views on how to run the company. He set high standards for himself and expected the same of others. The family shareholders were happy with the success to date but, as none of them was now involved in the company, they wanted to crystallise the value of their shareholding. Holden wanted the company to maintain its identity and not be absorbed into a competitor, but was also happy to receive the value for his work, and to commit to a two-year contract of employment if the company went to the stock market.

The problem

Holden's advisers reviewed the business and indicated that there would be a 12-month preparation time for a successful public offering. A number of building blocks had to be in place. These included ensuring the senior management was strong enough to sustain future earnings once Holden stepped down and that there was a plan to develop the most credible internal candidates and consider them alongside anyone from outside. It was noted that a number of the senior people would be quite rich after the flotation and that their subsequent commitment would be in doubt. The control environment had to be fit for purpose in a public setting, and the general standards of governance had to be high enough for new investors.

The advisers' investigation uncovered areas of weakness that had the potential to derail an IPO. Their main findings are summarised below.

- Holden was believed to be autocratic and not good at communicating internally. This had led to a high turnover among the management team. A coterie of only three people had remained loyal. They had been with Holden for an average of 11 years and had adapted to his style. Their holdings in total accounted for 15 per cent of the share capital. Holden, who took virtually all the decisions, would consult these three colleagues but very few others.

- The organisational chart was unusual in that Holden was CEO, chairman and sales director (public sector). The other directors headed technical, marketing and sales to the non-public sector, and group services (finance, human resources, legal and secretarial).

- While there were informal meetings of the four directors and the legal requirements were observed, regular board meetings were not held.

- The management information system produced quarterly results in total terms for the business, limited to profit and loss and balance sheet. Supplementary information included debtors, work in progress and contract billing against milestones in the various live contracts.

- The control environment was regarded as 'fair'. Books of account were in place, but there was no accounting manual, no segregation of duties and no procedures for agreeing bids. There were no client profitability accounts as the overall profitability was deemed to be very good.

- There was no formal process of risk assessment and control and, indeed, no formal process for creating and leading strategy (directional change was initiated by Holden and communicated, almost in passing, to his directors).

- The directors had paid little attention to their fiduciary duties as the group services director ensured compliance with the obligations of reporting.

- Salaries were decided by Holden and he also decided what he should be paid.

- Staff turnover was unacceptably high due to a lack of motivation: employees saw themselves as paid hands rather than partners in the success of the business. Salary levels were in the upper quartile to try to compensate for this.

- The overall philosophy was a focus on customer service and keeping costs well under control.

The programme

It was agreed that the first step was to find an outside person as chairman, someone capable of giving assurance to the City, of working constructively with the CEO and other directors, and of providing direction for the IPO to ensure a successful float in 12 months. The chairman was chosen from a selection of candidates provided by a small firm of search consultants, and the corporate advisers were represented in the selection process.

The division of duties between the chairman and CEO was agreed, and the chairman initiated a search for two additional non-executive directors, one with a background in finance and the City, the other with a background in general management and the service industry.

The new chairman's priority was to mould the board into an effective unit. After some discussion, it was agreed that the board would consist only of two executive directors, the CEO and the group services director. This not only reflected the abilities of the executive directors but also provided the appropriate balance.

Audit, remuneration and nomination committees were set up and their terms of reference decided. The matters reserved for the board were agreed, along with the authority levels for decision-making. Work began on the accounting manual, with some outside help.

The CEO was encouraged to have monthly executive meetings to review the business with the appropriate members of his team and to find the right conduit to communicate with the staff beneath this group. Information for the board was evaluated, and it was agreed that monthly information based on the balanced scorecard should be prepared; and that this information would go to all directors by the 20th of the month following the month being reported upon.

A schedule of eight regular board meetings was prepared, and the coverage of all items throughout the year was agreed. Special topics such as strategic review, management development and succession plans and risk assessment and review were built in. A plan was made for a risk assessment workshop to identify high-level risks.

The accounting firm reviewed current controls and made recommendations for improvement.

The outcome

Putting the programme in place took longer than expected, and it was 18 months before the IPO was made.

That 18 months was an often painful transition, with Holden

mourning the 'good old days' when he didn't have to bother with all 'this process' and had no need to seek agreement to initiatives or 'waste time talking about them'. There was often a lot of friction between the executives and non-executives. However, respect between the two groups and a strong focus on their mutual goal overcame the issues, and the company did successfully float.

At the time of flotation, the market was volatile, and pricing was lower than had been hoped. Nevertheless, the company had a market capitalisation of £90 million, and seven months later breached the £100 million mark.

Holden was quick to point out that the transition was of great value. The non-executives helped him and the other directors make better decisions and lifted a lot of the worry from his shoulders. Today, staff morale is better, helped in part by improved communication and in part by the fact that Holden, before the float, put 10 per cent of his shareholding into an employee share trust, used as a reward for good service.

The lessons

▦ Good governance adds value and is therefore essential for any company planning an IPO.

▦ Better information makes for better decisions.

▦ Multilateral decision-making helps a company spot and act on opportunities and minimises the risks of strategic failures.

▦ Greater involvement of staff makes for better performance.

▦ Focus on the talent in an organisation helps the board get a better picture of the talent pool and develop it in a more comprehensive way.

▦ A private company considering an IPO needs to plan well in advance and address warning signs that it's not fit to float.

Summary

It's difficult for anyone now to deny the case for good governance. In-depth research by Deutsche Bank, published in 2004, found a clear link between standards of governance and share-price performance and equity risk among members of the FTSE 350. It concluded that companies with the highest standards of corporate governance and behaviour outperformed those with the lowest financially. A search on the internet will uncover a number of other studies with the same message.

The principles of and provisions for good governance laid down by the UK Corporate Governance Code, and used as a frame of reference by stock market analysts, are a useful starting point for any board that wants to establish good practice. Organisations in the public sector have used them as the basis for their own codes. (See, for example, the Governance Code of Practice for Universities and the Monitor Code for NHS Foundation Trusts.)

The challenge for organisations of all types is to first ensure that they are clear about the required standards and that they have clear values that inform their decision-making. They must then find an effective way of communicating this to the public at large.

Governance is a board responsibility; and the board must ensure its standards are properly supported by management. The organisation must live by and live up to its values.

Boards around the world should, at least annually, objectively review their standards of governance.

The Role of the Chairman and the Non-executive Directors

Introduction

The UK Corporate Governance Code calls for the separation of the roles of chairman and chief executive. The chairman is the person who leads and runs the board; the chief executive, by contrast, leads and runs the company. The UK Corporate Governance Code says that no more than two company chairmen roles should be undertaken by one individual.

In some organisations, the leader of the board may be known as 'the chair'. This has the advantage of 'gender neutrality', but I dislike the term. To me, a chair is a piece of furniture – an inanimate and often wooden object; the very antithesis of an effective leader of the board! I prefer the term 'chairman' and have stuck to it throughout this book. It should be read as referring to any incumbent in the role – male or female.

The chairman

Demands of the job

Even before the 2009 Walker review of the corporate governance of banks, expectations of part-time chairmen and non-executive directors, especially those serving on the committees of the board, were high. The Higgs Report of 2003 on the effectiveness of non-executives underlined their role as 'custodians of the governance process'. The idea that chairmen will be more effective if they are able to spend sufficient time on the company's direction and business is now a sine qua non.

There will inevitably be times when urgent meetings must be called to tackle specific challenges – ranging from a takeover approach to dealing with funding levels in a downturn. The chairman needs to ensure they will be able to respond to the company's needs – that is, have the time to provide the leadership required.

Appointment of the chairman

The chairman is elected by the board and has the same legal duties as other directors. However, given the importance of the role, in public companies a chairman will usually be appointed after a wide professional search overseen by the nomination committee.

It's essential to match the candidate to the specific needs of the company. The first stage is to set out the recruitment criteria. These will include the experience and knowledge desired and the specific competencies that will augment and complement those already on the board. Due regard will be paid to the challenges and direction indicated in the forward strategic plan.

Matching the skills set with those of the chief executive will be a particularly important consideration. The chief executive of one FTSE 100 company, for example, was an excellent operations person with good marketing credentials, but was inexperienced in strategy creation and had little direct knowledge of the industry. The company therefore decided to bring in a chairman with good knowledge of the industry and its key participants, and with the vision and flair to develop strategy. This was not in the expectation that the chairman would *lead* the strategic process but that they would offer the chief executive the benefit of their experience.

The banking crisis provided a stark reminder of the need for relevant experience among non-executive directors and chairmen. Many products in the financial services sector are highly complex: they and, crucially, their associated risks, must be understood at board level.

Key qualities

Chairmen are individuals and bring a measure of personal experience and special knowledge to the board, but there are some *general qualities* necessary for the role. Effective chairmen:

▦ have the intellect and ability to grasp complicated issues, distil from them the most important elements and identify the areas for decision-making;

▦ show leadership by word and deed;

▦ deliver the best from the team of directors, ensuring that each is able to contribute fully;

▦ build relationships within the company, the industry and at large in the community;

▦ have the integrity to champion the values of the organisation;

▦ are challenging of but empathetic towards the executive team;

▦ encourage debate and discussion of the key areas, making decision-making more robust and conclusions more satisfactory;

▦ are aware of trends and issues in the community;

▦ are respected by and known to the financial community.

The chairman's responsibilities

The most fundamental part of the chairman's role is to run board meetings and any special one-off meetings of directors effectively and efficiently. They must also conduct the annual general meeting, and any other public meetings such as an extraordinary general meeting. In listed companies, responsibilities will include attendance at the annual and half-yearly results meetings, occasional contact with significant shareholders and meeting with advisers and bankers.

Chairmen should not stray into the responsibilities of the executive, but they will want to have their finger on the pulse and be informed of and aware of trends and issues early on. When trust is built up between the two individuals, the chief executive will be relaxed about the chairman spending time with senior executives to talk about important issues or initiatives for the company. The ability to take a close interest in the business without usurping the chief executive's authority is an important attribute for the chairman.

Areas of added value

The Financial Reporting Council (FRC), which oversees the UK Corporate Governance Code, recognises the pivotal role of chairmen. The Code makes clear their job is to help get the best from the board. Chairmen can add value by:

- being available to mentor the top team or provide the input needed when special circumstances arise;

- ensuring that the board gives the entrepreneurial leadership the company needs – that it has a clear vision, that it sets the direction and the standards by which the company operates;

- being clear about the roles of chairman and chief executive and where they diverge;

- ensuring that the board has the right balance of executive to independent non-executive directors and of skills and experience to work effectively.

The chairman will have an appraisal system for the non-executive directors and a succession plan for them that ensures an orderly transition to 'new blood' to meet new challenges. The chairman will also pay due regard to the timing of their own departure.

The board, as already stated, needs to work effectively and efficiently. While this starts with its composition, the *chemistry* between members is also important. The chairman will observe the interaction at meetings and will take the necessary action to draw out the best from the team.

Information, communication and consultation

The chairman will ensure that the board receives the right information at the right time. At least annually, they will ask the board if the information it receives is clear, in the right form, produced in time to be effective and relevant to the areas that the board needs to monitor.

The importance of a good supply of good information is hard to over-emphasise. Relevant, concise, well-presented information that reflects the total health of the business is the best model. The board's role is not just to monitor the executive and ensure compliance with strategy and regulation and the law; it exists to set the objectives and the direction of the organisation, and it must observe the progress towards these goals.

Communication with the stakeholders through annual reports and other publications must be informative, accurate and reflect the values of the company. The chairman's responsibility does not begin and end with their own statement in the annual report: they should be interested in the entire communication.

Last but certainly not least, the chairman has an important role in ensuring that there are development plans to identify the brightest and best talent for promotion and, perhaps, for consideration as future executive directors. The chief executive should ensure that the chairman has a good knowledge of the top talent and a detailed understanding of both emergency and planned succession for the senior team.

Board committees

It is the chairman's responsibility to see that the committees of the board (examined in some detail in the next chapter) are properly constituted, with clear terms of reference and the right balance of members. Given that they have the primary responsibility for board composition, the chairman will in most circumstances chair the nomination committee.

Chairmen will not chair the other committees, as this is not considered best practice, but they may attend committee meetings at the invitation of the committee chairman. (It's common to see them at remuneration committee meetings; less so at audit committee meetings.) When they do attend sub-committee meetings, they must remember their role is not to attempt to control the meeting or indeed to unduly influence it. (This is sometimes a challenge!)

The chairman and the chief executive

The first task is to be clear about each other's roles and to express this in formal job descriptions. Transparency about their roles and responsibilities will help build trust between the two individuals – and between them and internal and external stakeholders.

With trust, the chairman will be able to act as an informal sounding board for the chief executive before going to the directors. The wise chief executive knows that it is best to have a well-prepared chairman, with no surprises sprung at meetings. Trust breaks down when things are hidden and when there is a lack of openness.

There will inevitably be times of friction and disagreement between the two people, but their duty is to rise above them and resolve the issue that has caused the conflict. If chairman and chief executive compete with each other they will be unable to act in the best interests of the company.

The style of the two individuals will dictate how and when they communicate. Some will want an hour together each week to provide an update on current issues and to discuss the future plans of the chief executive. In larger international organisations, they may meet less frequently but for a longer period – providing the opportunity for a two-way 'download'.

For any organisation, it's essential that the two individuals at the top discuss the agenda for board meetings beforehand. Such discussions help make sure meetings are well run and provide the opportunity to share views in good time.

Is there a practical list of items that should be discussed between the chairman and the chief executive? While there is no universal template, given the differing styles of working, there are some universal 'themes'. Set out in Box 4.1 is a suggested list of headings.

Box 4.1
Items normally discussed by the chairman and the chief executive before a board meeting

Regular items – discussed monthly

■ Significant items requiring decisions.

■ Comments on current trading compared with expectations.

■ Any sensitive issues that may be commented upon by the board.

■ Warning signs of failure to meet strategic milestones.

■ Organisational changes at the level of senior management and above.

■ Changes in the competitive environment.

■ Major developments affecting customers – for example, a decline in service levels.

Special items – discussed when necessary

■ Key issues arising from the strategy review; the stages when the chairman and the board should become involved.

■ Mergers and acquisitions, sales of parts of the company and major joint ventures being considered by the executive.

■ Parameters being considered for the annual plan or budget.

■ The key points likely to be included in the appraisal of executive directors and members of the management committee.* (This allows the chairman's comments to be taken on board in advance of the interview.)

■ The rating to be given to key executives and executive directors.

■ Objectives and personal goals for the top team.

■ The development plans of the top team.

■ Significant changes to the structure of the organisation.

■ Any major projects, especially those involving ICT.

■ Any proposed changes to key advisers.

* The chief executive's own appraisal is a key set piece between the two, as is the setting of their objectives and personal goals.

The chairman and the senior independent director

When the investment banker Derek Higgs conducted his 2003 review of corporate governance (hot on the heels of the Worldcom and Enron scandals in the US) he said that boards of publicly listed companies should appoint a senior independent director (sometimes know as the 'SID') from among their independent non-executives. The proposal initially caused controversy, with claims that it made governance more cumbersome and weakened the role of chairman, but it made it through to the revised version of the Combined Code brought out in 2003, and, today, is included in the UK Corporate Governance Code.

As time has moved on, the role has become generally accepted. The principle is that the senior independent director provides a safety valve in times of conflict or in cases where shareholders believe that their concerns may not be brought to the boardroom table. Where chairman and chief executive act as one and do not communicate fully with shareholders, the senior independent is able to step in and provide a link. Where relations between chairman and chief executive break down, the SID can intervene, identify the issues that have caused the rift and try to build a consensual path back to normality.

Where the best efforts of the senior independent non-executive fail, the non-executive directors may have to rule on the way forward. In extreme cases, one of the two people at the top might need to be replaced.

The independent non-executive director

Not all non-executives are the same. There is a difference between the non-executive director and the non-executive independent director. The UK Corporate Governance Code sets out a number of tests for independence. Non-executives will, for example, normally 'fail' if:

■ they've been appointed by a major shareholder;

■ they hold cross-directorships or have significant links with other directors (ie, they're part of an old boys' network);

■ they have close family ties to the business, including ties to its advisers;

■ they receive remuneration and rewards from the company other than their fees or have been an employee of the company within the past five years;

■ their term of office exceeds nine years.

Appointment of the non-executive director

Key considerations

Independent or not, the non-executive will, as we've already seen, have the same obligations and the same potential liabilities as the others on the board. *Directors, in other words, are equal under the law.*

A non-executive directorship is not a job to be taken lightly, either by an individual or by a company. The responsibilities have, as mentioned earlier, intensified over recent years, and it's crucial that selection is handled carefully. It's common sense to ensure that a potential candidate is committed to the company and free of any conflicts. Candidates must be prepared to make the necessary commitment of time.

Effective non-executives do more than turn up to meetings: they make sure they're adequately informed about the issues on the table; they take the time to refresh their skills; they build networks in the company; they keep up with key developments in the organisation.

Sir David Walker in his review of the corporate governance of UK banks concluded that, in order to fully discharge their duties, non-executive directors must spend more time sitting on the board, recommending a minimum commitment of 30 days a year in the financial sector. The FRC stuck to the spirit of his proposal by introducing a principle into the 2010 UK Corporate Governance Code that all directors must 'be able to give sufficient time to perform their responsibilities effectively'. Higher expectations mean more time with a company and therefore fewer directorships. (This will need to be reflected in the way non-executives are rewarded.)

The company must also look at what an individual will bring to the 'mix'. As Chapter 1 made clear, there is a need for balance on the board – not only in terms of the number of non-executives to executives but also in terms of skills and experience – and this should be a key consideration for nomination committees when recruiting.

At the same time, it's important to remember that selection is not a one-way street. The chosen candidate will want to do some due diligence of their own. This will include research on the company and its leading people, talking with advisers, reviewing current issues with the chairman and, separately, the company secretary, and, finally, assessing the chemistry at meetings to decide if they will fit in and enjoy the role.

New directors will want to feel they can contribute and add value. Importantly, they will need to be sure they will have the ability to stand back and look at the big picture rather than become immersed in management detail. For those coming straight from an executive position, this can be a difficult adjustment.

Key qualities

Non-executives are valued because they have a wider set of experiences that can be brought to bear on issues and decisions in the company. They are best seen as *empathetic* to management rather than *sympathetic*: they need to be quite challenging in their analysis and evaluation of proposals put to the board. Sometimes, the contribution of a non-executive may be blunted by the style in which the challenge or comment is made. Some have continually reminded the board of the way things are done at their main employer in their past or present executive role, and this is not always helpful.

Are there some key prerequisites for an effective non-executive director? The Chartered Institute of Personnel and Development (CIPD) website cites 25 skills. This is a comprehensive list, but it is a bit daunting and it will include skills that are not necessarily essential for all non-executives. Here is my list of 10 attributes, which will be seen to overlap with the key qualities for a chairman, listed above.

1. The ability to understand issues and to identify the central points requiring boardroom decisions.

2. Sound judgment.

3. The ability to challenge in a constructive way.

4. The ability to influence through clear communication and persuasiveness.

5. Good interpersonal skills and the ability to manage conflict.

6. Forward thinking; the ability to anticipate and be aware of new trends.

7. The ability to think strategically, and to understand the role of risk assessment and control.

8. Financial and commercial skills sufficient to ensure understanding of the organisation's progress against predetermined goals.

9. Integrity and high ethical standards, demonstrated in practice.

10. Self-awareness; a thirst to improve personal knowledge and personal performance.

Appraisal and review

As we've seen in Chapter 1, the UK Corporate Governance Code requires chairmen of FTSE 350 companies to meet with the non-executive directors separately each year, and the senior independent director to meet with the non-executive directors to appraise the chairman's performance each year.

All directors will want to see that the board operates well, and the tool that most boards use to establish this is an annual board effectiveness review. The review is inevitably a reflection of the performance of the chairman, which may be a sensitive issue. Recognising this, the process is often 'outsourced' to a consultant or a professional body such as the IoD.

The Walker Report placed greater prominence on the board evaluation review, and the Code now requires an externally facilitated review at least every three years at FTSE 350 companies. Set out in Box 4.2 is the list of headings used by a FTSE 100 company in its annual review of effectiveness. The answers are consolidated into a report for the board that receives sufficient 'airtime' to consider where improvements can be made.

Box 4.2
Board effectiveness review – the key elements

SECTION A – CORPORATE STRATEGY

■ Is understood by the board.

■ Is well understood by shareholders and employees.

■ Directors have collectively and individually brought their knowledge and experience to bear in the testing and development of group strategy.

■ Strategic options are effectively and systematically evaluated.

■ There is an effective and productive process for the review and updating of group strategy.

SECTION B – BUSINESS PRINCIPLES

■ Are owned and championed by the board.

■ Are underpinned by a set of clear and comprehensive group policies, approved by the board.

■ Are reviewed annually by the board and updated to ensure continued appropriateness, support and effectiveness.

■ Are explicit, unambiguous and practicable.

■ Are championed by the executive management group.

■ Provide appropriate guidance and motivation for all staff.

■ Are effectively communicated to shareholders and other stakeholders.

SECTION C – INTERNAL CONTROLS AND RISK MANAGEMENT

■ There is a clear and comprehensive framework of risk-based internal controls to implement the group policies adopted by the board and thereby manage significant risks.

■ Significant risks are effectively identified and evaluated.

■ The board effectively assesses and monitors the system of internal controls and the effectiveness with which risk is being managed.

SECTION D – SHAREHOLDERS AND STAKEHOLDERS

■ The group strategy is effectively communicated to shareholders and other stakeholders.

■ The board receives sufficient information about the views of shareholders and other stakeholders from relevant external sources.

SECTION E – COMMUNICATIONS

■ The timing, coverage and quality of shareholder and stakeholder communications are appropriate.

■ The board communicates effectively with the executive management group.

■ The organisation has the resources, skills and experience to manage the key risks and deliver the business plan.

SECTION F – ORGANISATION AND CULTURE

■ The group culture encourages continuous improvement.

■ Performance reporting is adequate and timely and ensures prompt capture of adverse trends.

- Variances from budget are clearly identified and corrective actions are detailed.

- Management performance is regularly and thoroughly reviewed, and rewards or sanctions are given promptly.

SECTION G – SUCCESSION, DEVELOPMENT AND REWARD

- There is an appropriate succession management plan for all board and executive management group positions.

- Training and development are encouraged and are focused on the delivery of the business plan.

- The range of rewards is suited to recruiting and retaining qualified, capable and high-quality staff.

- Rewards are structured to focus on short, medium and long-term performance.

SECTION H – BOARD COMPOSITION

- The present board membership and composition are the best for the company, given its current needs.

- The range of skills, knowledge and experience is appropriate.

- The process for identifying and recruiting new board members is transparent and appropriate.

SECTION I – BOARD INDUCTION AND TRAINING

- There is a comprehensive programme to provide new non-executive directors with an induction into the group.

- Directors are kept up to date with the latest developments in the regulatory and legal environment and how these affect their responsibilities.

- There is a comprehensive training programme for directors to refresh their knowledge and skills.

SECTION J – DELEGATION AND ACCOUNTABILITIES

- The matters reserved for the board are appropriate.

- The present range of committees is capable of addressing all areas that should be reviewed on behalf of the board.

- The committee chairmen report appropriate and timely information on their activities to the whole board.

- The board delegates appropriate authority to senior management.

SECTION K – BOARD MEETINGS

- The agenda includes only what is important.

- Agenda items and presentations are relevant and timely.

- The agenda allows the appropriate amount of time for the discussion of each item.

- The time allowed for each item is appropriately allocated to ensure proper consideration of key issues.

- The schedule of meetings, lunch and dinner allows adequate time for discussion, participation and reflection.

- Meetings are of high quality and are productive, with a full and open discussion of issues.

- Board visits to overseas assets are useful and effective.

SECTION L – SECRETARIAT SERVICE

- Board papers are received in sufficient time.

- Board papers are sufficiently clear and concise.

- The minutes accurately reflect the substance of the discussions.

- Minutes are distributed in a timely manner.

- Action points from the meetings are properly followed through.

▪ The board receives appropriate information on the activities of all its committees and sub-committees.

▪ The board receives timely and comprehensive advice on matters of governance relevant to items of discussion.

▪ The AGM venue and arrangements are appropriate.

SECTION M – OTHER

▪ In which area(s) do you believe the board operates most effectively?

▪ In which area(s) do you believe the board operates least effectively?

Summary

As the leader of the board, the chairman performs a pivotal role; the effectiveness of the board is a reflection, in large part, of their performance. The chairman sets the tone for the board and gets the best from the individuals, while ensuring that the executives have appropriate freedom to get on and deliver the plan.

It is crucial that the division of responsibilities between chairman and chief executive is clearly defined and that each understands and respects the other's role and objectives. In the best companies, these objectives are shared with the rest of the board. (The case study in Chapter 1 of Cosgrove Manufacturing plc is a good example of what happens when things go wrong between chairman and chief executive.) Openness and trust are the foundations of a good working relationship between the two people at the top.

The chairman's role includes ensuring that the agendas are right for each board meeting, and that all directors have the opportunity to express views.

The board needs to provide leadership to the organisation and make sure decisions by management are consistent with strategy. In pre-board meetings with the chief executive, the chairman will be alerted to management proposals where there may be a strategic conflict and where the board may need to say 'no'.

The success of the board will largely be a function of the quality and diversity of experience and skills of the non-executive directors. Great care should be taken in their appointment and in their annual appraisal to get the best individually and collectively from them.

The senior independent director can be a useful interface between investors and the company, especially where they feel that the chairman has not acted on their concerns. However, there are some residual fears that the role marginalises that of chairman. Again, appointing the right person as senior independent director will be crucial.

The board effectiveness review now receives greater emphasis and enables boards (and therefore chairmen) to show continuous improvement. It should be carried out in a systematic, structured way.

Key Committees of the Board

Introduction

The major and prescribed committees of the board are the remuneration, nomination and audit committees. Increased focus on the risk assessment and control process means that many larger and regulated businesses will also have a separate committee for risk. Others, meanwhile, continue to roll this up in the audit committee. This chapter looks at the work of the three prescribed committees and the risk committee.

Just as the board needs to be clear about those matters reserved for its authority, each committee must also have clear terms of reference, reviewed annually by the board to ensure their continued relevance. We will deal with each committee in turn.

The remuneration committee

Basic role

The principle here is that no director should decide their own remuneration. Non-executive fees are set by the executive directors, often on the advice of external consultants, and are usually paid in cash. (Some companies, however, will pay part or all of the remuneration in shares.) The remuneration of executive directors is set by a sub-committee of non-executives and will include performance-related elements.

Best practice says that the remuneration committee (or 'remco' as it's sometimes known) should be made up entirely of independent non-executive directors and be led by someone other than the chairman of the main board. Committee meetings are usually attended by the human resources director and, often, the chief executive. (Executives should, though, be excluded from discussions in which they have a direct personal interest.) The company secretary usually provides the secretarial back-up.

The remuneration committee is encouraged to have independent input on salaries, deferred income such as pensions, and incentives. *In setting rewards, the key rule is to avoid paying more than is necessary to attract, retain and motivate executive talent.*

The committee will want to ensure that there's a system for effective appraisals against objectives and that targets for bonuses are seen to be stretching but achievable.

The committee needs to identify the population it will look at individually. This will usually include directors of significant subsidiaries, members of the top executive committee and those who have breached a predetermined income threshold.

The chairman of the committee is responsible for the remuneration report, included in the annual report and accounts, and must be available at the company AGM to answer questions on remuneration.

Normally, the committee will meet three times a year.

Benchmarking

The members of the remuneration committee will seek objective assessment of competitors' pay from surveys and consultants.

They should, however, think carefully about their company's position in any comparator group. Remuneration policy should not be driven by 'me-tooism'. Committee members should, in the words of the UK Corporate Governance Code, avoid an 'upward ratcheting' in executive pay without a corresponding improvement in performance.

Rewards that exceed the upper limit for the cohort in the comparator group are hard to justify to shareholders.

Key considerations; current trends

Packages should be competitive but aligned with the delivery of the company's strategy. The UK Corporate Governance Code calls for a 'significant proportion' of performance-related elements, but the precise ratio of base salary to 'money at risk' – eg, annual bonus and longer-term plans – will differ from company to company.

The Financial Reporting Council paid special attention to the subject of performance-related pay in the light of the conclusions of the Walker review. Proposals have been made to ensure that performance conditions are in the long-term interests of the company and reflect its policy on risk. The UK Corporate Governance Code observes that 'performance-related elements of executive directors' remuneration should be stretching and designed to align their interests with those of the share-holders and the long-term success of the company'.

Bonuses paid to senior people have long attracted the attention of the media and politicians. Criticism was most fierce, perhaps, during the credit crunch, when rewards for performance were said to have con-tributed to a culture of excessive risk-taking among Britain's banks. While some of the anger may have been born of envy, the important point is that, in pursuit of the kind of short-term results that improve bonuses, individuals might be disassociated from the risks inherent in their decisions. This is most likely to happen when bonuses are paid annually, without the right of clawback in the event of future short-falls.

The trend now is to hold the money for longer before payout and for the remuneration committee to be more rigorous in scheme design to reflect the company's appetite for risk. (The 2009 Walker Report recom-mended that banks and financial institutions release cash bonuses over three years after they've been earned and that clawback should be allowed in the event of mis-statement or misconduct.)

Generally, there has been some debate as to whether the current pay model for directors is fit for purpose. Incentive payments based on share price often reward the executive when share prices move up but fail to penalise them when they move down. In other words, it's a one-way bid unless the executive also puts some of their own money into the company. Currently, executive directors in listed companies do not have significant investments at risk in the companies they run. The private equity model, on the other hand, requires the executive to invest at current prices into the company at levels usually around one or two times salary. Executives with a lot to lose are arguably more motivated to do well.

Increased scrutiny of pay packages inevitably puts greater pressure on the remco. The importance of getting the elements of remuneration right cannot be over-emphasised. Shareholders are entitled to an advisory vote on the remuneration report; and 'no' votes always attract adverse publicity.

Key challenges

In summary, the key challenges for the remuneration committee are to:

■ ensure that the remuneration policy is aligned with the requirements of strategy, is competitive and motivating;

■ ensure that the remuneration package is affordable, not excessive and not damaging to the reputation of the company;

■ ensure that the remuneration policy is aligned with the long-term interests of shareholders in delivering value;

■ avoid rewards for failure;

■ ensure that the criteria for payments at risk are stretching but achievable and based on the risk appetite of the company.

Terms of reference

The UK Corporate Governance Code requires the terms of reference for the defined committees to be formally laid down. Set out in Box 5.1 are the terms of reference for the remuneration committee of a FTSE 100 company.

Box 5.1
Terms of reference – remuneration committee of a FTSE 100 company

Membership

Members of the committee are appointed by the board, on the recommendation of the nomination committee in consultation with the chairman of the remuneration committee. The committee is made up of at least three members, all of whom are independent non-executive directors.

Only members of the committee have the right to attend committee meetings. However, other individuals such as the chairman of the board, the chief executive, the head of human resources and external advisers may be invited to attend for all or part of any meeting as and when appropriate.

The board appoints the committee chairman, who is an independent non-executive director. In the absence of the committee chairman and/or an appointed deputy, the remaining members

---

present elect one of themselves to chair the meeting. The chairman of the board may not be chairman of the committee.

The current members of the committee are: (*names are inserted here*).

Secretary

The company secretary or their nominee acts as the secretary of the committee.

Quorum

The quorum necessary for the transaction of business is two.

Meetings

The committee meets three times a year and at such other times as are appropriate.

Notice of meetings

Meetings of the committee are convened by the secretary of the committee at the request of any of its members. Unless otherwise agreed, notice of each meeting confirming the venue, time and date, together with an agenda of items to be discussed, is forwarded to each member of the committee and any other person required to attend, no later than three working days before the date of the meeting. Supporting papers are sent to committee members and to others as appropriate, at the same time or as soon as practicable thereafter.

Minutes of meetings

The secretary minutes the proceedings and resolutions of all committee meetings, including the names of those present and in attendance.

Minutes of committee meetings are circulated promptly to all members of the committee and, once agreed, to all members of the board, unless a conflict of interest exists.

Annual general meeting

The chairman of the committee attends the annual general meeting prepared to respond to any shareholder questions on the committee's activities.

Duties

The duties of the committee are to:

■ Determine and agree with the board the framework or broad policy for the remuneration of the company's chief executive, chairman, the executive directors, members of the executive management group and such other members of the executive management as it is designated to consider. The remuneration of non-executive directors is a matter for the chairman and the executive members of the board. No director or manager is involved in any decisions as to his or her own personal remuneration.

■ In determining such policy, take into account all factors that it deems necessary. The objective of such policy shall be to ensure that members of the executive management of the company are provided with appropriate incentives to encourage enhanced performance and are, in a fair and responsible manner, rewarded for their individual contributions to the success of the company.

■ Review the ongoing appropriateness and relevance of the remuneration policy.

■ Approve the design of, and determine targets for, any performance-related pay schemes operated by the company and approve the total annual payments made under such schemes.

■ Review the design of all share incentive plans for approval by the board and shareholders. For any such plans, determine each year whether awards will be made, and if so, the overall amount of such awards, the individual awards to executive directors and other senior executives and the performance targets to be used.

■ Review the ongoing administration and appropriateness of all share-based remuneration.

■ Determine the policy for, and scope of, pension arrangements for each executive director and other senior executives.

- Ensure that contractual terms on termination are fair to the individual and the company, that failure is not rewarded and that the duty to mitigate loss is fully recognised. (In the case of executive directors, the committee is to approve the amount of any payments made to ensure that they meet these criteria.)

- Within the terms of the agreed policy and in consultation with the chairman and/or chief executive as appropriate, determine the total individual remuneration package of each executive director and each member of the executive management group, including bonuses, incentive payments and other share awards.

- In determining such packages and arrangements, give due regard to any relevant legal requirements, the provisions and recommendations in the UK Corporate Governance Code, and the UK Listing Authority's Listing Rules and associated guidance.

- Review and note annually the remuneration trends across the group.

- Oversee any major changes in employee benefits structures throughout the group.

- Agree the policy for authorising claims for expenses from the chief executive and chairman.

- Ensure that all provisions regarding disclosure of remuneration including pensions, as set out in the Directors' Remuneration Report Regulations 2002 and the UK Corporate Governance Code, are fulfilled.

- Be exclusively responsible for establishing the selection criteria and the terms of reference for any consultants who advise the committee, for appointing consultants and for obtaining reliable, up-to-date information about remuneration in other companies. The committee shall have full authority to commission any reports or surveys that it deems necessary to help it fulfil its obligations.

Reporting responsibilities

The committee chairman reports formally to the board on its proceedings after each meeting.

The committee makes whatever recommendations to the board it deems appropriate on any area within its remit where action or improvement is needed.

The committee produces an annual report of the company's remuneration policy and practices that forms part of the company's annual report and ensures each year that it is put to shareholders for approval at the AGM.

Other

The committee, at least once a year, reviews its own performance, constitution and terms of reference to ensure it is operating at maximum effectiveness and recommends any changes it considers necessary to the board for approval.

Authority

The committee is authorised:

■ to seek any information it requires from any employee of the company in order to perform its duties; and

■ in connection with its duties, to obtain, at the company's expense, any legal or other professional advice.

The nomination committee

The UK Corporate Governance Code requires there to be a formal, rigorous and transparent procedure for the appointment of new directors to the board.

The nomination committee leads the process of selecting new board members, making recommendations or nominations to the full board. It will typically also ensure that succession plans are in place for the board and the executive level immediately below it. It is made up mainly of independent non-executive directors. The chairman of the main board is usually a key member and often chairs the committee (unless its main business is to appoint their successor).

In smaller companies, the duties and responsibilities of the nomination and the remuneration committee are combined. Box 5.2 sets out a model terms of reference used by a FTSE 100 company.

Box 5.2 Terms of reference – nomination committee of a FTSE 100 company

Membership

Members of the committee are appointed by the board. The committee is made up of at least three members, the majority of whom should be independent non-executive directors.

Only members of the committee have the right to attend committee meetings. However, other individuals such as the chief executive, the head of human resources and external advisers may be invited to attend for all or part of any meeting as and when appropriate.

Appointments to the committee are for a period of up to three years, which may be extended for two further three-year periods, provided that the majority of the committee members remain independent.

The board appoints the committee chairman, who should be either the chairman of the board or an independent non-executive director. In the absence of the committee chairman and/or an appointed deputy, the remaining members present elect one of their number to chair the meeting. The chairman of the board does not chair the committee when it is dealing with the matter of succession to the chairmanship.

The current members of the committee are: (*names are inserted here*).

Secretary

The company secretary or their nominee acts as the secretary of the committee.

Quorum

The quorum necessary for the transaction of business is two, both of whom must be independent non-executive directors.

Frequency of meetings

The committee meets at least twice a year and at such other times as the chairman of the committee shall require.

Notice of meetings

Meetings of the committee are convened by the secretary of the committee at the request of any of its members.

Unless otherwise agreed, notice of each meeting confirming the venue, time and date, together with an agenda of items to be discussed, is forwarded to each member of the committee, and any other person required to attend, no later than three working days before the date of the meeting. Supporting papers are sent to committee members and to other attendees as appropriate, at the same time or as soon as practicable thereafter.

Minutes of meetings

The secretary minutes the proceedings and resolutions of all meetings of the committee, including the names of those present and in attendance.

Minutes of committee meetings are circulated promptly to all members of the committee and the chairman of the board and, once agreed, to all other members of the board, unless a conflict of interest exists.

Annual general meeting

The chairman of the committee attends the annual general meeting prepared to respond to any shareholder questions on the committee's activities.

Duties

The committee:

■ Regularly reviews the structure, size and composition (including the skills, knowledge and experience) required of the board compared with its current position and makes recommendations to the board with regard to any changes.

■ Gives full consideration to succession planning for directors in the course of its work, taking into account the challenges and opportunities facing the company, and what skills and expertise are therefore needed on the board in the future.

▩ Is responsible for identifying and nominating, for the approval of the board, candidates to fill board vacancies as and when they arise.

▩ Before making an appointment, evaluates the balance of skills, knowledge and experience on the board and, in the light of this evaluation, prepares a description of the role and capabilities required for a particular appointment.

▩ In identifying suitable candidates, uses open advertising or the services of external advisers to facilitate the search, considers people from a wide range of backgrounds and on merit and objective criteria, taking care that appointees have enough time to devote to the position.

▩ Keeps under review the leadership needs of the organisation, including executive, non-executive and senior management, with a view to ensuring the continued ability of the organisation to compete effectively in the marketplace. In doing so, it will review management development programmes and the succession planning process for the executive management group and other senior management prepared by the chief executive.

▩ Ensures that on appointment to the board, non-executive directors receive a formal letter of appointment setting out clearly what is expected of them in terms of time commitment, committee service and involvement outside board meetings.

▩ The committee also makes recommendations to the board concerning:

 – plans for succession for both executive and non-executive directors and in particular for the key roles of chairman and chief executive;

 – suitable candidates for the role of senior independent director;

 – membership of the audit and remuneration committees, in consultation with the chairmen of those committees;

 – the reappointment of any non-executive director at the conclusion of their specified term of office, having given due regard to their performance and ability to continue to contribute to the board in the light of the knowledge, skills and experience required;

– the re-election by shareholders of any director under the 'retirement by rotation' provisions in the company's articles of association, having due regard to their performance and ability to continue to contribute to the board in the light of the knowledge, skills and experience required;

– any matters relating to the continuation in office of any director at any time, including the suspension or termination of service of an executive director as an employee of the company, subject to the provisions of the law and their service contract; and

– the appointment of any director to executive or other office (except that of chairman and chief executive, the recommendation for which would be considered at a meeting of the full board).

Reporting responsibilities

The committee makes whatever recommendations to the board it deems appropriate on any area within its remit where action or improvement is needed.

The committee makes a statement in the annual report about its activities and the process used to make appointments and, if external advice or open advertising has not been used, explains why.

Other

The committee, at least once a year, reviews its own performance, constitution and terms of reference to ensure it is operating at maximum effectiveness and recommends any changes it considers necessary to the board for approval.

Authority

The committee is authorised:

■ to seek any information it requires from any employee of the company in order to perform its duties; and

> ▪ in connection with its duties, to obtain, at the company's expense, outside legal or other professional advice.

The audit committee

Composition and basic role

The UK Corporate Governance Code says that the board should have formal and transparent arrangements for considering how it applies the corporate reporting and risk management and internal control principles. The board also needs to ensure that an appropriate relationship with the company's auditors is maintained.

The Code goes on to say that the audit committee should be comprised of at least three non-executive directors, one of whom should have recent and relevant financial experience. Current European proposals go further, suggesting that members should have accounting or auditing experience. For the time being in the UK, though, numeracy (financial literacy), good experience and good judgment can be enough to get you a seat. (Critics say the EU proposals define membership too narrowly and would exclude many people capable of making an excellent contribution to the committee.)

The finance director and the head of internal audit will always be in attendance, and the secretary is usually the company secretary or the head of internal audit. It's usual for the committee to meet quarterly. Naturally, two meetings will coincide with the publication of half-year and full-year results. Additional special meetings are held as necessary.

Scope

The role of the audit committee is commonly misunderstood. The quotes below were all recorded in a straw poll of small investors conducted by the author for a private seminar:

'It is there to ensure that published accounts are correctly drawn up.'
'The audit committee is a vehicle to prevent fraud.'
'The audit committee is there to keep management on their toes.'
'It gives shareholders assurance that controls in the organisation are robust.'
'It is there to comply with the UK Corporate Governance Code.'

While there is some element of truth in these views, they do not accurately reflect the work of the committee. Its scope is laid down in its terms of reference and is usually quite wide. Typically, it includes:

■ providing a direct link with the auditor;

■ approving the annual internal audit and external audit plan;

■ ensuring the auditor's independence and agreeing terms under which the audit firm can accept non-audit work;

■ appraising the auditor's effectiveness;

■ having a direct reporting relationship with the head of the internal audit function;

■ reviewing and monitoring the control environment, and in particular ensuring that an appropriate risk assessment and control process is embedded in the business (see the box on page 100);

■ reviewing and agreeing any changes in accounting policy;

■ scrutinising the accounts and financial reports to shareholders and, if satisfied, recommending them to the board for approval.

The chairman of the committee must, of course, attend the AGM to answer any questions put to them by the shareholders.

The terms of reference show clearly the scope of the audit committee, but the question audit committees need to ask is: 'How can we add value to the organisation?'

The basic tasks that need to be undertaken are compliance-driven, involving the review of accounts and financial statements and controls. The broader focus is risk assessment and control, the very foundation for internal and external audit. By playing a fundamental role in the control environment, the audit committee can bring real value and help the organisation meet its strategic goals.

The audit committee and risk assessment

Risks are an inherent part of business life; profits are, to some extent, the rewards of taking risks. As the UK Corporate Governance Code points out, the board is responsible for defining the nature and extent of the risks that the company is willing to take. The board needs to have a sound system of risk management and internal control to safeguard shareholders' interests and the company's assets.

The identification and management of risk has moved higher up the company agenda. Assessing the risks of a company strategy is now a well-defined procedure, most usefully tackled through risk workshops. Risks are evaluated for impact and probability, and ranked accordingly.

Where there is no separate committee for risk (see below), the audit committee plays, as has been stated, a fundamental role in risk assessment and control. It will need to satisfy itself that the process of evaluation is robust and that the high-level risks are being identified. High-level risks need to be 'owned'; there should be a person responsible for managing each one.

Risk management is not an annual and financial exercise: it's integral to operational life. In a 2006 report, the accountants and management consultants Ernst & Young defined it as 'a systematic and structured way of aligning an organisation's approach to risk and its strategy, helping the business to manage uncertainty more effectively, to minimise threats and maximise opportunity'.

External stakeholders want assurance that the organisation's leaders have the right systems, people and information to reduce exposure to risks and to realise value. Effective directors are not constitutionally risk-averse, but they're not reckless either.

Risk review

The high-level risks must be reviewed by the committee and the board, and a plan developed to manage and thereby ameliorate them.

The format by which the risks are reviewed is a matter of choice for the company concerned. However, rather than pretend that the value of the risks and the probability that they will occur can be calculated to an accurate mathematical formula, most follow a simple traffic light system. A generic format will have these headings:

Description of risk	Risk category eg strategic/ HR/ financial operation	Impact High Medium Low	Probability High Medium Low	Ranking	Net risk score High Medium Low	Ownership person/ people responsible for managing the risk	Action measures taken to mitigate risk

The process works well when there is a 'bottom up' approach in the trading divisions or separate companies, and a 'top down' approach from the executive committee. Risk workshops, which may involve the full board, can be a very effective way of assessing the risks, and are often led by outside practitioners.

The sources of risk can be both internal and external. Some examples under each category are set out in Table 5.1.

Table 5.1

External risks	Internal risks
1. Inability to implement strategy due to lack of funds and low-rated share price	1. Insufficient skilled people available to deliver the strategy
2. Government macro-economic policy reduces market size and affects margins	2. Impact of serious health and safety breaches
3. Change of government hurts business environment	3. Reputational damage through product failure or inappropriate actions in the business or community
4. Adverse exchange rate change has an impact on sterling earnings	4. Failure to innovate to keep product or service offering relevant
5. Demographic changes reduce market opportunity	5. Entry of new competitor with a significant cost advantage
6. Change in the indirect tax regime has negative impact on company profitability	6. Customer service failure due to IT or inadequate supply chain
	7. Credit rating is downgraded; cost of borrowing materially increases
	8. Exceptional failure of a large project due to inadequate project management
	9. Loss of IT systems due to a disaster
	10. Fraud or fraudulent accounting hits profits and affects reputation and market rating
	11. Changes in assumptions increase the pension funding deficit and the company rating

Ranking risks

The probability of an event happening and the impact that it would have on the business jointly determine how a risk is 'ranked'. Assessment of the latter needs to take into account any consequential loss not covered by insurance. There can be a 'domino effect' to adverse events; this can be seen in the crisis that hit Cadbury Schweppes in 2006. Following a salmonella scare, the company took the step of withdrawing more than a million confectionery products. The cost of the product recall was put at £5 million but total losses were later estimated at £35 million. The difference was reputational damage: customers lost confidence in the quality of the company's products and bought less chocolate.

The domino effect also works in reverse: companies can be hit by something that happens to or action taken by one of their suppliers. Supply-side risks are likely to be highest where the supplier base is small and limited to a few strategic relationships. In these circumstances, supplier failure is likely to have a particularly heavy impact on the company and on its customers. Companies need to know and understand the risk analysis and risk management plan of their critical suppliers.

Some risks can be covered or part-covered by insurance, but these need to be effectively managed, too – if competitive premiums and future insurance are to be available.

Terms of reference

Again, the audit committee's terms of reference need to be formally set down and annually reviewed and approved. Box 5.3 sets out the terms used by a FTSE 100 company.

The company featured had decided against a separate risk committee, in part because of the expertise on the audit committee, and in part due to the close connection between the risk environment and audit. Special care was taken to ensure that the board was also involved in significant discussions on risk strategy at least twice a year and in risk workshops held every two years.

Box 5.3
Terms of reference – audit committee of a FTSE 100 company

Membership

Members of the committee are appointed by the board, on the recommendation of the nomination committee in consultation with the chairman of the audit committee. The committee is made up of at least three members.

All members of the committee are independent non-executive directors, at least one of whom has recent and relevant financial experience. The chairman of the board may not be a member of the committee.

Only members of the committee have the right to attend committee meetings. However, other individuals such as the chairman of the board, group chief executive, group finance director, other directors, the head of group review and audit, and representatives from the finance function may be invited to attend all or part of any meeting as and when appropriate.

The external auditors are invited to attend meetings of the committee regularly.

Appointments to the committee are for a period of up to three years, which may be extended for two further three-year periods, provided the director remains independent.

The board appoints the committee chairman, who is an independent non-executive director. In the absence of the committee chairman and/or an appointed deputy, the remaining members present elect one of themselves to chair the meeting.

The current members of the committee are: (*names are inserted here*).

Secretary

The company secretary or their nominee acts as the secretary of the committee.

Quorum

The quorum necessary for the transaction of business is two.

Frequency of meetings

The committee meets at least four times a year at appropriate times in the reporting and audit cycle and otherwise as required.

Notice of meetings

Meetings of the committee are convened by the secretary of the committee at the request of any of its members or at the request of any of those individuals referred to above, or external auditors if they consider it necessary.

Unless otherwise agreed, notice of each meeting confirming the venue, time and date, together with an agenda of items to be discussed, is forwarded to each member of the committee and any other person required to attend, no later than three working days before the date of the meeting. Supporting papers are sent to committee members and to others as appropriate, at the same time or as soon as practicable thereafter.

Minutes of meetings

The secretary minutes the proceedings and resolutions of all meetings of the committee and records the names of those present.

The secretary ascertains, at the beginning of each meeting, the existence of any conflicts of interest and minutes them accordingly.

Minutes of committee meetings are circulated promptly to all members of the committee and, once agreed, to all members of the board.

Annual general meeting

The chairman of the committee attends the annual general meeting prepared to respond to any shareholder questions on the committee's activities.

Duties

The committee should carry out the duties below for the parent company, major subsidiary undertakings and the group as a whole, as appropriate.

Financial reporting

The committee monitors the integrity of the financial statements of the company, including its annual and interim reports, preliminary results announcements and any other formal announcement relating to its financial performance, reviewing any significant financial reporting issues and judgments that they contain. The committee also reviews summary financial statements, significant financial returns to regulators and any financial information contained in certain other documents, such as announcements of a price-sensitive nature.

The committee reviews and challenges where necessary:

■ the consistency of, and any changes to, accounting policies both on a year-on-year basis and across the company/group;

■ the methods used to account for significant or unusual transactions where different approaches are possible;

■ whether the company has followed appropriate accounting standards and made appropriate estimates and judgments, taking into account the views of the external auditor;

■ the clarity of disclosure in the company's financial reports and the context in which statements are made;

■ the treatment of any items in the financial statements that differs from the views of the company's external auditor;

■ the going concern assumption; and

■ all material information presented with the financial statements, such as the business review and the corporate governance statement (insofar as it relates to audit and risk management).

Internal controls and risk management systems

The committee:

■ keeps under review the effectiveness of the company's internal controls and risk management systems; and

■ reviews and approves the statements to be included in the annual report concerning internal controls and risk management.

Whistle-blowing

The committee reviews the company's arrangements for its employees to raise concerns, in confidence, about possible wrong-doing in financial reporting or other matters. The committee ensures that these arrangements allow proportionate and independent investigation of such matters and appropriate follow-up action.

Internal audit

The committee:

- Monitors and reviews the effectiveness of the company's group review and audit in the context of the company's overall risk management system.

- Approves the appointment and removal of the head of group review and audit.

- Considers and approves the remit of group review and audit and ensures it has adequate resources and appropriate access to information to enable it to perform its function effectively and in accordance with the relevant professional standards. The committee also ensures group review and audit has adequate standing and is free from management or other restrictions.

- Reviews and assesses the annual internal audit plan.

- Reviews promptly all reports on the company from the internal auditors.

- Reviews and monitors management's responsiveness to the findings and recommendations of group review and audit.

- Meets the head of group review and audit at least once a year, without management being present, to discuss their remit and any issues arising from the internal audits carried out. In addition, the head of group review and audit has the right of direct access to the chairman of the board and to the committee.

External audit

The committee:

- Considers and makes recommendations to the board, to be put to shareholders for approval at the AGM, in relation to the appointment, re-appointment and removal of the company's external auditor.

- Oversees the selection process for new auditors; and if an auditor resigns, investigates the issues leading to this and decides whether any action is required.

- Oversees the relationship with the external auditor, including (but not limited to):

  - approval of its remuneration, whether fees for audit or non-audit services, ensuring that the level of fees is appropriate to enable an adequate audit to be conducted;

  - approval of its terms of engagement, including any engagement letter issued at the start of each audit, and the scope of the audit;

  - assessing annually its independence and objectivity, taking into account relevant professional and regulatory requirements and the relationship with the auditor as a whole, including the provision of any non-audit services;

  - satisfying itself that there are no relationships (such as family, employment, investment, financial or business) between the auditor and the company (other than in the ordinary course of business);

  - monitoring the auditor's compliance with relevant ethical and professional guidance on the rotation of audit partners, the level of fees paid by the company compared with the overall fee income of the firm, office and partner, and other related requirements;

  - assessing annually the auditor's qualifications, expertise and resources, and the effectiveness of the audit process, which shall include a report from the external auditor on their own internal quality procedures; and

  - developing and implementing a policy on the supply of non-audit services by the external auditor, taking into account any relevant ethical guidance on the matter.

- Meets regularly with the external auditor, including once at the planning stage before the audit and once after the audit at the reporting stage. (The committee also meets the external auditor at least once a year, without management being present, to discuss its remit and any issues arising from the audit.)

▪ Reviews and approves the annual audit plan and ensures that it is consistent with the scope of the audit engagement.

▪ Reviews the findings of the audit with the external auditor. This shall include but not be limited to, the following:

 – any major issues that arose during the audit;

 – any accounting and audit judgments;

 – levels of errors identified during the audit; and

 – the treatment of any item in the financial statements that differs from the views of the external auditors.

▪ Reviews any representation letter(s) requested by the external auditor before they are signed by management.

▪ Reviews the management letter and management's response to the auditor's findings and recommendations.

▪ Reviews the effectiveness of the audit.

Reporting responsibilities

The committee chairman reports formally to the board on its proceedings after each meeting. The committee makes whatever recommendations to the board it deems appropriate on any area within its remit where action or improvement is needed.

The committee compiles a report to shareholders on its activities to be included in the company's annual report.

Other matters

The committee:

▪ has access to sufficient resources in order to carry out its duties, including access to the company secretariat for assistance as required;

▪ is provided with appropriate and timely training, both in the form of an induction programme for new members and on an ongoing basis for all members;

■ gives due consideration to laws and regulations, the provisions of the UK Corporate Governance Code and the requirements of the UK Listing Authority's Listing Rules;

■ is responsible for co-ordination of group review and audit and external auditors;

■ oversees any investigation of activities that are within its terms of reference and acts as a court of the last resort; and

■ at least once a year, reviews its own performance, constitution and terms of reference to ensure it is operating at maximum effectiveness and recommends any changes it considers necessary to the board for approval.

Joint ventures and associated companies

Where the group has investments in joint ventures or associated companies that do not confer control, the committee reviews, so far as practicable, the arrangements relating to the duties described above.

Authority

The committee is authorised:

■ to seek any information it requires from any employee of the company in order to perform its duties;

■ to obtain, at the company's expense, outside legal or other professional advice on any matter within its terms of reference; and

■ to call any employee to be questioned at a meeting of the committee as and when required.

Improving audit committee effectiveness

The audit committee will periodically review how it can be more effective and add greater value to the enterprise; it will continuously seek to improve its performance. An important tool for achieving continuous improvement is an annual review of effectiveness. This can be carried out in several ways:

▓ by having a detailed questionnaire that is agreed with the chairman of the committee and circulated to committee members, members of the senior executive team, other board members and the partner of the audit firm;

▓ by having an independent qualified person carry out structured interviews;

▓ by having the audit firm review the committee, using external best practice as its benchmark.

In each case, the 'results' are consolidated and actions agreed to improve performance. Box 5.4 reproduces the questionnaire devised for the audit and risk committee of the IoD.

Box 5.4 Draft questionnaire, audit and risk committee, Institute of Directors

1. Terms of reference

▓ Has the committee clear, approved terms of reference?

▓ Are these reviewed annually?

▓ Is there a clear policy on whistle-blowing?

▓ Is there clarity on the engagement of the auditors for non-audit work?

2. Membership and appointments

▓ Does the audit committee consist of independent members?

▓ Are members appointed by the board, or the nomination committee in consultation with the audit committee chair?

▓ Does at least one member have recent and relevant experience?

▓ Is there a relevant balance of skills on the committee?

▓ Are terms of office restricted to three years?

▓ Does the committee have succession plans?

▓ Is there an induction programme for new members?

▓ Do members take steps to update their knowledge and skills?

---

3. Meetings

■ Does the committee meet regularly and at least three times a year?

■ Are the meetings well attended?

■ Is sufficient time allowed for discussion?

■ Are agendas well prepared, with relevant information, and on time?

■ Are arrangements made for the committee to meet alone with the auditors?

■ Does the chair keep in touch with key staff and the audit partner?

■ Are appropriate non-members invited and encouraged to attend?

■ Is the committee adequately served by the staff?

4. Review of accounts

■ Does the committee review all significant financial reporting issues and judgments made?

■ Where there is a difference of view between the auditors and the IoD does the committee formally consider what is appropriate?

■ Is there a committee review of the clarity and completeness of statements?

■ If there is any significant aspect of disagreement with the accounts are changes made, or is this reported to the board?

■ Does the committee review any significant differences between accounts produced by the IoD and the auditors' workings?

5. Internal controls and risk assessment

■ How well is risk assessment embedded in the IoD?

■ Does the committee have a list of high-level risks?

■ How well are the risks managed at the IoD?

■ Does the committee monitor the integrity of the controls?

■ Is the committee satisfied that the information available to the board enables it to monitor the business effectively?

■ Is the annual assessment made on establishing an internal audit function?

6. External auditor

■ Is the committee responsible for overseeing the auditor?

■ Does the committee recommend the appointment or removal of the auditor?

■ Is the annual auditor's work plan agreed by the committee?

■ Does the committee monitor the skills and independence of auditors?

■ Is the committee aware of the auditor's processes to preserve quality and independence?

■ Has a level of materiality been agreed with the auditors?

■ Does the committee monitor the management letter and ensure that follow-up is timely and appropriate?

■ Is there a formal review of the effectiveness of the audit?

7. Other matters

■ Are copies of the minutes distributed to members and to the board in a timely manner?

■ Does the report of the committee go to the board?

■ Is the chair of audit available at IoD council meetings/the AGM?

8. Finally ...

■ What does the committee do really well?

■ What areas must be improved to achieve best practice?

■ Are there areas you are concerned about because you see the IoD at risk?

Relationships and communication

The role of the chairman of the committee is pivotal. They can build trust between the committee and the auditor, the internal audit team, the finance director and the key general managers of the main businesses, including the CEO. A spirit of openness is essential for effective working: no party should surprise another.

The committee chairman needs to make the time to maintain the important relationships in the company, to keep up to date with changes in accounting and auditing standards, and to support and interact with the internal audit leader and team. Chairing an audit committee is thus a difficult task that places significant demands on an individual. The Smith Guidance on audit committees, annexed to the UK Corporate Governance Code, says this should be reflected in the chairman's remuneration.

The audit committee's understanding of the business is enhanced by presentations from executives that focus on the control environment and, perhaps, significant organisational change. Specific areas to consider include:

■ tax strategy;

■ foreign exchange hedging policy;

■ the risk assessment and control process;

■ an evaluation of past capital projects.

This last exercise is a valuable one for the business as it looks at significant capital expenditure and compares the outcome with what had been planned. It is not just another financial exercise: it will reveal strengths and weaknesses in project management and help build a bank of knowledge to improve decision-making. It's vital that lessons are learnt from the process. Again, a spirit of openness will be helpful: executives should face up to honest mistakes; this is not the time for self-justification or defensiveness.

The internal audit team will have an annual approved work plan for the year ahead. Audit reports are shared with the audit committee, and dates are agreed for implementing recommendations. The audit committee can learn a lot from the organisation's responses to the recommendations. Defensiveness may point to further weaknesses in the control environment, or indifference by the staff concerned.

Agreed actions should be monitored by the committee and, where important recommendations have not been implemented to time, the executives concerned should be called to account.

The internal audit plan should complement work by the external auditor so that duplication is avoided and so that the external auditor can rely on work by the internal auditor.

Risk committee

Role

As the introduction made clear, some larger companies choose to have a separate committee to handle the risk review and management processes described above. The crucial point here is that they don't do so in the belief that the topic of risk can be sidelined or 'ghettoised' but because they want to enhance the control environment.

As already indicated, risk assessment and control is an important area for the board, its sub-committees and for the executive too. If risk management is deemed to be a 'separate' issue that can be handled in a silo, then the process is limited and more akin to box-ticking. Risk management must be an important part of the management of the organisation. The process must be embedded in the psyche and practice of management.

Terms of reference

At the outset, the risk committee must be clear about its responsibilities and its role in governance. Its terms of reference must specify the following:

1. Membership: the expected membership must be set out; the names of the chairman and the current members and their terms of office must be stated. (Membership should be broadly based and not over-burdened by those with a financial background.)

2. The secretary and support for the membership.

3. The number for a quorum.

4. Frequency of meetings.

5. Notice of meetings and the documents expected to support the agenda.

6. Minutes of the meeting and the fact that these will be sent to the full board for circulation.

7. Duties, including assuring that:

   – the management of each high-level risk has been assigned to the right individual;

- each high-level risk is being monitored and reported to the board as well as being shared with the audit committee;

- there is a rigorous system for scanning the environment for new risks and responding to unexpected ones;

- risk assessment and control is embedded in the decision-making of the company.

If the committee is to fulfil the obligations of its terms of reference, there must be a process that:

■ identifies the risks in the business;

■ evaluates their impact;

■ assesses the probability of the event happening;

■ grades the risks.

Embedding risk assessment in the organisation

Effective risk control goes beyond compliance. It is not 'bolted on' as a superstructure: it is part of the everyday management of the business or organisation.

Even where the exercise to 'tick the governance box' is diligently carried out and reviewed during the year it means little without the culture to support it. But how do you embed risk assessment and control in the organisation? Here are a few pointers.

■ Risk control starts with, and should be aligned with, leadership and strategy. The direction the company has chosen must be assessed for risk; each risk must be identified and graded. As the strands of the strategy unfold, they will need to be assessed in the same way.

■ The broader environment in which the company trades should be annually assessed; the risks that have grown should be identified; so should those that have receded. The result may be a new 'pecking order' of risks.

■ 'Sensing mechanisms' for changes in the broader environment make risk management more effective; companies are more resilient if they can act on early warning signs of increases to risk profiles.

- The subject of risk should feature on the agenda of the management committee each quarter, enabling the management of the high-level risks to be regularly reviewed and the impact of any newly discovered ones to be regularly assessed.

- Individual operating boards should follow the same risk management steps as the group board.

- The risks of capital projects should be routinely examined; project managers should be especially pragmatic about executional risk.

- The audit committee should be the champion of risk assessment and control.

Ernst & Young in its 2009 business risk report divides the risks into four main domains: financial, compliance, operations and strategic. Of course, within such broad categories there are subsets and I have listed these in Box 5.5.

Box 5.5 Top 10 risks for global business

Financial, includes:

- impact of recession;

- ability to get funds.

Compliance, includes:

- regulation across the entire business;

- compliance to specifically imposed regulations such as those under supervision of the FSA.

Operations, includes:

- addressing the cost base;

- possible redundancy of the business model;

- managing the talent;

- ■ reputational risk;

- ■ managing major projects successfully.

Strategic, includes:

- ■ non-traditional entrants;

- ■ radical greening;*

- ■ executing alliances and transactions.

From the interviews by Ernst & Young, the ranking of the top 10 2009 business risks across all sectors for international firms was as follows (2008 positions are shown in parentheses):

1. The credit crunch (2)

2. Regulation and compliance (1)

3. Deepening recession (new)

4. Radical greening* (9)

5. Non-traditional entrants (16)

6. Cost cutting (8)

7. Managing talent (11)

8. Alliances and transactions (7)

9. Business model redundancy (new)

10 Reputation risks (new)

* The impact of radical environmental standards on a business's or country's ability to compete.

Source: The 2009 Ernst & Young business risk report

Summary

The UK Corporate Governance Code prescribes three subsets of the main board – the audit, nomination and remuneration committees. The requirements of the Code are clear that the permanent members of these committees should be non-executive directors, with executives invited to attend when necessary. (In smaller companies, the work of these committees is often absorbed into the total programme for the board, with all members participating.) Each committee works to terms of reference, and these should be clearly laid down and regularly reviewed.

We have seen the increasing importance of understanding the risks in the business and ensuring that a proper process is in place for this. Many, especially larger companies, will establish a separate risk committee.

Risk is not necessarily negative, and indeed profits are often the reward for risk-taking. The key point is that the company needs to understand the risks implicit in the strategy and make sure they are compatible with the risk appetite and not disproportionate to the potential rewards. It is for this reason that the risk process needs to start with the strategy process and be an important part of decision-making across the business.

The audit committee has a pivotal role in governance and in providing assurance to the board. Its work is inextricably linked to risk assessment and control and can help optimise the value of projects.

Non-executive directors need to give a substantial and increasing amount of time to the work of the key committees such as audit, risk and remuneration. Organisations need to consider carefully the fees paid to the chairmen of these important committees.

Building Effectiveness

The world we live in

We live in an imperfect world – or at least in a world made imperfect by some of its inhabitants. Many of the business leaders I speak to feel frustrated by today's environment and question whether they can derive the desired degree of satisfaction from their roles.

Elements of society take great delight in exposing the feet of clay of worthy institutions or those leading them. Self-interested elements of the media thrive on the negative, on sensational stories that generate more heat than light.

The antipathy of the public and the press towards business often seems matched by that of the legislators, who thrust yet more rules and regulations on already overburdened organisations. The Companies Act 2006, meant to consolidate and simplify preceding laws, is still the longest piece of legislation on the UK statute book. While Section 172 spells out directors' duties in some detail, it's far from the last or only word: the Health and Safety at Work Act 1974, the Corporate Manslaughter and Corporate Homicide Act 2007, the Insolvency Act 1986, the Bribery Act 2010 and the Sarbanes-Oxley Act 2002, are among those pieces of legislation that also affect the role of director.

It is, though, all too easy to blame external factors for the increased pressures and constraints. In some ways, business has been its own worst enemy. Through financial failure, malfeasance, or simply by being asleep on their watch, directors have let down themselves and their shareholders and stakeholders. The media did not make up Robert Maxwell. And they did not invent the debacles that were Enron, WorldCom, Tyco, Satyam and Parmalat; or tragedies such as the Hatfield rail crash in the UK, where management negligence led to the loss of lives.

The recent credit crunch and associated failures of once proud financial institutions have thrown up rogues and criminals who defrauded, and leaders who seemed not to understand or care about the risks their companies had assumed. The cast of the guilty reside around the world; and trade and income have contracted around the world, directly affecting people and communities.

Strategic failures

In addition to the spectacular scandals that have hit the headlines over recent years are many more failures where significant shareholder value has been lost through flawed or poorly executed strategy. A Booz Allen study of 1,200 firms, each with a market capitalisation of $1 billion or more, found that:

■ more shareholder value has been wiped out by mismanagement and poor strategy execution than by all the worldwide corporate scandals;

■ among the 360 worst firms, 87 per cent of the lost value was due to 'strategic mishaps';

■ only 13 per cent of lost value was due to regulatory compliance failures.

Booz Allen concluded that codes such as Sarbanes-Oxley in the US are really no more than quality-control mechanisms. They do nothing to protect strategic and executional elements of the business.

The Sarbanes-Oxley Act and the UK Corporate Governance Code have been put in place to give assurance to the public and to stakeholders and to improve transparency. The irony is that some companies are now so preoccupied with ticking boxes and minimising the risks of being sued that *focus on building value through the right strategy and right ethos has been lost*. It seems to me that trying to repair damage from breaches in professional standards or failures of integrity through application of a code is a bit like repairing the broken hinges on the stable door when the horse is long gone!

Trust has been diminished. And it will take more than a box-ticking approach to governance to rebuild it.

Reasons for low trust

The effect of corporate scandals, such as those mentioned above, has been to give the whole of business a bad name. With every company that unravels, the public becomes a little more cynical, trusts a little less. Trust has also been eroded by:

▪ Executive greed – a number of top executives have, over the years, received rewards wildly disproportionate to the value they've created and to the pay increases that have been awarded to more junior staff.

▪ Executive reward for failure – public confidence is lost if large bonuses are paid when the company has not progressed or if large payments are made when an executive is removed from office.

▪ Failure to reflect risk as an important part of strategy and in the remuneration 'at risk' for senior people.

▪ 'Spin' – the refusal to 'straight talk', perceived to be prevalent among politicians, has arguably made the public more cynical about leaders in all walks of life.

▪ A number of cases of fraud and deception on a massive scale – for example, the £38 billion scam pulled by New York financier Bernie Madoff and the 'accounting gimmick' that allowed the now defunct bank Lehman Brothers to keep £33 billion of debt off its balance sheet (see Chapter 12, page 215).

▪ Underinvestment in people – many organisations have failed to spend time on the HR practices that build trust and value.

This last factor is, in my view, particularly important and particularly relevant to our discussion here. It is linked to the recent and current preoccupation with compliance and codes – in many organisations, *the human resource function has receded into the background while compliance and audit have been pushed to the fore.* Perhaps worse still, HR departments have sometimes become so bogged down in rules, forms and procedures that they've failed to get a voice at the top table, which has therefore severely compromised the contribution they could make.

In both the US and the UK, there is strong evidence that the psychological contract between worker and employer has been broken. Results from three separate surveys in the US, recorded by the management guru Stephen M R Covey, showed that:

■ only 51 per cent of employees have trust and confidence in senior management;

■ only 36 per cent of employees believe their leaders act with integrity and honesty;

■ 76 per cent of employees observed illegal or unethical conduct at work over a 12-month period.

A British report by the Council for Excellence in Management and Leadership (CEML) is similarly depressing. In summary: only 11 per cent of leaders are deemed to be inspiring by their staff; and one third of all managers and half of junior managers rate leadership in their organisation as poor – with the public sector recording the worst scores.

Building blocks of better performance

Organisations need to place trust high on their agendas if they're to deliver value to their shareholders over the long term and make the greatest possible contribution to society.

All organisations will perform better if they're clear about their vision, mission and values. These are the building blocks of effectiveness.

Vision and mission statements are often criticised for being vague or for having limited value. Although they're ultimately only as effective as the strategy and action plans that support them, to dismiss them as imprecise is to fail to understand their motivational value.

Some companies will talk about their *purpose* rather than their vision; they will give a central, motivational reminder of why the organisation exists. Hewlett Packard, for example, sees its purpose as 'to be respected by our customers, our people and society'.

Vision, mission and strategy are interdependent. *Without a clear idea of the destination, the strategy of the organisation has limited meaning.*

Values set out the behaviours expected of employees in an organisation. They are the style, the character and the philosophy of the organisation: its *ethos*. A clear idea of values is very important in organisations where decisions are delegated as close as possible to the point of impact.

Getting the *right people* in the *right role* through effective recruitment techniques will deliver results. But people need to be challenged if they're to find their work stimulating and rewarding (see Table 6.4 on page 125). Evidence suggests that one of the greatest motivators for the talent in an organisation is the ability to grow and develop, to use initiative and judgment within clearly defined boundaries. To make the right decisions, people will need to have as their frame of reference the values of the organisation.

Values are not vague notions held in the locker of good processes for the sake of political correctness. They are an invaluable aid to the right behaviour. More than that, for the ethical director, they're consistent or compatible with their own personal values.

There is an increasing trend in the boardrooms of the western world to have sensing and monitoring systems that test whether values are embedded in the organisation. (See Chapter 1, under 'Testing the statement of values'.)

Strategy must be communicated effectively, and clear, supportive objectives must be given to the staff. In the best organisations, appraisals are an essential part of the vision, mission and values mix.

Trust enhances value

When there is mutual trust between members of an organisation, things happen more quickly and more cost-effectively. When there is mutual trust and a clear focus and purpose, and an effective system for delivery, an organisation creates optimum value for its shareholders.

High levels of trust lead to high morale, which in turn makes it easier to recruit, motivate and retain the best people, which in turn improves performance. The 'high-trust organisation' therefore develops a virtuous circle of value; it satisfies shareholders and stakeholders and the communities in which it operates.

Understanding trust

The most comprehensive approach to understanding trust is found in Rebecca R Merrill's and Stephen M R Covey's 2006 book, *The Speed of Trust*. Covey talks about the five waves of trust – the five levels or contexts in which we establish trust.

The first wave is *self-trust* or confidence and the ability we have to demonstrate our own trustworthiness and to inspire trust in others.

The second is *relationship trust*, building and maintaining trust with others.

Third is *organisational trust* – how leaders can generate trust to make the organisation more cohesive and effective.

Fourth is *market trust* – the reputation of the individual or a brand or the organisation itself.

The fifth wave is *societal trust*, the value the organisation creates by making a broader contribution or giving back to society.

Covey's approach is a very useful reminder of the dimensions and far-reaching nature of trust.

Whichever dimension we concentrate on, we should be clear that we will be judged on our actions and not our words. Words are useful pointers to or a precursor of behaviour but their meaning must be embedded in our every action. Hypocrisy and inconsistency destroy trust. Openness within an organisation enhances trust, aids communication and improves performance. It's easy to set down and publish our values in a booklet; more difficult to follow them in practice. An organisation's values must be reflected in decision-making at every level.

I want to spend time in this chapter looking at the personal skills individuals need to develop trust and be more effective in the workplace.

Trust and integrity

Warren Buffett has said he looked for three things when he hired people: personal integrity, intelligence and a high energy level. He emphasised the first as the most important.

Employers wishing to follow his advice should note that you do not have to rely on the CV or résumé, or on your subjective judgment during the interview. There are objective measures that can give greater certainty of a candidate's suitability and highlight the areas where more information will be needed. Good psychometric tests have been developed for integrity, where consistency of responses can be verified.

A useful starting point is to understand what the word 'integrity' means. The literal definition is helpful: integrity is a state of completeness, wholeness and *unbrokenness*. It is about *deeply held principles and beliefs*. It is not a rules-based model, and it cannot be captured in the depths of corporate manuals or governance procedures. It is about having a personal code and a set of values that don't break or disintegrate under pressure.

We need to demonstrate integrity because if we don't, reputation, our most valuable resource, is weak. Integrity is not about words and lofty ideals. It is about our actions and the *pattern of consistency* that we can find in them. It is the opposite of duplicity; it is about being open and transparent. Integrity, in other words, is synonymous with trustworthiness.

Trust is at its highest when there is a spirit of openness and where challenge is invited. Integrity and hubris do not go together; leaders should have no difficulty in sharing goals and the progress towards them, in listening to and accepting, where appropriate, input from all levels. In this environment, the team will implement agreed actions effectively, efficiently and enthusiastically.

Directors are in a prime position to create an organisational environment where integrity is the primary value. They do this by leading by example. Lofty words and powerful speeches to the workforce are simply a noisy gong unless directors live by them.

Basing a culture on integrity builds reputation, and this is a cornerstone of personal and organisational effectiveness. Leaders will spend time ensuring they have the right ethical standards for the company and that they have a reference framework to assess at board level that they are being maintained. The key barometers include employee feedback, evidence from the whistle-blowing process and the way decisions are made at operational level. The importance of spending time at every site cannot be over-emphasised.

Skills and self-awareness

To build trust and confidence among followers and their peer group, a person needs not only integrity but also competence. This makes an objective assessment of the skills set of the individual against the requirements of the job essential. In the best organisations, the competencies of each individual are reviewed annually against the needs of their role, and development plans are drawn up and implemented to address any shortfalls.

In my experience, the employee who undertakes a personal review, ahead of development discussions, has the advantage. The personal review must, however, be pragmatic; early on in a career it can tend to revert to wishful thinking. The analysis will need to review the technical skills required now and for future promotion, broader competencies such as strategic knowledge, communication skills, ability to influence, track record of delivery, and personality.

A simple self-awareness checklist is set out in Box 6.1.

Box 6.1
Self-awareness checklist

1.
What is my preferred style of working?
What are the positive aspects of this?
What are the negatives?
What actions do I need to take?

2.

How much do I really know about:
- the industry (*or wider voluntary sector in the case of a charity*);
- the organisation;
- the products;
- technology and processes;
- customers;
- competitors;
- the drivers of value?

3.

What is my level of understanding of external factors that affect my current role?
Am I curious?
Do I search out new trends that might have an impact on my role?

4.

How deep and how extensive is my professional knowledge?
Have I kept up to date?
How do I rate against my peers inside and outside the current employer?

5.

What progress have I made in personal learning and development over the past 12 months? (*Give specific examples.*)

6.

How are my relations with:
- superiors;
- subordinates;
- peers;
- networks?
Do I work well as a team member?

Have I authenticated these views through 360 degree feedback?

To build trust at the personal level, we need to know ourselves and be prepared to develop the areas where improvement is needed. *Learning is continuous, no matter what level we have reached in an organisation.*

Directors, too, have a need to regularly refresh their knowledge and skills. In other professions there is a requirement to devote a minimum number of hours to professional development over a year. Those directors who have qualified with the IoD's chartered director programme are required to record their professional development hours to maintain their C.Dir. accreditation. Yet in many board surveys, directors seem resistant to a formal approach to training and development. It is almost as if they think they're a bit above the requirement for continuous professional development. This is a pity, and an attitude that needs to change.

The UK Corporate Governance Code points out that new directors should have an appropriate induction programme on joining the board and should regularly update their skills and knowledge. The chairman is encouraged to agree and regularly review a personalised approach to training and development with each director.

Trust requires knowledge and performance that earn the respect and confidence of those we work with and those who follow us. In the armed forces, the ranks are instilled with the need to trust their officers and, in return, officers need to demonstrate that that trust is well placed.

It is helpful to have a tool that enables us to look at competencies in a consistent, objective manner. Thinking from a prospective employers' view is not a bad approach. Table 6.1 is a competency-based interview rating form for the position of marketing manager. Here, the job requirements were judged by the employer to be:

▓ strategic thinking;

▓ creativity;

▓ knowledge of market research methods;

▓ analytical orientation;

▓ oral communication skills;

▓ the ability to influence.

Individuals can think of their current job description, their current roles and 'duties', and provide the evidence that they would give in an interview situation. Objectivity is the key: the self-assessment should be informed by 360 degree feedback.

Table 6.1

Candidate	....
Date	....
Interviewer	....

Position: Marketing manager

Criteria	Evidence	Rating
Organising/planning		
Strategic thinking		
Creativity		
Knowledge of market research methods		
Analytical orientation		
Oral communication skill		
Other information		

Scale:

5 Well above

4 A little above

3 Meets the standard requirement

2 A little below

1 Well below

Teams

Organisations value teamwork and the ability of individuals to work well together. Team-playing does not stifle creativity or the entrepreneurial spirit: it enhances them.

The effective team is made up of a rich combination of experiences and personality types and, often, diverse backgrounds. More than this, its collective talents are harnessed towards clear, common goals.

Katzenbach and Smith, in their book *The Wisdom of Teams*, see the basic prerequisites as skills, accountability and commitment. Effective teams, they say, are performance-driven and offer significant opportunities for personal growth. One of their most important conclusions is that 'teams strengthen the performance capability of the individuals'.

Understanding how the individual personality types work and their preferred styles of working is essential for team members. There are several tools to help with this, but, in my experience, one of the best is the Belbin team roles. Table 6.2 provides a brief summary of these and the 'allowable weaknesses' in those who play them.

Table 6.2

Roles and descriptions Team role contribution	Allowable weaknesses
Plant: Creative, imaginative, unorthodox Solves difficult problems	Weak in communicating with and managing ordinary people
Resource investigator: Extrovert, enthusiastic, communicative Explores opportunities Develops contacts	Loses interest once initial enthusiasm has passed
Co-ordinator: Mature, confident and trusting A good chairman Clarifies goals, promotes decision-making	Not necessarily the most clever or creative person in the group
Shaper: Dynamic, outgoing, highly strung Challenges, pressurises and finds ways around obstacles	Prone to provocation and short-lived outbursts of temper
Monitor evaluator: Sober, strategic and discerning Sees all the options Judges accurately	Lacks drive, speed and the ability to inspire others
Teamworker: Social, mild, perceptive and accommodating Listens, builds, averts friction	Indecisive in crunch situations
Implementer: Disciplined, reliable, conservative and efficient Turns ideas into practical actions	Somewhat inflexible; slow to respond to new possibilities
Completer finisher: Painstaking, conscientious, anxious Searches out errors and omissions Delivers on time	Inclined to worry unduly; reluctant to delegate

Specialist:

Single-minded, self-starting, dedicated	Contributes only on a narrow front
Provides knowledge or technical skills in rare supply	

Communication and personal influencing skills

The ability to communicate is a core competence for managers today, whatever their role in the business or organisation. Motivating teams, controlling important projects, reinforcing strategy and values, and implementing part of a change programme, all require excellence in communication.

Excellence in communication brings with it greater self-confidence. It therefore improves results. Through the virtuous circle of confidence, self-belief, more experimentation, greater success and, in turn, greater confidence, performance is improved. The ability to communicate is one of the key aspects of personal influencing skills; see Table 6.3.

Table 6.3

Area	Description
Knowledge	Technical knowledge, appropriate to the role Organisational knowledge Knowledge of industry or sector competitors, customers, suppliers
Communication style	Uses facts and figures to persuade Technically competent in relevant forms of communication Listens, evaluates and then responds
Awareness	Curious and alert to new trends that might have application Visible in the organisation
Attitude and approach	Avoids the use of hierarchical power; breaks down barriers across layers, teams and functions
Appearance and manner	Appropriate to the occasion

Directors' attributes

As we've seen in earlier chapters, there must be a balance of skills and experience on the board that reflects the needs of the organisation. There is great benefit in understanding individuals' preferred styles of working, in understanding the dynamics of teams, in communicating well and creating the power to influence effectively.

One of the paradoxes of directorship is that it requires both independence of mind and the ability to collaborate with others to arrive at the right decisions. The wealth of experience and different backgrounds of the directors are brought together and *applied to* an issue before the board. (Effective boards avoid stultifying 'group think' but that doesn't mean their members work in a vacuum.)

The Institute of Directors has identified several qualities and skills that are important for the board, irrespective of the type of the organisation. The IoD publication *Standards for the Board*, last revised in July 2006, lists a research-based set of personal attributes. The importance of each one will, of course, vary by organisation, but *Standards for the Board* says that 'each of those deemed necessary by a particular board should be possessed by at least one director'.

The attributes can be found among chairmen, managing directors, executive directors and non-executive directors. The list is long and should be read as a template for the balanced board rather than the skills set of any individual member.

Standards for the Board divides the attributes into six groups:

1. strategic perception;

2. decision-making;

3. analysis and use of information;

4. communication;

5. interaction with others;

6. achievement of results.

A number of these are components of leadership, dealt with more fully in the next chapter. *Standards for the Board* breaks each one down into sub-categories – see Box 6.2.

It's important to remember that there are objective measures for the extent to which a director has the attributes identified here. The indicators include 360 degree feedback, psychometric tests and information gleaned from development workshops or from competency-based appraisals.

Box 6.2
Directors' attributes
Strategic perception

Change orientation
Alert and responsive to the need for change.
Encourages new initiatives and the implementation of new policies, structures and practices.

Creativity
Generates and recognises imaginative solutions and innovations.

Foresight
Is able to imagine possible future states and characteristics of the company in a future environment.

Organisational awareness
Is aware of the organisation's strengths and weaknesses and of the likely impact of decisions on them.

Perspective
Rises above the immediate problem or situation and sees the wider issue and implications.
Is able to relate disparate facts and see all relevant relationships.

Strategic awareness
Is aware of the various factors that determine the company's opportunities and threats (for example, shareholder, stakeholder, market, technological, environmental and regulatory factors).

Decision-making

Critical faculty
Probes the facts, challenges assumptions, identifies advantages and disadvantages of proposals, provides counter-arguments, ensures discussions are pertinent.

Decisiveness
Shows a readiness to take decisions and take action in the time-frame needed.

Judgment
Makes sensible decisions or recommendations by weighing evidence; considers reasonable assumptions, the ethical dimension and factual information.

Analysis and the use of information

Consciousness of detail
Insists that sufficiently detailed and reliable information, appropriate to the decision being taken, is considered, evaluated and tabled.

Eclecticism
Systematically seeks out all relevant information appropriate to the decision from a variety of sources.

Numeracy
Assimilates numerical and statistical information accurately; understands its derivation and makes sound interpretations.

Problem recognition
Identifies problems and possible or actual causes.

Communication

Listening skills
Listens dispassionately, intently and carefully so that key points are recalled and taken into account, questioning where necessary to ensure full comprehension.

Openness
Is frank and open when communicating; is willing to admit errors and shortcomings; is willing to take on board the views of others.

Verbal fluency
Speaks clearly, audibly and has good diction.
Concise, avoids jargon; pitches the content to the audience's needs.

Presentation skills
Conveys ideas and images with clarity, with words appropriate to the audience and in a memorable way.

Written communication skills
Conveys ideas, information and opinions accurately, clearly and concisely; writes intelligibly.

Responsiveness
Is able to invite and accept feedback.

Interaction with others

Confidence
Is aware of personal strengths and weaknesses.
Is assured when dealing with others.
Is able to take charge of a situation when appropriate.

Co-ordination skills
Adopts appropriate interpersonal styles and methods in guiding the board towards task accomplishment.
Fosters co-operation and teamwork.

Flexibility
Adopts a flexible (but not compliant) style when interacting with others; takes their views into account and modifies a position when appropriate.

Presence
Has a strong, positive presence on first meeting; has authority and credibility; establishes rapport quickly.

Integrity
Is truthful and trustworthy and can be relied upon to keep their word.
Does not have double standards and does not compromise on values, on ethical and legal matters.

Learning ability
Seeks and acquires new knowledge and skills from multiple sources, including board experience.

Motivation
Inspires others to achieve goals by ensuring a clear understanding of what needs to be achieved and by showing commitment and enthusiasm, encouragement and support.

Persuasiveness
Persuades others to give their agreement and commitment; in face of conflict uses personal influence to achieve consensus and/or agreement.

Sensitivity
Shows an understanding of the needs and feelings of others, and a willingness to provide personal support or to take other actions as appropriate.

Achievement of results

Business acumen
Has the ability to identify opportunities to increase the company's business advantage.

Delegation skills
Distinguishes between what should be done by others and by themselves. Allocates decision-making or tasks to appropriate colleagues or subordinates and monitors their progress.

Exemplar
Sets challenging but achievable goals and standards of performance for self and others.

Drive
Shows energy, vitality and commitment.

Resilience
Maintains composure and effectiveness in the face of adversity, setbacks, opposition or unfairness.

Risk acceptance
Is prepared to take action that involves calculated appropriate risk in order to achieve the desired benefit or advantage.

Tenacity
Stays with a position or plan of action until the desired objectives are achieved or require adaptation.

Work-related stress

Work-related stress is a big issue for countries in the developed world. Estimates of its impact on economies are not easy to make. The cost of days not worked is easy to compute, but the opportunity cost of lower productivity is much more difficult. In the UK, the Health and Safety Executive (HSE) puts the number of days lost to work-related stress, depression or anxiety at 10.5 million a year. The annual cost, according to the HSE, exceeds £10 billion.

The changing economic and commercial context in which people work is frequently reported and well understood. The emphasis on cost reduction, downsizing (or 'right sizing' as it is now euphemistically called) and the impact of new technology and offshoring are all adding to the pressures.

The recession and the credit crunch have increased anxiety among employees at every level. The increase in the number of people out of work affects not only the economy but also feelings of personal security.

For those making the key business decisions, the stresses can be acute, particularly if accompanied by a sense of loneliness or isolation. There are occasions when so many issues seem to be pressing down on the director that it is far from easy to cope.

The effective director understands how to identify and deal with both personal stress and the stress of others in the organisation. When the effects of stress are ignored or underestimated, directors and senior managers, in my view, put themselves and their organisations at risk.

Dealing with personal stress

Given the wonderful complexity of people and the different ways they react to stress, there is no magic or foolproof formula. Common sense and experience, however, suggest a general approach to managing stress. Some of the key elements of this are listed below.

■ Get a balance in life. Make time for family, friends and outside interests. Have a personal fitness regime and ensure you stay healthy.

■ Understand your natural susceptibility to stress. People who are naturally analytical may be particularly stressed by deadlines and the unavailability of information.

■ Prioritise. Understand the difference between urgent and important tasks.

■ Delegate where possible and appropriate. Give space for the delegate to perform but do not abdicate responsibility for the final task. Accept support from others.

■ Have a mentor or trusted person to talk to.

■ Make time at work for reflection, prioritisation and feedback from staff. 'Diarise' thinking time and treat it as a priority.

■ Trust your judgment: once a decision is made, get on with implementation. Nothing is more debilitating than continually questioning past decisions; mistakes are learning experiences.

■ Have a personal development programme to ensure new and improved skills, and make sure there's a process to keep you fully up to date on key areas.

The point about the importance of work-life balance needs amplification. For some people in business, a sense of proportion seems to have been lost. The service industries, for example, can mean long hours Monday to Friday, meeting the needs of clients, and then time spent at the weekends catching up on the creative work the week-days have pushed out. This is acceptable in short bursts of periodic pressure, but it should not be the norm. When your job seems permanentlyto have taken over your life, something's wrong: either the workload hasn't been delegated enough (or to the right people), or you need more staff.

To firms struggling in the current economic climate, taking on more people might seem an unrealistic option, but it should not be dismissed out of hand. If the business model, properly staffed, does not deliver profitability then the levers of profits need to be re-examined.

There remain some directors and senior managers who are so busy that they seldom take their holidays, and this, too, is dysfunctional behaviour. Holidays refresh and recharge the batteries and are an essential part of balance in life. Holidays are an important part of the contract we have with those close to us, with our partners and families: we have an obligation to them, too.

Stress in the organisation

The chief executive of a large international company believed that the best way to discover the true talent in an organisation was to maintain what he called 'creative tension' among his senior executives. He would deliberately have loosely described and overlapping objectives; he would put a task out and see who would pick it up and perform best: 'I like to throw a bone on the floor and see which dog gets to it first.'

The organisation did not perform well, there was a lot of friction, and those who rose to the top were all of a similar 'dog eat dog' style. Clashes at the top were inevitable, as was sub-optimal performance. Things were made worse by the fact that this CEO was a dominant, controlling person, largely a 'shaper' in Belbin terms, and his top team were similar in psychometric profile. With this kind of structure an organisation can implode; and, after a major conflict, half the top team left.

Effective leaders understand that excessive, continuous stress in the organisation will not deliver the best results or retain the best talent. While it is recognised that stress can have a positive effect in delivering a project to a predetermined timetable, and that self-induced stress pushes a person to higher levels of attainment, the evidence is that prolonged stress is unhelpful and that deep-seated stress in an organisation will adversely affect performance.

Directors need to be aware of the things that have the potential to create the kind of stress that will damage the business and the organisation and increase costs. Prevention is better than cure.

There is much to commend ongoing monitoring of the work environment in staff surveys. Some of the topics to be covered may include:

■ management style and credibility;

■ people's understanding of their roles and what is expected of them;

■ pressures of work;

■ the effect of change and uncertainty;

■ the potential of the business, the industry or sector;

■ the impact of strategy on work prospects;

■ the potential of people to influence management and the ability to discuss personal issues;

■ opportunities for self-development;

■ pay and conditions;

■ conflicts between personal values and perceived organisational values;

■ personal issues; a person's own wellbeing and health.

Indicators of stress

SHL Group, a leading consultant in psychometric methods and evaluation, recognised the criticality of the individual's personality in relation to their ability to cope with stress. Indeed, it has built a model that is an accurate predictor of stress by personality types. In general, it found certain key indicators of stress; Table 6.4 lists the high-probability factors.

Table 6.4

Highest	
Level 1	Lack of power
	Lack of clear objectives
	Teamwork and peer-group pressures
	Repetitive, routine work
Level 2	Lack of autonomy
	Poor promotional prospects
	Thwarted ambition
	No creative opportunity
	Severe time constraints; always under pressure
Level 3	Bureaucratic structures
Level 4	Lack of status
	Complex problem solving
Lowest	
Level 5	Dealing with the public
	Lack of consultation
	Few intellectual demands

While these represent the norms found in the SHL sample, the relevance of each one will, of course, vary from person to person. It is helpful in stress control to try to identify those factors or events that are the root cause for each individual.

It is interesting for directors to note that 'change and uncertainty', 'delivering bad news', or 'making tough decisions' scored lower than those triggers included in Table 6.4.

Summary

Building effectiveness is not just about getting the basic competencies the organisation needs. It is about developing a high level of trust between members of the board – and, crucially, between them and all shareholders and stakeholders. Trust takes time to build but is easily lost. Trust implies consistent behaviour, to standards set by the organisation and by the individuals within it.

In today's sceptical world, directors have a continuing role to show not only that they act in the best interests of their organisations but also that they pay due regard to employees, customers, suppliers and the wider communities in which they operate. Sarbanes-Oxley and the UK Corporate Governance Code are really only quality-control checks; compliance with them is not proof of effectiveness.

There are good building blocks to better performance, and these include having clarity of purpose and embedding values at every level of the organisation. Individual directors will wish to continually improve their skills and knowledge, and the first step is to truly understand themselves. The self-awareness checklist in this chapter (Box 6.1) is a useful starting point. It is also helpful to pay attention to the team members' preferred methods of working: understanding the diversity on the board will improve its collective performance.

Getting the right people into the right roles requires rigour in the selection process, and the organisation needs to think about the existing director skills set carefully. Box 6.2 lists desired director attributes. An organisation can use this as a template for the composition of its own board, deciding which attributes are essential for its particular needs and circumstances.

Prolonged and deep-seated stress – for example, that resulting from poor management of people – is the enemy of effectiveness. Directors need to be able to identify the root causes of stress for both themselves and the organisation and take steps to ameliorate them.

Leadership

Introduction

Leadership seems to be one of those things that is easy to spot but difficult to describe. You know it when you see it; but what exactly is it?

Many people start the search for a definition by thinking of the difference between management and leadership. Managers focus on tasks such as planning, organising, staffing, directing and controlling; they are often 'back stage'. Leaders influence others and inspire people to follow them; they are clearly visible in the organisation.

Looking elsewhere, Wikipedia offers: 'Leadership has been described as the process of social influence, in which one person can enlist the aid and support of others in the accomplishment of a common task.' But neither this nor other succinct definitions help us to understand the behaviours that need to be exhibited by good leaders. Similarly, the distinction between management and leadership provides only limited help.

What does influencing others and inspiring people actually mean? What are the *practical components* of effective leadership?

The fundamental qualities

As search consultants will affirm, there is a wide array of leaders across the diverse organisations serving the world's communities. They have different styles and, in many cases, different skills sets. But they share the same fundamental ingredients of leadership. Ian Odgers of the international executive search firm Odgers Berndtson sees these as:

■ a vision that drives strategy and shapes the future;

■ a pragmatism that translates the vision into strategic objectives;

■ the ability to assess a situation accurately and absorb information quickly;

■ the ability to set priorities that are aligned and focused, and implemented decisively.

Finally, he observes that 'the best practitioners have a sound analytical ability matched by creativity and inventiveness'. Understanding and demonstrating leadership is of critical importance for the effective director but the same fundamental principles apply at all levels of management in all organisations.

For leadership to flourish throughout an organisation, the ultimate leader must be trusted by those they would seek to influence. As the previous chapter made clear, trust is achieved when the leader is faithful to the values of the organisation, when he or she practises them. It is actions one is judged by, not fine words.

This thought is endorsed by the leadership guru Warren Bennis, who observes in his book *On Becoming a Leader:* 'Managers are people who do things right, while leaders are people who do the right thing.'

Approaches to effective leadership

There are two distinct approaches to effective leadership. The first is to observe the behaviour of leaders, so that we can identify and promote those actions that are seen as value-adding, that will, if widely implemented, help get the best from the talent in the organisation. The second is to examine the underlying attributes of leaders in order to improve the identification, selection and development of leaders for the future.

The ability to lead is essential for those who are, or aspire to be, effective in management roles. It is also at the top of the list for organisations looking for promotable talent or for top executives.

Leadership behaviours

There are five main behavioural components of leadership; these are summarised in Box 7.1.

Box 7.1
Five dimensions of leadership

1. Define the vision.

2. Commit to success.

3. Communicate freely, share goals, insights and approaches.

4. Challenge the status quo.

5. Develop personal characteristics of leadership (learn the skills).

Defining the vision gives the team a common goal. The leaders' passion for this goal must be seen in their actions as well as good motivating words: their support and belief in it must be unequivocal.

The second requirement of leadership is *commitment to success*. The leader will typically need to demonstrate energy, drive and the will to win. Effective leadership, however, is not about blind ambition: it requires the building blocks of success to be identified and monitored. As a New Zealand rugby coach said to his team, 'the will to win is important but the will to practise and perfect is essential'.

Third is the need to *communicate openly and share goals*, adjustments made to them and the progress being made. When leaders see the need to depart from the prescribed course but fail to communicate the new direction to the troops, performance is sub-optimal. In extreme cases, the troops have been left marching to old orders, lemming-like to the cliff top, while the leader has found a better pathway down.

Fourth is *challenging the status quo*. The secret here is to have a culture where challenge is welcomed and invited and where new, more productive pathways are sought. The best leaders are capable of thinking the unthinkable and championing innovations that are aligned to the strategy, whether they originated with them or not. They never dismiss ideas purely on the grounds that they weren't 'invented here'; they don't demotivate young managers and graduates by saying, 'We don't do things that way here.'

The *personal characteristics of leadership* include curiosity and thirst for knowledge; effective leaders draw on networks of information inside and outside the organisation and are widely read. The other key attributes are discussed in detail on the next page.

Behavioural characteristics; attributes

A number of writers have, from their research, listed leadership attributes or behavioural characteristics that promote understanding of effective leadership. Bill Mabey and I have identified specific behavioural characteristics frequently found among successful leaders; these are summarised in Box 7.2.

Box 7.2
Behavioural characteristics of successful leaders

■ Ability to inspire others.

■ Enthusiasm.

■ Flexibility.

■ Intellect, and the ability to grapple with complex issues.

■ Ability to build relationships.

■ Trustworthiness; integrity.

■ Ability to communicate; ability to influence.

■ Ability to delegate.

■ Willingness to experiment.

■ Frankness.

This can be compared with Box 7.3, Howard Gardner's and Emma Laskin's list, based on observations of US leaders. After studying a large number of US organisations and leaders, Gardner concluded that the person capable of leading in one situation could probably lead in another. He identified common threads connecting effective leaders. Some of the main ones are listed here.

Box 7.3
Gardner's leadership attributes

▪ Physical vitality and stamina.

▪ Intelligence and action-oriented judgment.

▪ Eagerness to accept responsibility.

▪ Task competence.

▪ Understanding of followers and their needs.

▪ Skill in dealing with people.

▪ Need for achievement.

▪ Capacity to motivate people.

▪ Courage and resolution.

▪ Trustworthiness.

▪ Decisiveness.

▪ Self-confidence.

▪ Assertiveness.

▪ Adaptability/flexibility.

A personal emphasis

One of the key attributes that distinguish success in leadership is intellectual curiosity. Great leaders challenge the status quo. They are looking for newer and better ways of doing things and ensure that they're aware of new trends and developments. In many ways, they display the characteristics and style of the Resource Investigator in the Belbin team role model (see Chapter 6, page 115).

I have always sought to have people around me who are challenging yet supportive and who bring different dimensions to problem solving. It's possible to turn on its head the concept of *problem solving* and to think about *problem finding*. This is fully compatible with the concept of the inquiring mind that I find so helpful in defining great leadership. Michael A Roberto in his book *Know What You Don't Know* reinforces this point in a very clear way:

Problem-finding requires a certain amount of intellectual curiosity. You must have a restless mind, one that is never satisfied with its understanding of a topic – no matter how much expertise and experience you have accumulated on the subject. You must have the instinct to explore puzzling questions that may challenge the conventional wisdom. You have to resist deferring to the experts who may feel that a particular matter is closed, that the knowledge base on that subject is complete and certain. Perhaps most importantly, you must be willing to question your own prior judgments and conclusions.

To make better decisions in the future, we need to learn from past decisions. Reviews and objective assessments are essential. Lessons from capital expenditure projects, for example, must be learnt – what went well, what went badly, and why. Organisational knowledge is built up from the negative as well as the positive. The same could be said of personal development. The concept of personal learning is very different from that of continuously looking over your shoulder to see if past decisions were correctly made. It's consistent with the idea of personal integrity, explored in detail in the previous chapter.

Sources of authority; types of leaders

The licence to lead is sometimes found in the power of the position the individual holds. This is particularly true in organisations that are naturally hierarchical. The military is, perhaps, the most obvious example, and some of the earliest references to leaders and their actions are rooted in a war theatre. Leadership can also be emergent: the person 'bubbles to the top' or emerges with the consensus of the group. The mandate of the leader is a significant determinant of their effectiveness. I like the description of the types of leaders proposed in R A Dale's 2002 translation of the *Tao Te Ching*:

There are four types of leaders. The best is indistinguishable from the will of those that selected her.

The next best enjoys the love and praise of the people.

The poor leader rules through anarchy and fear, and the worst leader is a tyrant despised by the multitudes who are victims of his power.

What a world of difference between these leaders.

In the last two types, what is done is without sincerity or trust. In the second type, there is harmony between the leaders and the people. In the first type, whatever is done happens so naturally that no one presumes to take the credit.

Robert Townsend, co-author of management book *Up the Organisation*, observed that 'true leadership must be for the benefit of the followers, not the enrichment of the leader'. While we may not agree 100 per cent with this concept, preferring to see leadership as being for the benefit of the organisation, the idea that followers must be the focus and that the leader must not be motivated by self-interest is right.

Followers

Leadership, as the quote from the *Tao Te Ching* implies, is more effective when followers have a clear sense of direction and are loyal and committed to the cause. Loyalty cannot be commanded; it must be earned and constantly reinforced by continuous bond-building between the leader and follower.

James Kouzes and Barry Posner recognised this in their study of more than 15,000 people from around the world. They found that the 10 words most used by followers to describe a good leader were:

1. valued;

2. motivated;

3. enthusiastic;

4. challenging;

5. inspired;

6. capable;

7. supported;

8. powerful;

9. respected;

10. proud.

High-level performance requires followers who are involved and informed. To maintain the high level of motivation that is characteristic of a well-led organisation, the thinking leader is constantly helping the constituents to improve their skills base and to develop as individuals. Personal development is one of the most important motivators of employees of all organisations.

Inspirational and perspirational leadership

Are leaders born or made? The ability to inspire is often seen as linked to personal charisma. Minds are drawn to charismatic or high-profile people who have achieved prominence in their chosen fields. Charismatic leadership is often synonymous with heroic leadership, where the emphasis is very much on the individual and their achievements, rather than those of the team.

Experience has shown, however, that leadership skills can be learnt, improved and mastered, provided there is the time and the resource devoted to this. You do not have to be a born charismatic to lead an organisation well. And 'star quality' does not guarantee success; leadership, as will be clear from other chapters, has to be worked at. Effectiveness depends on both inspirational and perspirational leadership.

Inspirational leadership

The key features of this are:

▪ The leader is very visible. They take every opportunity to see people in their own workplaces and use these opportunities to reinforce values and culture, and clarify objectives.

▪ The leader is the role model and 'symbol' for other leaders in the organisation and is transparent in decision-making.

▪ The leader is the living ethical standard, aware that their actions are always under scrutiny, aware that actions validate the fine motivational words.

▪ The leader is agent provocateur, the non-conformist, the challenger of the status quo and agent for change.

▪ The leader has apostles who are energised and committed to the same cause; they rely on feedback that is direct and unbiased.

▪ The leader recognises the importance of excellent internal and external communications designed for the specific audience.

▪ The leader fights bureaucracy but does not destroy essential control.

Perspirational leadership

Perspirational leadership makes sure the energy and enthusiasm created by the inspirational leader are properly channelled. Without it, there will be a highly charged, motivated organisation that is directionless, that lacks the ability to deliver. Perspirational leadership, in other words, is about action; the practical steps that are necessary to realise the vision. The tools needed for delivery will include:

- a vision, mission and set of values that have been clearly communicated throughout the organisation;

- clarity of objectives that cascades down;

- organisational clarity that enables delivery;

- reward systems that are aligned with goals;

- compatibility of resource allocation and clarity of priorities;

- reporting mechanisms and controls that will enable the organisation to be measured correctly against suitable and predetermined goals.

Successful leadership in practice

Great leaders not only have the power to inspire but also the ability to link their vision to the practical, more mundane tools of achievement. Leaders don't just lead: they also need to manage. This is the point that Ian Odgers makes in the earlier quote.

The leader achieves success through team-building, inculcating a spirit of openness and seeking out feedback from followers. They are committed to effective communication both inside and outside the organisation; successful international top-level managers spend between 20 and 25 per cent of their time communicating internally and with external stakeholders.

The leader knows the power of continuous learning and the importance of refreshing their personal skills. They demonstrate this by placing a high priority on self-improvement and ensuring that management development is a key objective for all leaders in the organisation.

The particular style of leadership will, however, reflect the individual's own aptitudes and strengths. Leadership does not require reinvention: the leader does not have to become some 'ideal' new personality, unrecognisable to those they lead; leaders can remain true to themselves. (Transformation or reinvention could, indeed, suggest a lack of personal integrity.)

Leadership and the board

The chairman, as leader of the board, sets the tone and ensures the best contribution from directors. In addition to this, the board provides leadership to the company through its direction, and through values that are reflected in its decision-making.

The UK Corporate Governance Code reminds us that the company should be headed by an effective board that is responsible for the long-term success of the company and that acts in the company's best interests. Directors, it makes clear, provide entrepreneurial leadership within a framework of prudent controls, set the company's standards and values, and ensure that its statutory obligations are met.

In addition, the board has a leadership role in communicating with shareholders, both at the AGM and at other meetings. Clarity and openness are the watchwords – with the proviso, of course, that detailed commercially sensitive information needs to be protected.

Perhaps the key point to remember is that, as Boxes 7.2 and 7.3 show, effective leaders are far more than figureheads. Directors are not just at the top of the tree: in many important respects, they are the tree.

Newly appointed directors

Thankfully, newly appointed directors today will in almost all cases have a bespoke induction programme. Where there is an agreed need, this will include special elements tailored to the individual and their role.

Executive directors are likely to have strong knowledge of the company and its operations; a non-executive director will need to develop this over time, starting during the induction phase. An understanding of the articles of association, and of the rights, duties and obligations of directors, is essential. In addition, new members will need to familiarise themselves with current issues for the board. Agendas and minutes for meetings over the previous 12 months, and discussions with the chairman and the secretary, will help them to understand the 'live' and important issues for the organisation.

For listed companies, another good source of information is the broker's notes and those of competing analysts. Discussions with the advisers, especially the auditor, are also advisable. A development plan should emerge and be agreed with the chairman, reflecting individual needs.

In Box 7.4 there is a suggested checklist for new directors.

Box 7.4
New director's checklist

- Am I clear about the legal requirements of the role of a director? In particular, do I have a good knowledge of the duties and liabilities of directors?

- Have I read and understood the powers in the articles of association?

- Am I clear about the company's strategy and how it will be delivered?

- Have I received and understood the vision, mission and values of the company?

- Have I reviewed the agenda and minutes over the past 12 months; am I satisfied that the right items are discussed and covered at the board?

- Have I drawn up a schedule of visits or meetings, where needed, to improve my knowledge?

- Have I made the time to talk to key advisers and, where appropriate, some of the key shareholders?

- Is the information provided to directors concise and valuable; does it present a balanced view of the health and progress of the business against predetermined goals?

- Are the minutes informative, listing areas for future action by individuals and issued quickly after each meeting?

- Are the minutes of the main sub-committees of the board available to the directors?

At their first board meeting, new directors will spend most of their time observing and learning, contributing special knowledge as needed. Where appropriate, the sensitive chairman will take time briefing a new director on the context for significant items, or provide background information at the meeting. Given the time constraints, however, the wise new director will make a note of any areas they need more information on and follow them up later.

The first meeting is a golden opportunity to observe the style and chemistry of the board. Networking is an important element, and this, together with informal discussion, often takes place over a lunch afterwards, or, increasingly, in a pre-board dinner the night before.

Summary

Much has been written about leadership by business book authors and consultants. However, it's important to stress that leadership is not an abstract or theoretical concept to be analysed and reduced to a formula. It cannot be packaged into capsules or 'taken daily'; it is a living and inherent part of the director's role.

This chapter has not aimed to capture the concept by refined definition, but to talk about the relevant aspects of leadership as directors go about their business lives. There is great merit in thinking about how followers feel about leadership and what words they would use to describe a 'good leader'. These point to the attributes and characteristics of effective leadership, listed in Boxes 7.2 and 7.3. There must be both 'inspirational' leadership and 'perspirational' leadership if the organisation is to succeed.

New directors or those who aspire to being a director must be equipped with the practical tools for leadership. These include knowledge, understanding and information.

People Advantage

Introduction

Talent has the potential to create value and improve collective performance. A key responsibility of directors is to ensure that the powerful force of people is released for the benefit of the organisation.

From our work for the book *The People Advantage*, Bill Mabey and I were clear that 'putting the right people in the right jobs and encouraging the right development will enhance organisational efficiency, productivity and, where appropriate, profitability'. Two of the most important elements of a successful organisation (whether it's a business, a charity or NPO) are the right strategy and the right people. In other words, right strategy + right people = outperformance.

'People are our most important asset' has become a mantra of leaders. In many organisations, however, it remains unsupported by the building blocks to manage people effectively. That's why I'm including this chapter in this book.

Directors must have a clear view of the processes behind the selection, motivation and development of their people. They must also make sure that the organisation will not be left vulnerable when top talent goes: that succession plans are robust and include both planned promotion and emergency 'cover'.

Key areas for improving the people resource

Before setting out to improve the talent in an organisation, the director must understand how the recruitment process works. There is clear evidence that greater productivity and better performance start here.

Too often, the recruitment process is sloppy and over-reliant on subjective elements such as the interview and the CV. When a final decision has been made, references are taken from people nominated by the candidate. With this approach, only about one in three appointments is thought to be successful. The cost of poor candidate selection is too high – for both the employer and the employee – to take these kinds of risks.

How do you make the selection process more robust? The starting point is to spend time and effort thinking clearly about the key elements of the role and how these may change over the next few years, and from them prepare a job description.

Once the profile of the ideal candidate is established, there is a better chance of selecting someone suitable. Objective competency-based tests and personality profiles for the final candidates will help identify the closest 'matches'. If the results of these are available before the final interview, the interviewer can do a more rigorous job, exploring any areas of inconsistency or asking for more information to substantiate the candidates' claims.

More rigour and time need to be put not only into the selection process but also into the development of people. When 'successful managers' claim to spend less than 4 per cent of their time on personal development and training and devote only 8 per cent of their time to development of the people resource, something has clearly gone wrong.

Non-executive directors are not expected to be HR experts, but they should be keenly interested in the selection and development of people and in making sure 'human capital' is an issue for the board. Box 8.1 is a checklist of areas to focus on and principles to remember when improving HR performance.

Box 8.1
Key principles for performance improvement
Select the right people

- The recruitment process should attract the most appropriate candidates.

- Job analysis is essential.

- The effectiveness of the recruitment process should be monitored.

- Recruiting internally (where possible) can motivate others and improve efficiency.

Train and develop people in the right way

- Raise expectations in recruits; give people the tools (support, training and experience) to achieve their personal best.

- Match skill development to the business needs for today and for tomorrow.

- Draw up personal development plans for each employee and make sure these are regularly reviewed and amended at appraisal time.

Communicate effectively

- The mission and strategy should be clearly stated and widely communicated.

- Values must be clear, comprehensible and practised.

- Key messages, including success stories, should be communicated through a structured programme.

- Individual and organisational performance should be clearly communicated.

Make sure everyone is clear about their roles

- Personal objectives should cascade down from corporate objectives and must be understood; performance against these should be objective and clear.

- Appraisals are for all – from the chairman to the staff members.

Motivate employees at all levels

- Employees must feel valued, empowered to act, and they must be competent in their roles.

- Reward systems must be aligned to the needs of the business and be competitive as well as motivating.

- Employee 'ownership' (responsibility and initiative) is a good thing and should be encouraged.

Create a spirit of curiosity in the organisation

- Always be outward-looking.

- Encourage experimentation – there is always a better way.

Management development and succession planning

This is one of the most important items the directors will discuss. It should rank alongside the strategy session, risk assessment and controls, and the annual budget exercise. However, from feedback that I have received in recent years and from my own observations, it's not given the weighting it deserves.

Where a process for management development and succession planning exists (eg, in larger companies) it tends to be inadequate and heavily biased towards *form*. The importance of having a meaningful discussion at the board is often missed.

Directors have a responsibility to understand the basis on which management potential is identified and how it's followed up with individual development programmes. They will also be keenly interested in the implications of the management review for succession planning. This is a top-level overview for the board that is usually undertaken annually, following on from the strategy discussions. It is built up from individual actions and appraisals but, crucially, is set in the context of the changing environment. Trends and implications are evaluated, as are opportunities and threats that are likely to have future impact. Directors will have some key questions.

- Have the external trends been identified and evaluated in the strategy process; have the implications for skills been properly reflected?

- Looking at the strategy, have the implications for the quantity and quality of the people been correctly reflected?

▩ What are the steps being taken to identify the managers of significant potential?

▩ Are the right development opportunities being offered to managers with potential? Does their personal development plan take full account of the opportunities that are likely to be offered?

▩ Are the 'peaked managers' (usually a high proportion, see Figure 8.1) being given opportunities to improve?

▩ How does the organisation propose to deal with the 'blockages' – people who will impede progress and possibly destroy value?

▩ What are the succession issues both on a planned basis and on an emergency basis? (Special and individual attention must be paid to the roles at the top of the organisation and those that are one level beneath them.)

Model of executive potential

In many organisations, identifying the very top talent is far too subjective an exercise. Inconsistencies arise when different managers make assessments in different ways. Input from the human resource director can create a level playing field for all the people proposed, and having a common assessment template helps.

In smaller firms, perhaps where there is no human resource director, the managing director is likely to have a good, rounded view. Assessment centres where young managers take predetermined 'tests' under observation are a good way of introducing more objectivity (see further under 'assessing potential', below).

There are two important elements to consider: performance and potential. The former can be assessed through a high-quality appraisal process. The latter is best assessed through special assignments and multiple programmes that simulate work/management situations, the results of which are summarised in a form that can be understood by the board and allows comparisons to be made over time.

Set out in Figure 8.1 is the model of executive potential, which gives a good picture of the shape of the talent pool. The key to understanding it is given below.

▩ *High flyers* are the people of high performance and high potential. Here the imperative is to find roles that motivate them, give further insights into their potential and challenge their abilities in new areas. (This may involve some risk taking.)

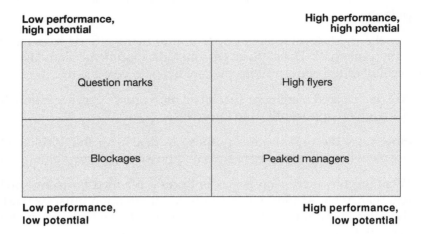

Figure 8.1

■ *Question marks* are people who are not performing well in their current roles but have high potential. Often, the organisation will be failing them. There is a need to ask, 'Are they in the right role? Are they sufficiently motivated or well managed?'

■ *Peaked managers* make up the bulk of employees. They perform well but have little or no extra potential. Here the task is to add to their skills to improve their effectiveness in their current role or a role that is similar.

■ *Blockages* are those of low potential and low performance. They need to be removed from their current role – and, probably, from the organisation.

Foundation for managing people more effectively

We have seen the importance of aligning the people plan with the strategy, so that the current and future needs of the business are met. Fundamental to this is clarity of corporate objectives and then clarity of the derived objectives and personal goals for employees. Aligned to these is the reward system, which should reinforce the importance of delivery.

It will, therefore, be readily seen that the foundation on which good management development and succession plans are built is the *appraisal system*. The approach to appraisals will vary not only according to the needs of the organisation but also the position the person holds. For some people, the competency-based appraisal is best. Here, the focus will be on the extent to which the individual has the key competencies for his or her job; a personal development plan will then evolve.

At higher management levels, the focus is commonly on achieving objectives and personal goals that may have a bonus entitlement attached to them. I set out in Table 8.1 a suggested template for a simple but effective approach to this type of appraisal.

Table 8.1

Element	Description
1. Background	A brief description of the key factors that may have influenced performance for the period under review, paying special regard to external factors.
2. Comments on objectives	Identification of the key achievements in the review period and any not achieved or partially achieved.
3. Management development and team-building	The part of the appraisal that underlines the absolute importance of the manager's priorities and discusses progress towards goals.
4. Comments on overall performance	This is the summary that encapsulates the overall performance and highlights any areas of weakness/disappointment.
5. Comments on style and job competencies	This part of the appraisal is made more objective by 360 degree feedback. Discussion should be two-way and should include interpersonal skills, qualities of leadership, time management and areas where additional or improved competencies are needed.

6. Training and development plans	After 5 above, development areas are identified and a plan agreed that will be followed up by the HR department. The training needs of all will be summarised for the board overview report.
7. Career aspirations	A full career review is best carried out at a separate time from the appraisal, but a brief discussion here is helpful. There should be an opportunity to talk about aspirations (and their validity), along with training needs and the competencies to be acquired or developed in the agreed timeframe.
8. Additional items	This allows time for any other relevant item.

People not processes

For appraisals to be effective, they must be more than token, box-ticking exercises. If they degenerate into mere 'data gathering' they will cause anger and frustration and do little to enhance the reputation of the human resources department.

Regrettably, some professional human resource directors and consultants focus more on the process than the results. In one company I've worked with, the instructions to managers for the appraisal process ran to more than 10 pages, with the emphasis on conformity: data had to be easily document-read into the computer. This was an unsuccessful model; employee development should never be this impersonal.

My approach is to keep things simple but to avoid superficiality. Both the appraiser and the person being appraised should thoughtfully prepare for the discussion, after which the appraiser should prepare notes in the form shown in Figure 8.1. These will then be signed by both parties. Based on the grandfather principle, the appraisal will be reviewed and noted by the appraiser's boss, who will be invited to add comments.

The individual should be at the heart of the appraisal system. And there should be clear recognition that the process is two-way. The training and development of a member of an organisation is a dual responsibility. While the organisation has a real obligation, the initiative should be with the individual. A person's development and career are too important to be left solely to the employer.

Assessing potential

Directors will need to be satisfied that the spotting of talent is not left to chance and that no one is being overlooked.

In smaller companies, it will be relatively easy to have a comprehensive view of the potential of individuals. The senior managers will know their work habits, observe their styles, and measure their ability to handle new tasks.

In much larger organisations, the task is trickier. The most basic approach is for top management to meet with the human resource director and discuss the names that each manager has put forward. Since each manager may be looking for different things, this has the disadvantage of being random and subjective. It can be given more rigour and be made more 'scientific', however, by a sound appraisal system; the evidence of appraisals can be used to *inform* discussions.

Increasingly, given the vital importance of having the right people in the right roles, employers are using tools to make the approach more effective. These include 360 degree feedback exercises and psychometric tests that assess personality and the qualities needed for the top. A more rigorous approach still can be found in assessment centres. These use psychometric tests and management simulation exercises that can be tailor-made to test the competencies that the employer sees as essential for future executive talent. They usually require an investment of a couple of days.

In Box 8.2 is a list of desired competencies for managers capable of rising to board level within three years. It was set out by a FTSE 350 company.

Box 8.2
Competencies for managers of potential

▧ Has the ability to think and act strategically; sees the big picture.

▧ Inspires a shared vision, a common set of goals and lives out the values in decision-making.

▧ Has the ability to lead others, motivates individuals and teams to deliver agreed objectives.

▧ Provides stability and direction.

- Delegates tasks appropriately and effectively, leaving specifics to others.

- Shows organisational awareness in decision-making.

- A team person.

Summary

Performance will always be sub-optimal if the talent in the organisation is under-developed and under-exploited.

'Human capital' should be a priority for the boardroom. Developing and motivating people should have equal 'billing' with strategy creation and implementation. As well as spending sufficient time on their own development, directors should spend sufficient time on the development of others.

Box 8.1 suggests a checklist of areas to focus on to improve HR performance. There is a need for clear personal objectives that are aligned with the overall strategy and for a robust appraisal system.

The board will need to review the appraisal process and a summary of the results from it. The model of executive potential in Figure 8.1 can be used to create a snapshot of the talent at a particular time.

Because an organisation will depend upon the managers of potential for future leadership, Box 8.2 gives an example of the competencies looked for by a FTSE 350 company.

Small and Medium-sized Companies

Introduction

Much of the content of this book applies to organisations of all sizes. Small and medium-sized enterprises (SMEs) are, however, worthy of a chapter in their own right.

Smaller businesses are inevitably overshadowed in the public consciousness by the big household names that hit the headlines, but they make a vital contribution to the economy. In 2008 they employed, according to figures from the Department of Business, Innovation and Skills (BIS), 59 per cent of all private sector workers in the UK and accounted for 50 per cent of private sector turnover.

The shape of the SME sector

The BIS defines a small business as one employing fewer than 50 people and a medium-sized company as one employing between 51 and 250 people.

Within these brackets is great diversity. The SME sector spans very small owner-manager businesses with only a handful of employees, small but dynamic enterprises that have high-growth potential (eg, biotech spin-outs), family-owned and family-operated businesses incorporated as limited liability companies, and growing but relatively mature companies that are closer to the larger public company model.

Nonetheless, members of the SME sector face common issues. This chapter looks at the key areas of consideration. It also discusses the particular challenges faced by family businesses.

Legal duties of directors

All SMEs operate in the same legal and regulatory framework. The rules governing directors (and their equivalents) have been examined in some detail in Chapter 2. For the sake of context, some of the most important points are repeated here.

▨ A company is a *separate legal entity* from those who run it or put up the capital. It has both shareholders and stakeholders and exists in the communities where it operates. Directors owe it responsibilities.

▨ The legal obligations of directors apply whether they hold executive or non-executive roles.

▨ The company's constitution (articles of association) comprises its by-laws. It will define what the company can and cannot do, specify the number of directors and how they can be appointed or removed, and set out the rights between shareholders. Changes to the constitution need shareholder approval.

▨ In the UK, the Companies Act 2006 sets down much of the legal framework for directors. It includes a code of director's duties, central to which is the principle that a director must act in a way considered most likely to *promote the success of the company for the benefit of its members as a whole.*

▨ Directors' duties and liabilities arise under common law as well as the Act, and from UK or EU regulations covering areas such as health and safety, the environment, employment and tax.

▨ A copy of the constitution must be available to the public at Companies House. In addition, directors of limited companies and limited liability partnerships must file annual returns and accounts with the registrar of companies. There are penalties for late filing.

■ Companies must keep proper records, including minutes of meetings, books of account and financial statements. *The accounts must be audited if the profit exceeds £500,000.*

■ Shadow directors, people who have a history of influencing the board's decision-making, can be subject to many of the same legal obligations as the formally appointed members. (*The chairman must make the status of those attending meetings clear in the minutes.*)

■ Directors need to pay special attention if the company is at risk of becoming insolvent – ie, of having insufficient assets to cover its liabilities or being unable to meet payments as they fall due. (This is comprehensively discussed in the final chapter of *The Director's Handbook*, sister publication to this book.)

Governance

SMEs (like all organisations operating today) are increasingly expected to go beyond their strict legal obligations. Good governance is not just about operating within the law; it is about observing best business practice.

The importance of good governance has been underlined in Chapter 3. Worldwide, there is clear evidence of a high correlation between poorly performing companies and low levels of governance. Enron, Worldcom, Parmalat and Satyam in India collapsed dramatically after spectacular failures in governance. The corollary is that companies with high standards of governance receive a higher rating from investors and from lenders.

But is there really a *business case* for smaller companies to pursue good governance, given that they are usually less dependent on the good opinion of institutional investors and have very different ownership structures from the big, public corporates? The answer depends partly on what you understand by 'good governance'. If you think of it purely in terms of box-ticking and compliance, it's a no. If, as I do, you see it as creating standards and behaviours that add value, it's an unequivocal yes.

The next question, therefore, has to be, 'Are SMEs as interested in governance as they should be?' I've been genuinely impressed by the number of directors of small businesses who want to do the right thing for their companies in terms of governance. In the 2005 IoD Scotland survey, 84 per cent of SME directors considered corporate governance as 'essential to their company's prospects'. However, from the feedback I get, understanding of the principle that governance is good for business is not always matched by an understanding of how and why.

Before we examine the role of governance in adding value, we need to know a bit more about how SME directors see the state of governance in their companies.

Governance: what SME directors think

Feedback from IoD members who are directors of SMEs makes it clear that they take their responsibilities seriously and try to ensure that standards of governance in their companies are at a level commensurate with their size and ownership. A special survey of 3,774 directors, from which 189 usable replies were received, revealed a high level of satisfaction with governance structures and control environments. At these SMEs:

■ boards meet regularly (65 per cent of respondents said quarterly or more often), and agendas and board conduct generally are viewed as positive;

■ the board is seen to have the right balance of skills and is not seen to be dominated by one individual;

■ topics such as strategy, succession planning, risk assessment and control, the control environment, and health and safety are all seen to be an important part of the board agenda.

The results also showed that:

■ 78 per cent prepare audited accounts and think they provide value to stakeholders;

■ 91 per cent have channels for communicating the company's progress to staff;

■ 65 per cent think independent directors add real value.

While these findings are very positive, they are no cause for complacency. They are but a snapshot of the state of governance in Britain's SMEs; they are not the full picture.

Respondents to surveys like these are naturally more likely to be positive in their approach to these issues. There will be many other companies that have much further to go. And, importantly, the results are not really a *qualitative* measure of governance. They don't tell us how the personal standards of the respondents compare with best governance practice, and they say little about the value good governance actually creates in their organisations.

Building a governance framework for SMEs

What should be the priorities for SMEs that want to improve performance through better governance? Given the diversity of the sector, there is no universal 'one size fits all' approach.

It's also the case that the governance needs of SMEs (and other companies that are not listed on major stock markets) have historically been relatively neglected by governance experts. In particular, most officially endorsed corporate governance codes relate to listed rather than unlisted enterprises.

To fill this gap, a new set of guidelines has recently been published by the European Confederation of Directors' Associations (ecoDa), *Corporate Governance Guidance and Principles for Unlisted Companies in Europe*. The ecoDa guidance stresses that good corporate governance at an SME is not primarily concerned with the relationship between boards and external shareholders (as in listed companies), nor is its focus on compliance with formal rules and regulations. Rather, it's about establishing a framework of company processes and attitudes that add value to the business, help build its reputation and ensure its long-term continuity and success.

Another important observation from the guidance is that the shareholders of SMEs have limited ability to sell their ownership stakes. They are therefore committed to staying with the company for the medium to long term. This increases their dependence on good governance.

EcoDa defines 14 principles of good governance for unlisted companies (see Box 9.1). Although many of these will be familiar from earlier chapters of this book, particular emphasis is placed by ecoDa on how the implementation of each one should take into account the size, complexity and maturity of the company.

Box 9.1
EcoDa corporate governance principles for unlisted companies

Phase 1 Principles: Corporate governance principles applicable to all unlisted companies

Principle 1: Shareholders should establish an appropriate constitutional and governance framework for the company, eg, in the articles of association.

Principle 2: Every company should strive to establish an effective board, which is collectively responsible for the long-term success of the company, including the definition of the corporate strategy. However, an interim step on the road to an effective (and independent) board may be the creation of an advisory board.

Principle 3: The size and composition of the board should reflect the scale and complexity of the company's activities.

Principle 4: The board should meet sufficiently regularly to discharge its duties, and be supplied in a timely manner with appropriate information.

Principle 5: Levels of remuneration should be sufficient to attract, retain and motivate executives and non-executives of the quality required to run the company successfully.

Principle 6: The board is responsible for risk oversight and should maintain a sound system of internal control to safeguard shareholders' investment and the company's assets.

Principle 7: There should be a dialogue between the board and the shareholders based on a mutual understanding of objectives. The board as a whole has responsibility for ensuring that a satisfactory dialogue with shareholders takes place. The board should not forget that all shareholders have to be treated equally.

Principle 8: All directors should receive induction on joining the board and should regularly update and refresh their skills and knowledge.

Principle 9: Family-controlled companies should establish family governance mechanisms that promote co-ordination and mutual understanding among family members, as well as organise the relationship between family governance and corporate governance.

Phase 2 principles: Corporate governance principles applicable to large and/or more complex unlisted companies

Principle 10: There should be a clear division of responsibilities at the head of the company between the running of the board and the running of the business. No one individual should have unfettered powers of decision.

Principle 11: Board structures vary according to national regulatory requirements and business norms. However, all boards should contain directors with a sufficient mix of competencies and experiences. No single person (or small group of individuals) should dominate the board's decision-making.

Principle 12: The board should establish appropriate board committees in order to allow a more effective discharge of its duties.

Principle 13: The board should undertake a periodic appraisal of its own performance and that of each individual director.

Principle 14: The board should present a balanced and understandable assessment of the company's position and prospects for external stakeholders, and establish a suitable programme of stakeholder engagement.

Further details are available from the ecoDa website: www.ecoda.org

Creating value, not bureaucracy

In all of this, it's important to emphasise that the *essence* of the organisation (see vision, mission and values, below) is what matters. The detailed process can be relatively light. Indeed, the ecoDa guidance stresses that a firm's governance framework should be implemented in a way that is both proportionate and realistic. It should also evolve over the company's lifecycle.

For example, there's no sense in introducing 'big company' corporate governance, boardroom committees or highly formalised procedures, if they're inappropriate to the individual circumstances of the business. SMEs that associate governance with bureaucracy have missed the point. Box 9.2 is a practical governance checklist that can be used to focus on the main governance issues in a smaller business.

One of the key challenges is to demonstrate to stakeholders that you can be depended upon to maintain high standards and avoid nasty surprises. This makes a review of the accounts and the control environment of vital importance. In smaller companies, this is often carried out with the full board, including the executives. There is, though, a strong case for a concurrent review by an audit committee, led by an independent non-executive.

Box 9.2 Governance checklist for SMEs

The key questions

■ Is there a division of duties on the board; is power shared? Is there 'objective challenge' – either by a non-executive director/ non-executives or, perhaps, a mentor?

■ Is there an audit committee led by a financially literate non-executive director that can objectively review the accounts and the control environment?

■ Have we appointed an auditor to give assurance to all stake-holders? If not, can we justify this?

■ Does the board review the health and safety environment at least annually?

■ Does the board understand its legal obligations? Is compliance monitored by directors?

The key processes

Compliance with the UK Corporate Governance Code or ecoDa principles does not, as Chapter 6 made clear, provide assurance against failure. It will mean little without the building blocks of good governance. For the vast majority of SMEs, these will include:

■ a strategic plan – a document that sets out the direction of the company, the milestones to be achieved and the resources and structures necessary for successful execution and delivery;

■ risk assessment and control – a system to identify high-level risks and the steps to ameliorate them;

■ a budget or annual operating plan for the strategy;

■ a values statement that is communicated so clearly to staff that it informs every important decision made in the organisation;

■ an annual succession and employee development plan – vital if the company is a fast-growing business or one where the owner-manager is planning their exit;

- a pragmatic appraisal process rooted in effective two-way communication;

- a management information system that provides regular relevant information on the progress and health of the business. (For some, this will mean monthly accounts and key performance indicators that move beyond financial measures; for others, it will mean quarterly reporting on the state of the business.)

Vision, mission and values

Studies of successful directors in SMEs show that they have a clear idea of where they want their company to be in the future and that they have a business plan to get there.

The best, most rigorous, approach is to commit ideas to writing. The business plan, essential for securing government grants or other funding, should include a *written statement* of the company's mission. Further, there should be a clear vision for the organisation, communicated effectively and clearly to employees and other stakeholders, and a clear set of values. Again, these should be committed to writing.

In setting the vision, mission and values, directors distil the essence of the business and communicate it clearly with the minimum of fuss and process. The model of distinguishing vision, mission and values discussed in Chapters 1 and 3 is a useful way to get discipline here. For owner-managers, the process of setting vision, mission and values can, of course, be problematic. The goal of selling the business within a prescribed timeframe or handing it on to a family member may not be the most motivating for staff. The solution is to have a business-oriented mission and a set of values that transcend any ownership changes.

The owner-manager will also want to discuss the ownership aim openly with other directors and key employees, making sure that there will be a process of consultation and that the future of the organisation's people will be an important consideration in any decision.

Information to manage the business

Owner-managers are usually much closer to the business and typically need less information, less regularly. This is especially true where there are no other significant shareholders or independent directors on the board. However, it is still desirable to review the regular information needed for managing the business.

Set out in Table 9.1 is a list of questions that should help identify and decide the information needs of the business. For illustrative purposes, I've included hypothetical answers.

Table 9.1

Question	Response
1. How often will the board meet?	Quarterly
2. What financial information is needed for these meetings?	P&L against budget and last year, balance sheet and cashflow Analysis of stock and debtors, forward order book
3. What non-financial information is needed?	An update on the trading environment and on productivity and human resources
4. What input do we need before we file statutory accounts?	Reports and statements from the auditor, who should attend the relevant board meeting(s) Review of the control environment
5. What information and reports do we need annually?	The strategic plan, with milestones The annual budget Management development and succession plans Health and safety review Risk assessment and control review The board effectiveness review
6. What do we need to ensure continued compliance with statutory obligations?	Annual review; annual checklist
7. When will we review remuneration?	Annually, with recommendations made to the board

Family companies

Family companies are worthy of special consideration. The challenges they face can be particularly tricky where more than one branch of the family has shareholdings and where several family members are involved in the management of the business.

Shareholders who have no part in the management of the company may well have the objective of crystallising the value of their shareholding and may, therefore, be focused on an exit strategy. Management, on the other hand, may wish to preserve the heritage of the company and, indeed, their own executive roles. Good communication is essential in these circumstances, and a more formal and disciplined approach to meetings and governance may be necessary.

Crucially, family politicking should not be allowed to damage the business. To counter this danger, the ecoDa guidance argues that family discussion forums – such as a family assembly or a family council – may be a useful means of disseminating company information and heading off conflicts among family members. However, if such a path is followed, it's important to retain a clear distinction between family institutions and the formal decision-making structures of the company. The central role of the board and shareholder meetings in the governance of the firm must not be undermined by the existence of these additional family structures.

The most important step for ensuring the long-term survival of a family company is the introduction of independent non-executive directors to the board. They will help keep the family factions in check, and bring an essential outside perspective to bear on the activities of the company.

Set out in Box 9.3 are some questions that will help clarify the position for family companies and make the relationships easier. The following case study of a private, family business in Scotland, which, for the purposes of this book, I've called McTavish Ltd, further highlights the key issues.

Box 9.3
Questions for the family business

- Is everyone clear about the vision and mission of the company; have these been committed to writing and communicated to all shareholders and managers?

- Are there family members who wish over time to realise the value of their shareholdings? If yes, is there an agreed plan for achieving this?

- Is there a succession plan that shareholders as well as the board can commit to?

■ Has the board appointed one or two independent directors who have the trust and respect of all shareholders?

■ Where different branches of the family are involved in the management of the company, are job descriptions clear? Are there clear objectives and an appraisal process?

■ Is there a clear policy for the resolution of family disputes?

■ Is there a clear, competency-based approach to employing new family members in defined roles that will add value to the company?

■ Is there a distinction between business and family issues?

Case study: McTavish Ltd

The background

McTavish is a manufacturer of die castings for a variety of customers and industries. It was founded in 1985 by the then 30-year old Hamish McTavish, who had worked in the metal bashing industry for 10 years.

McTavish saw the opportunity to make money in the die casting business, where the applications were relatively wide and labour costs relatively low. (Creation of the dies could be outsourced.) With initial capital of £5,000, half of which was borrowed, McTavish was able to set up a small operation consisting of an electric furnace and a four-slide small-product die casting machine. He already had a customer, who was prepared to give a long-term contract.

McTavish set up the plant in a small rented shed on an industrial site and outsourced the manufacture of the specialist dies to Germany. Once the dies were made and the machines were set up, the production was automated. The ingots of zinc were conveyed to the furnace, melted and presented to the casting machine. Finished product was cooled and conveyed into packaging boxes.

The company supplied metal valves for bicycles and motorcycles, household goods and small components for motor industry contractors.

McTavish was a good employer who commanded the loyalty of his staff. Soon, the large manufacturers in the motor industry, which had heard about his expertise and the quality of his products, offered him the chance to expand. They wanted bigger components, produced by bigger machines, and they wanted them to be supplied from key plants around the world.

Although McTavish was technically very able and read widely to keep up with new developments in the industry, he was an intuitive manager with no international experience. If the expansion were to succeed, the company would need not only new capital but also new skills.

The expansion programme

In 1997, McTavish made the decision to expand overseas and increase capacity in the UK. He drew up a seven-year expansion plan, which involved:

- a new, larger UK site;

- a plant in Germany;

- a plant in Mexico to feed the US motor vehicle market.

The funding gap was filled by a combination of private equity, debt and family money. Filling the skills gap was arguably trickier. Hamish McTavish had a 17-year old son Angus, who, he hoped, would one day take over the business. It was agreed, however, that Angus should first go to university to read business studies or economics.

It was clear that Hamish needed a right-hand person to manage the installation of the new operations and then to run the overseas interests. Further, it was felt that a wise non-executive director, who understood the industry and had experience of running international businesses, should be brought in. The private equity house also appointed a non-executive. The other directors were Mr McTavish and his wife. Hamish McTavish and his immediate family held 60 per cent of the shares; private equity 25 per cent; the wider family 15 per cent.

The stumbling blocks

During the seven-year plan the business developed, but the learning curve was steep. Poor project-management skills meant delays and problems at each expansion. It was pretty much a case of 'learning on the job' and dealing with the most pressing issues first. There were supply-chain and production problems. McTavish's passion for quality, new technology and customer service remained, however, and probably saved the business.

McTavish drew satisfaction from the development of his business, but was growing increasingly more uncomfortable in the boardroom. Board meetings had changed beyond recognition. They were more formal, requiring papers to be prepared in advance and they were much more confrontational. The private equity investor interrogated Hamish, driven by the need for cash generation and the desire to exit the business in seven years, with a tax paid internal rate of return of between 25 and 30 per cent. The other non-executive director also proved incisive, keen to see proper standards of governance and to fulfil his role as business mentor. Board meetings were not looked forward to by Mr and Mrs McTavish and, indeed, Mrs McTavish eventually stopped going to them.

Angus joined the company in 2002 after a business degree from Heriot-Watt University, but he seemed to lack the commitment and drive of his father. His role in the business was not clearly defined, and he was given a number of more short-term projects. His strength lay in information technology; he disliked negotiation and confrontational meetings with the hard-nosed buyers in the motor industry. Hamish continued to believe that when he reached the age of 65 in 2015, Angus would take over the reins. He put his son's uncertainty in the business down to youth and inexperience.

By 2004, however, the private equity holder was keen to realise its investment and it was clear that the McTavish family would not be able to make an attractive offer. The business had doubled in value over the past seven years and was, according to the accountant, now worth between £40 million and £50 million.

The private equity company had found a potential buyer in a major UK-based engineering conglomerate, which was expected to have significant synergies with McTavish Ld. On the basis of published information, the new company offered to buy out all shareholders at £60 million. A two-year contract would be given to Hamish; but there was nothing on the table for Angus.

The outcome

Hamish was initially very resistant to the offer, keen to keep the business in the family. After considerable discussion with the independent director, however, he understood that the offer was generous, and in the best interests of all shareholders, and that he had no right of veto as to who should run the company.

The offer was accepted, but Hamish stayed on less than six months. The manager he had appointed to run the overseas parts of the business was delighted that (with Angus out of the picture) he now had the opportunity for promotion, and stayed with the new owner. Angus, who wanted to leave to join an IT firm, was equally happy.

The lessons

■ Expansion plans create the need for a new capital structure.

■ Moving from a small owner-manager model is a painful process; the skills required are seldom found in the company.

■ Senior staff may be demotivated by a succession plan of keeping the top job in the family.

■ The children of founders do not necessarily have the skills for the future development of the business.

■ More formality and process inevitably follow a widening of the shareholder base, and more time spent on governance and communication is necessary.

■ A good independent director, who has the right skills and who is empathetic to the business, is valuable in the boardroom and as a mentor.

■ Private equity holders will want an exit route and a high return in a defined period. This needs to be discussed up front, and the implications understood.

■ Private equity houses may actively seek buyers for your business.

■ A majority shareholding does not mean the right of veto.

Taking advice

Running a small business, of whatever type, is extremely demanding. The range of tasks is broad; the regulatory burden huge. Issues have to be faced that may have a fundamental impact on the business – and the owner-manager, founder or majority shareholder may often feel that they're facing them alone.

External advisers such as accountants, lawyers and banks are useful sources of specific information but they fall short of the more general 'mentoring' or 'coaching' role. They do not usually provide the kind of sounding boards SME directors need. The gap can be filled in a number of ways.

■ Experienced non-executive directors can be an invaluable addition to the board. As well as contributing to meetings, they will be available for off-the-record discussions and will provide the kind of input that makes executive decision-making more robust. As the UK Corporate Governance Code puts it, they will 'constructively challenge' the board.

■ The accounting firm can provide valuable insights. The partner concerned should have knowledge of the company, its competitors, the industry and the challenges that are faced. Relationships need to be built over time if they are to provide the maximum value. (At the same time, of course, they must remain professional. Accountants and auditors who get too close to their clients or 'go native' pose serious threats to internal control. This point is underlined in the Smith guidance annexed to the UK Corporate Governance Code, which says that the provision of non-audit services by the auditor should not be allowed to impair their independence.)

■ Directors can gain the benefit of wider experience by being involved in industry groups or representative bodies such as the IoD and the Federation of Small Businesses.

■ Taking a non-executive role in another, unrelated industry can help broaden the director's personal experience and increase their self-confidence.

Husband-and-wife teams

In some companies, the directors are husband and wife. Often, one runs the business as managing director; the other handles or assists with administration. This model may have tax benefits: if the less-involved party has no other income, they will be able to take tax-free cash up to the level of the personal allowance.

Sometimes, the husband will run the business, and the wife will be a non-executive director. In these circumstances, it is important to remember that their duties and obligations will be the same under law.

The future of the business

For many small and family-run companies, change and growth can be painful. Those used to having and running their 'own' businesses can find it difficult to adjust when a larger and different group of share-holders and stakeholders becomes involved. Nonetheless, the temptation to treat the company as their own personal fiefdom must be resisted. A fundamental principle of the law governing directors, remember, is that a company is a separate legal entity. There will need to be an understanding that there are important standards that apply with increasing weight as the business continues to grow.

Many owners of family businesses aim to develop the business over their working lives and then pass it on to their 'heir'. Indeed, children often grow up with the idea, carefully planted and repeated by the parent, that 'one day all this will be theirs'. The trouble is, the ideas and aspirations of parents and children often diverge. Inheritance does not, as the McTavish case study shows, constitute a good succession plan.

Where there is a happy congruence between the aspirations of parent and child, the child should still be encouraged to work outside the family business first. There is considerable merit in the ability to bring fresh ideas to the table, rather than simply copy the behaviours of the parent. In my view, the 'heir' should be sent away for at least five years.

Some family owners recognise the frailty of the 'inherited' management and look for professional outside managers to fill the top roles. This may well expand the company more readily and provide better balance and sub-division of responsibilities. Here, the owner manager needs to learn the art of delegation, an important component of effective leadership, discussed in detail in Chapter 7.

Exit routes

During the strategic planning process, the owner needs to ask what the exit strategy is likely to be. If the answer is to continue trading for the next 20 years, then the question becomes, 'How do we build value on the agreed basis set out in the strategic plan?' If the business is capable of expanding at a faster rate but lacks the management and/or cash resource to do so, further questions need to be asked:

◼ Will the additional cash resource mean a dilution of family share-holdings, or, if debt is used, more restrictions by the lender?

◼ Can new blood be brought into the business, motivated and retained to plug skills gaps?

◼ How will the owner adapt to working in a new way, with new people?

Some SME owners I've spoken to plan to exit the business in a much shorter timeframe, say between 5 and 10 years. Here the focus should still be:

◼ adding value in the time available;

◼ setting and following good standards of governance;

◼ having a management team that is capable of taking the business forward once the current owner has left.

Summary

The health of the economy is inextricably linked to the health of the SME sector. That's why SMEs have been given a separate chapter in this book.

There is real value to be harvested from good governance, no matter what the size of your organisation. Effective directors of SMEs understand how the principles of best practice and good governance can be applied to add value to their companies.

The ecoDa code is a well thought out approach to providing the appropriate areas of focus for smaller firms. Adoption of its principles will mean greater transparency and standards that will, over time, be reflected in the business's reputation.

Growth and expansion phases can expose management and structural weaknesses. Addressing these requires pragmatism and the ability to adapt. Family businesses face particular challenges. Balancing the interests of family shareholders and those of the family members who run the company can be difficult. A clear strategy, clear communication and a disciplined approach to governance will help. Succession plans must provide for the possibility that family members will be unwilling to take over the business or will lack the necessary skills. Pragmatism and adaptability are, again, key requirements.

Charities and Not-for-profit Organisations

Introduction

The idea that charities and other not-for-profit organisations (NPOs) are quaintly amateurish and run by volunteers of good intention but little ability is increasingly outdated. Charities are big business. The 179,000 in the UK (as of the end of 2009) have an annual income in excess of £51 billion.

Over the past 10 or so years, the very large charities, perhaps the top 5 per cent, have adopted working practices similar to those of the commercial sector. There is a good reason for this: those that follow the principles of good corporate governance out-perform their peers.

A focus on good governance essentially means three things for charities and NPOs:

1. the strategy, vision, mission and values to make decisions clearer and inspire employees, existing supporters and potential donors;

2. the tools that provide objectivity for the board and help it to fulfil its role and to measure and monitor the organisation's progress;

3. the transparency and integrity to win public and stakeholder trust and reassure donors that most of what they give goes directly to the cause they support.

Good governance, in other words, is as important for charities and NPOs as it is for commercial organisations.

This chapter aims to offer insights into the practices and processes that will add value and, crucially from the point of view of building trust, improve risk assessment and management. It will be a useful reference point for those who lead charities and NPOs or are thinking of joining them or setting them up. It should not, however, be read in isolation. The principles of good governance are one of the main frames of reference for this book; there will be much of relevance elsewhere – particularly, perhaps, in Chapters 1 to 5. The board effectiveness questionnaire for pension fund trustees, included in Chapter 14 (see Table 14.1), can be adapted for any charity or NPO.

The legal framework

Charity law and regulation

Before they look at the governance aspects of charities and NPOs, the trustees or directors must be clear about their legal duties and responsibilities.

A charity can take a number of legal forms, from a trust to an unincorporated organisation, or a company limited by guarantee. In addition, some are formed by Royal Charter or an Act of Parliament. However, in most cases the legal framework is defined by the Charities Act 2006, which amended the earlier 1993 Charities Act. Under the Act, all charities are required to demonstrate that they have objectives that will benefit the public rather than private investors (the so-called 'public benefit requirement').

Charities in England and Wales are supervised by the Charity Commission (those in Scotland and Northern Ireland have their own regulatory bodies). All charities with annual income in excess of £5,000 are required to register with the Commission. Where there are suspected irregularities, the Charity Commission, which has significant powers, can conduct detailed investigations into charities' activities.

The regulatory framework for charities is tailored to their size and complexity. For example, only charities with annual income in excess of

£10,000 must submit an annual return to the Charity Commission (within 10 months of year end). However, larger charities, with annual income above £25,000, must also submit their trustees' annual report and accounts. The annual accounts of the largest charities, with income above £500,000, must be independently audited.

Just as companies have a written constitution – in the form of their articles of association – charities have some form of governing document, which may be a deed of trust or articles of association. Like companies, charities also have some form of governing body, although it may be known as a council or a board of trustees rather than a board of directors.

A key legal point for charity trustees or board members is that they do not automatically benefit from limited liability (unlike, for example, the shareholders of a limited company). They can potentially be held personally liable for the debts of a charity. However, the Charity Commission has the power to relieve them of this liability in cases where they have acted 'honestly and reasonably and ought fairly to be excused'. This provides charity trustees with a strong incentive to practise 'good governance'.

Further information on the legal position of trustees and directors of charities is given under the sections 'the controlling body' and 'incorporated charities', on pages 181–82. For a comprehensive guide to the legal and regulatory framework, the reader should consult *The ICSA Charity Trustee's Guide* by Jane Arnott, an excellent handbook for trustees.

Community Interest Companies

Since 2005 it has been possible for public interest organisations to adopt the form of Community Interest Companies (CICs). This new legal framework permits socially-oriented enterprises greater flexibility in their operations than traditional charities, and is governed by company rather than charity law.

CICs do not have the same tax advantages as charities, but they are permitted to generate a surplus and may even provide a limited return to investors. It is also easier for them to pay a salary to board members. However, potential CICs must still pass a community interest test. This requires them to demonstrate that their primary objective is to operate for the benefit of the community rather than for the benefit of the owners of the company. They are also required to submit to a statutory 'asset lock', which restricts the distribution of their profits or assets to private companies or individuals.

As of the beginning of 2010, around 3,340 UK enterprises had chosen to incorporate as CICs.

The need for good governance

It is useful to examine the case for good governance in a more precise and detailed way.

Government and private-sector expectations

Charities and NPOs will perform an increasingly important role in the developed economies as the credit crunch and the recession lead to cuts in government spending.

Already, the lines between the public sector and the not-for-profit sector are blurred. Recent trends from around the world show, almost without exception, that governments are using NPOs to provide services in special areas such as healthcare and education. In the UK, for example, government had tackled inequalities in healthcare through Lottery-funded healthy living centres, which serve disadvantaged communities.

What's more, the worlds of NPOs and charities often collide with the worlds of big business and private enterprise. More and more companies are using charities as their interface with the community. Their CSR agenda increasingly includes joint projects with charities or support for specific initiatives within a charity's overall mission. Some companies release employees for community work – for example, helping children in local schools. (US clothing company Timberland lets people take up to a week in paid leave for volunteer work.) Some will nominate a 'charity of the year' and organise fund-raising events. Others will liaise through high-profile sponsorship deals.

Funds provided by the government or by the commercial sector are increasingly dependent upon high levels of governance and total transparency. They are unlikely to be given where there are serious concerns about the way a charity or NPO is being run.

Charities will need to reassure large-scale benefactors and the government, through transparent audit trails, that funds have been efficiently used for the designated cause. They will also need to reassure them that the quality of the board is high and that the key governance processes are in place.

Public expectations

The demand for good governance is also 'consumer' or community-led.

Public concerns about organisations and their leaders have serious implications for a sector that depends on goodwill. Potential donors and volunteers (the public at large) will have asked themselves a number of questions.

▮ Why do we see examples of failures when there is no apparent warning?

▮ How can audited accounts be so far from the reality? How can frauds and misreporting be possible?

▮ Why do charities sometimes lose value through investment policies?

▮ Why do charities seem to spend our donations on a very narrow aspect of the work they've committed to?

▮ Why do payments to directors sometimes seem excessive and unrelated to the value they create?

▮ How do we know that most of what we give to a charity will go to the charitable cause?

Some of these concerns can be addressed by better communication; others require appropriate standards to be set and supported within the organisation. It is clear, though, that failure to address them is not an option. Without public support, funds dwindle, volunteer numbers shrink and charities fail.

Senior-employee expectations

The not-for-profit sector is increasingly hiring its senior people from the private sector. Disillusioned executives are finding that greater satisfaction can be derived from a sector designed to improve people's quality of life. Directors from commercial backgrounds increasingly serve both in an executive or non-executive capacity in government-sponsored quangos or agencies. These people expect, and will be used to, good standards of governance.

The IoD is finding increased demand for its chartered director programme among not-for-profit organisations and is providing tailor-made development programmes for the sector. Organisations that don't recognise this trend, that don't have the correct systems and governance structures, will find it more difficult to compete in the labour market.

Macro-economic trends

Charities and NPOs are not immune to economic fluctuations. An effective monitoring system, one of the cornerstones of good governance, will pick up negative trends early and allow remedial action to be taken. Those that have followed this practice in the recent recession have been best able to protect their organisations and anticipate problems.

What makes for good governance?

The core principles

Good governance is clearly the lifeblood of charities and NPOs. But what exactly *is it?*

Although the precise degree of application and the formality of the processes will depend on the size and complexity of the charity, there are certain key, universal principles. These have been stated many times in this book: governance is about understanding and managing risks, ensuring that there are the right checks and balances for boardroom and executive power, and that the values of the organisation are fully supported and practised.

There are still many in the commercial sector, the government and the not-for-profit sector who see governance as something that they need to conform to, as a box-ticking exercise. This is negative and limited thinking. Good governance adds real value. This applies in all sectors.

Good governance is not just about setting down a framework of rules and regulations. It is about the *essence and the culture of the organisation.* It's only effective when it's second nature, when it's an attitude of mind.

The problems for charities and NPOs

Although good governance is a challenge for all types of organisations, experience suggests that certain governance problems might be particularly common in the voluntary and charitable sector.

■ *Stagnation of governing board membership:* when founders establish themselves as permanent members, it can become difficult to introduce new ideas and perspectives.

■ *Partisan behaviour:* the governing body might be composed of 'representatives' of different sections of the community, each with their own interests; individual board members might not necessarily have been selected for their potential to make a meaningful contribution.

■ *Lack of expertise:* though committed and highly motivated, board members might lack experience.

■ *Poor induction and development programmes:* limited resources or restrictions on administrative expenditure might mean board members fail to get sufficient training and information.

- *Inadequate control systems, performance measures and other means of monitoring the activities of managers.*

- *Sub-optimal performance on the board:* the chairmanship and leadership may need development.

In many instances, governing bodies might consist entirely of unpaid non-executives (in other words, exclude the CEO and management team). In such circumstances, there is a danger that the board becomes distant from the operation of the charity and assumes the status of a 'guardian angel' or advisory committee rather than a true governing body.

The solutions

Problems can be kept to a minimum and risks reduced if the foundations of good governance are there from the start. This is discussed in more detail in the following two sections, but the essentials for this sector may be summarised as:

- a clear sense of purpose and focus on the space the NPO occupies;

- clarity of strategy and certainty of values;

- a clear constitution, highlighting the purpose, powers and obligations of the organisation;

- a clear understanding of the role of the board of trustees and those items reserved for its decision-making, and of the division of responsibilities between chairman and CEO;

- a control environment that gives assurance to the trustees that the accounts are correctly drawn up, and that the risk of fraud or other loss is kept to acceptable levels;

- agreement about the information the board needs to monitor the health of the NPO and the frequency with which it should be provided;

- the appointment of a suitably qualified and independent auditor;

- an annual process for assessing risks and ensuring that they are being managed in an appropriate way;

- where investments are held, an investment policy agreed by the trustees that recognises the financial needs of the NPO and the risks attached to different classes of assets.

Putting the building blocks in place

Standards and values

As with most things, good standards of governance start at the top. They must be an agenda item for the board of trustees; they must be enthusiastically embraced by the chief executive; and they must be reflected in the values of the organisation.

The actions of members of the board must be consistent with the values and the standards of governance of the organisation. Box 10.1 lists the areas that the board and chief executive should address.

Box 10.1
High-level areas of focus

■ Does the constitution clearly state the areas for charitable support?

■ Is the distinction between the roles of chief executive and chairman of the board clear and understood?

■ Has the board debated and agreed the values for the organisation?

■ Does the board have a clear schedule of items reserved for its decision-making?

■ Does the board regularly review its membership, its effectiveness and the contribution it makes?

■ Is there a satisfactory segregation of duties, especially in relation to financial matters?

■ Have management and the board undertaken a risk assessment and control exercise? Is the board satisfied that the high-level risks have been identified and managed?

■ Is there a clear policy on investments and the monitoring of their performance? Has relative risk been factored into this? Does the board regularly review this?

■ Does the board have sufficient information to enable it to monitor progress against a predetermined plan? And is this information received promptly?

■ Has an independent auditor been appointed, and is there a direct interface between the board (or its audit committee) and the auditor?

■ Are there clear procedures for ensuring that all income is banked and payments correctly paid?

■ Is there a transparent arm's-length process to review the remuneration of the staff?

■ Is there a 'whistle-blowing' procedure?

■ Have all the statutory requirements been met?

In many organisations, the level of commitment to values is low. Yet values, if set down, communicated and practised, are the soul of the organisation and provide guidance to employees and volunteers about how they are expected to act. The most helpful sets of values are clear and concise. Box 10.2 sets out a statement of values for a hypothetical charity in the field of cancer research.

Box 10.2
Values for a charity

1. Our primary focus is cancer research. We will be well informed about the trends and the opportunities in this field and understand the extent of (and limitations to) the contribution we can make.

2. In all that we do we will hold ourselves accountable to the highest standards, so that we can be sure we are maximising our effectiveness and reassure the community. We will be professional in all that we do.

3. Our lifeblood is the contributions we receive from the community. We will communicate freely, and treat every donor as special.

4. The impact we make within the aims of our charity depends upon the people in our organisation. All our people must feel valued and enabled to contribute to the highest level possible.

We will provide training and development for them, ensuring that no one is disadvantaged on the grounds of sex, race, or disability.

5. Our organisation must be open and honest, sharing information that will help us be more effective. High integrity is an essential for all our people; and must be demonstrated in our actions.

6. We must be cost-effective in our operations, delivering the maximum proportion possible of funds raised to our chosen cause.

7. Our reputation in the community is critical, and we will do all that we can to enhance it.

Clarity

Clarity is needed to avoid a muddled organisation and weakened governance. The organisational structure should lead to effective and efficient decision taking: it should be no more complicated than is necessary to deliver the strategy. (See 'Choosing the organisation', page 181.) Where the structure is top-heavy, there can be confusion, duplication, indecision and waste – all factors, of course, that alienate stakeholders and potential investors and, crucially, make the organisation unable to do its work effectively.

I have seen a number of charities, from the very large to the more modest, where historical tensions between the central and regional branches and between the council or the board of trustees have posed serious threats. In larger charities, the problem is compounded by the perceived need to have every branch represented on the governing body. If a body is to be effective the rule is: the smaller the better.

The board of trustees needs to be clear about those items reserved for its approval or consideration. There should also be a clear division of responsibilities at the top. The first step is for the board to set down a list of 'reserved matters'. These will vary according to the exact requirements of the organisation, but Box 10.3 can be used as a starting point.

The second step is to set out the roles of chairman and chief executive in clear job descriptions that are approved by the board. It is inefficient to have overlap, and potentially harmful to have underlap of duties and responsibilities. (Effective leaders complement each other: they don't encroach on each other's territory, but they never work in 'silos'.) The job description should, for the sake of clarity, avoid unnecessary detail. Box

10.4 sets out a sample job description for the chairman of a charity, based on the essential requirements of the role.

Box 10.3
Matters reserved for the board of trustees

- The board shall consider and agree the strategy and the resources needed to deliver it.

- The board shall agree the operating plan and the budget for each year.

- Any material changes to the scope of the charity or the direction of its support will be agreed by the board.

- The board will agree changes to board membership and the top executive team in advance.

- The board will monitor and evaluate the performance of the chief executive, and ensure that the top team has an appropriate process for setting and monitoring objectives.

- The board will monitor the progress of the charity against the predetermined plan. It will satisfy itself as to the adequacy and timeliness of the information it receives to do this.

- The board will approve major investments and capital items, and will review the delivery of them against the original plans.

- The board will consider the high-level risks and the plans to control them.

- The board will approve the published accounts.

- The board will consider any major communication programme with the public to ensure that the tone is consistent with the ideals and values of the charity.

- The board shall be satisfied that the control environment is appropriate and robust.

Box 10.4
Job description for the chair of a charity
Primary objective

■ To provide the overall leadership, in close co-operation with the chief executive, in a way that maximises the contribution of the trustees and the staff, and donations from the target community. To ensure that all concerned are focused on achieving the charity's goals.

Specific duties

■ Ensuring that there is balance on the board, with the right mix of skills and experience.

■ Establishing clear procedures for rotation on the board, for the identification of new trustees and for their appointment.

■ Ensuring that there is a succession plan both for the board and for the senior executive team.

■ Participating actively in strategy formation prior to it being presented to the board.

■ Monitoring and acting as a mentor to the chief executive.

■ Establishing appropriate sub-committees.

■ Assisting, where appropriate, with contact with key donors or potential donors, and with any other PR activities.

■ Chairing the board.

■ Ensuring that there is an annual board appraisal process.

Other duties

■ Appraising the chief executive annually, and ensuring that there is a process to set objectives for and appraise all staff.

■ Ensuring that there is an induction and a training programme for new trustees and that they are fully aware of any areas where improvement is needed.

■ Ensuring that the control environment is satisfactory.

Investments

Many charities and NPOs choose to invest substantial donations, for example, bequests from wealthy benefactors. This is not the place to offer a detailed treatise on the management of investments and the various options available. However, there are some key principles that need to be borne in mind.

First is the need to spread risk. Having a block of shares in one company designed to provide both a stream of dividends and capital appreciation is fine if the company outperforms the index, less so if the reverse occurs. Selling the shares at a good time in the market can allow for a more balanced portfolio: the proceeds can be reinvested in a group of companies.

Second is the need to hold an appropriate balance of types of investment. Although equities have outperformed fixed-interest investments (eg, gilts) over time, they present a higher risk to both income and capital. There is always a risk/reward trade-off; the trustees will have to decide just how safe they want to play. The cash needs of the organisation will be a primary consideration. If a life insurance company were providing an annuity or a pension, for example, it would buy fixed-interest assets to ensure the annual liability would be matched by the income receivable.

In the past few years we've seen charities' spending plans slashed due to a decline in income or asset values. Balancing investments to match the charity's needs, and paying careful consideration to the risk profiles of investment vehicles, is essential.

Starting up

Requirements

The developed world is well served by charities and it's hard to think of a cause that isn't represented. Therefore, the first question that any would-be charity promoter should ask is, 'What space will this charity occupy?' The promoter needs to understand the competitive environment and how the proposed new charity will differentiate itself. Early analysis will reflect the appeal of the key aims and objectives, as this will directly influence the ability to raise money.

The size of the fund needed to carry out the work and the 'back-office' support to run the organisation will influence the key cost-to-serve (expenses-to-revenue) ratio, and this, too, will influence a potential donor. No one wants to make gifts to charities that spend a high proportion of their income on support costs.

Once the operating space has been identified and agreed, it is helpful to set down an operating charter covering the *vision, mission and values of the charity*. Vision, mission and values have been discussed in detail elsewhere in this book (see Chapters 1 and 3). Arguably, though, they have additional force and meaning when applied to an organisation that exists to do good.

The vision is the inspiring view of what the charity can become. It is the visualisation of its future shape and success. It describes the reason for the organisation's existence. It should be an inspirational statement that explains the purpose of the charity and how it expects to achieve excellence and competitive differentiation. The very best statements start with a clear idea of where the organisation is today and where it wants to be tomorrow. People and potential donors have a greater chance of being inspired if the statement is short, clear and represents a rallying cry.

The mission describes what needs to be done to achieve the envisioned state. It is a directional road map and sets milestones for the 'strategic journey.'

The values are the glue that holds the organisation together. They are the things that are really important in decision-making for the charity. In other words, they are the principles and standards of conduct that need to be embedded in the organisation.

Formalities

Setting up a charity, like setting up a business, requires groundwork and preparation.

One of the first tasks is to draw up a constitution. Typically, this will describe the scope of the charity and the rules by which it will be run. It should make clear where the charity's main interests lie without imposing rigid constraints.

The constitution is a key document in obtaining charitable status; a key point of reference for the charity commissioners. Once charitable status has been granted, the organisation will need to be registered with the tax authorities so that tax breaks can be claimed. It will also need to choose a bank – on criteria such as cost, service and interest paid on cash balances.

The appointment of an auditor should be given serious consideration. A good auditor will give assurance to stakeholders and add value by making recommendations for improving the control environment.

Premises should be selected on the basis of organisational need as well as cost. While it is important not to spend more than is necessary and to keep fixed costs and overheads down, choosing the cheapest option may be false economy. We all need a reasonable and effective environment for our staff. While I do not support unwarranted cost, I do believe that charities sometimes err on the side of what's frugal rather than what's pragmatic.

Choosing the organisation

Aims and aspirations can only be achieved by having the right people in the right place – in other words, by having an organisation that is shaped to deliver. The right organisational structure is one that:

■ is simple, clear and commensurate with the size of the charity;

■ meets strategic and operating needs effectively;

■ has short lines of decision-making, workable spans of control for the key job holders;

■ is cost-effective;

■ has a clear division of power at the top, with checks and balances that provide an effective framework for governance.

The controlling body

All charities will need a governing body and this, as we've seen, is often called the 'board of trustees'. Trustees of charities differ in kind from directors of commercial enterprises – the great majority will be volunteers and receive no payment for their work – but their basic duties and responsibilities are strikingly similar.

The Charity Commission describes their role like this:

> Trustees must accept ultimate responsibility for directing the affairs of a charity and ensuring that it is solvent, well-run and delivering the charitable outcomes for the benefit of the public for which it has been set up.

Substitute 'charity' with 'company', 'charitable outcomes' with 'strategy' and 'public' with 'shareholders and stakeholders' and you could be talking about the role of company directors.

Just like company directors, the trustees are fiduciaries. They must only use the funds and assets of the organisation in furtherance of the objectives laid down in its constitution. And just like company directors, they must ensure compliance with relevant law and regulation, and prepare reports and annual returns and accounts. The board of trustees will:

■ set the long-term strategy for the organisation and monitor the performance of the chief executive and the executive team in the attainment of the agreed milestones;

■ agree senior appointments and remuneration of the key employees;

■ ensure that the key people enhance the reputation of the charity and live by and live up to its values.

A chairman will need to be appointed to lead the trustees. (See 'Choosing trustees', below, for more details on board composition, etc.)

Incorporated charities

In the past, some charities have chosen to register as a company with Companies House as well as the Charity Commission. This has allowed the charity to incorporate as a separate legal entity. (Charities incorporated by Royal Charter or statute are not registered with Companies House.)

Registration as a company offers the advantage of limited liability; it means the trustees will not be asked to make up the shortfall if the charity's liabilities exceed its assets. This has often been the preferred model for larger charities with more complex asset bases. However, such a dual registration process has added to the cost and complexity of running a charity. Incorporated charities have been subject to both the regulatory regime of charities (as defined by the Charities Act) and that of companies (as defined by the Companies Act).

One of the innovations of the Charities Act 2006 is to introduce the concept of the Charitable Incorporated Organisation (CIO). This new legal form allows the creation of a separate corporate personality for the charity, but without the need for a dual registration as a company at Companies House. CIOs are registered solely with the Charity Commission, and not subject to the specific regulations and reporting requirements defined by company law.

Information for the board

The reporting system must be capable of providing information that enables both the executive team and the board of trustees to monitor progress. The information must be supplied in good time, allowing warning signs to be given and corrective action to be taken when plans go awry. And it must cover more than the straight financials – the board, for example, will want to measure:

■ donor attitudes (for example, through surveys);

■ market share;

■ conversion rates for donors;

■ the effectiveness of charitable spending.

In larger organisations, there should also be measures for employee satisfaction – eg, staff turnover and absenteeism rates – and reports on training and development.

Choosing trustees

Composition of the board

Choosing the individuals who will act as trustees and be members of the board is a serious and important business. The trustees must be sympathetic to the aims of the charity, and between them have the various skills sets that make an effective team. The best teams avoid 'group think' and invite challenges but are mutually supportive, with a good balance of skills and experience. The members should be well informed and work effectively together. The performance of the team as a whole should be greater than the sum of its parts. The points on boardroom effectiveness made in Chapter 1 and elsewhere in this book apply equally well here.

The size of the board will obviously depend on the size of the organisation. The rule of thumb, though, is for there to be a minimum of three members, two of whom should be independent.

Ideally, the composition of the board should be balanced not only in terms of the members' skills and experience but also their independence and non-independence. There are some foundations where the benefactor wishes to have a significant say in the running of the charity and wishes to be on the board. Other trustees are often appointed because they know the benefactor well and are likely to be supportive of their wishes. While there is nothing inherently wrong with this approach, it does carry risks: support and sycophancy sometimes get confused. In my experience, there is great value in having trustees who are truly independent, who can exercise sound judgment, who collectively have wider experience than the benefactor and their 'circle', and who can provide constructive criticism.

A chairman will be appointed to lead this well-balanced board of trustees. Best practice suggests that the appointments of the chairman and all trustees should be for a finite period. The norm for commercial independent directors in a company is a term of three years, with the prospect of renewal for a further three-year period. This is a reasonable model for the not-for-profit sector too, but the chairman should ensure that there is a sensible rotation of trustees. There is great inefficiency if all trustees have common terms and all need to be rotated at the same time.

Skills sets on the board

A fundamental requirement will be an understanding of the steward-ship role of trustees. The members of the board need to ensure that the charity stays true to the principal cause for which it has been formed, and protect the longevity of the charity and its aims, objectives and principles, and ensure that the charity and its ethos outlast its founders/ key people.

At the same time, however, there is a requirement on the board for financial literacy. The trustees must (collectively if not individually) also be able to protect the efficiency of the organisation so that it is run in a cost-effective way and, crucially, so that the maximum amount of money raised is spent on the good cause.

More and more donors, especially the larger benefactors, are demanding transparency, value for money and clear risk control. They want the board to achieve maximum value from hard-won funds. A parallel trend is for a greater proportion of trustees to come from the commercial sector.

The incorporation of business principles has caused disquiet in some quarters, with chairmen of charities claiming that it risks alienating existing and potential donors. The observation I would make is that the remit of business people is not to *commercialise* charities but to help them to operate to the highest possible standards.

Charities are different from profit-making businesses but they have many of the same needs: clear direction and leadership, effective over-sight and efficiency. A diversity of backgrounds among trustees is a strength, leading to better and more informed decisions.

Expect more from your trustees

There is a feeling in some quarters that charities should automatically be grateful to anyone who provides their services for free. While this is, perhaps, an understandable attitude, it leads to sub-optimal perform-ance. It also fails to understand someone's motives for working as a volunteer trustee.

In a small straw poll survey, trustees or trustee directors of different UK charities were asked to give the reasons why they served on a board where there was no remuneration. The main four reasons (from a sample of 20 replies) were:

■ I believe in this charity's work (85 per cent).

■ I want to make a difference (65 per cent).

■ I benefit personally from this contact (55 per cent).

■ I have the time and want to use this productively (50 per cent).

Charities should never feel they should apologise for having high expectations of their trustees. A chairman with the right leadership skills will demand more from those serving on the board and committees of the charity, and they will all be enriched by the experience. This applies as much to those who are executive directors on other boards as it does to people who are approaching retirement or 'between jobs'. Being a trustee of a charity should not be seen as 'second best'. If it is, the organisation is at risk.

A trustee's perspective

Selection should, of course, be two-way. The role of trustee is demanding, onerous and, as we've seen, usually unpaid. The candidate will want to feel that this is an organisation that they believe in and will be proud to work for. Before taking on the job of trustee, I ask myself a number of questions.

■ Do I fully understand the scope of the charity and am I enthused by its work?

■ Do I really think that I can make a difference? Or is the organisation just looking for someone to make up the numbers?

■ Can I give the required time?

■ Does the board provide the leadership required and have an agenda that is relevant?

■ Will I look forward to the meetings and to the information flow from them?

■ Are the professional standards high, is good governance in place, and is the organisation's reputation good?

■ Do I like the team of people and respect their views? Do they find time for fun?

Candidates will also want to establish what their liabilities will be – ie, whether or not the charity is incorporated/a limited liability company. In deciding whether to continue with their role, trustees will need to think about the effectiveness of the organisation.

Table 10.1 provides a health check for not-for-profit organisations. It is meant as a general template and may have to be adapted to reflect the specific needs of the organisation. It has a scoring mechanism based on established norms.

Table 10.1

Scoring		
+3 for definite yes; +1 for qualified yes; –2 for definite no	**Mark**	**Comments**

Purpose

1. Is there a clear understanding of the purpose, direction and values?

2. Can the trustees identify with the charity's aims?

3. Is the charity sufficiently differentiated from others in its field?

The board of trustees

4. Is the balance on the board right? (Skills and experience)

5. Does the board provide the required leadership?

6. Is the agenda comprehensive and appropriate?

7. Is sufficient information available?

8. Does the board pay sufficient attention to its own governance? (Authority levels and self-appraisal)

The management

9. Are there clear objectives, and is progress against them monitored?

10. Are appraisals open, effective and two-way?

11. Are managers selected objectively against the job requirements?

12. Is training available to meet needs identified?

The workforce and voluntary workers

13. Do they feel valued and fully involved?

14. Is there good communication with all sectors, and are key messages fully understood?

15. Does this charity select the most suitable people rather than those who happen to be available?

16. Is there an open culture, where challenge and improvement are sought out?

General

17. Does the organisation allow people to contribute to the full level of their ability?

18. Is there a clear understanding of the purpose, direction and values?

19. Is management alert to new trends and external factors that will influence future direction?

20. Is the organisation seen as a great place to work?

Evaluation: **40 and above** *exceptional;* **33-39** *excellent;* **26-32** *good, but there are areas that need attention;* **19-25** *significant improvements are needed;* **less than 19** *unsatisfactory*

Smaller charities

Definition

Small charities are those with income or expenditure of less than £25,000 a year. They are subjected to a relatively light regulatory regime by the Charity Commission and may file abbreviated reports and accounts, and simplified annual returns.

The smallest charities, with an annual income of less than £10,000, are, as we've seen, exempted from formal reporting requirements, but are required to keep their register details up to date and submit an annual update form.

'Smaller' charities can be defined as those with income up to £500,000, which is the lower threshold for submitting annual audited accounts.

Is there a difference?

In the course of preparation for this book, a wide range of not-for-profit organisations have been approached for their views. The smaller charities had concerns about the cost implications of following what is perceived as best practice.

The key to effectiveness is to ensure that the essential building blocks are in place but that red tape and processes are kept to a minimum. Governance need not be a cost or administrative burden. The founder or current head should decide which things are vital for the efficient and effective running of the charity. Box 10.5 lists the processes that are regarded as the minimum for smaller charities.

Box 10.5
Essentials for smaller charities

- An up-to date constitution.

- Registration with the Charity Commission and the HMRC.

- Clarity of purpose and direction, set down formally and reviewed annually. (A values statement is only optional where there are only a few employees or volunteers.)

- A board of no fewer than three trustees, two of whom should be independent.

- An independent auditor (obligatory for charities with income in excess of £500,000 pa).

- Accounting and legal controls commensurate with the organisation's size.

- A strategy for fund raising.

- An annual budget and operating plan.

- Financial reporting which, at least every six months, compares actual results against the plan.

> ■ Compliance with legal and regulatory obligations, including Charity Commission filing requirements.
>
> ■ Where income from investments helps fund the charity, a formal investment policy.

Some of the entries in Box 10.5 need further comment.

The governing document, the constitution, will have been drawn up at the time of the charity's formation. There will, however, be a periodic need to review it for continued relevance.

Charities with only a few staff often question the need for a formal laying down of their purpose, direction and values. Stating the vision and mission of the organisation not only adds to clarity and focus but is also a valuable communications tool for potential donors. Stating the values can be put off when the charity is in its infancy, but will be essential once more staff and volunteers start to be recruited.

The accounting system need not be complex but it must be robust and allow progress to be monitored accurately. Although smaller charities are not legally required to appoint an independent auditor, best practice suggests they should. As we've seen, an auditor can add value and provide the assurance so crucial for stakeholders and donors.

The auditor will need to be satisfied that all income received is properly accounted for, that expenditure is within the terms of the constitution, and that all charitable disbursements are for the causes specified. The assets and liabilities will be scrutinised so that the balance sheet can be certified as presenting a true and fair view at the specified date. The controls will be reviewed to ensure that they are satisfactory.

Summary

Charities and NPOs make an increasingly important contribution to both society and the economy. Successive governments have placed more responsibilities on their shoulders.

The growth in size and importance of the sector has led to new standards of 'professionalism', the core of which are the principles of good governance. Following these principles will give assurance to stakeholders, benefactors and supporters that the appropriate controls and checks and balances are in place.

Governance demands certain formalities and procedures – for example, effective supply of information for the board – but these should reflect the needs and size of the organisation. Unnecessary process and complexity are the enemies of good governance. Governance should add value to the organisation, not impede its progress. The critical areas that will add value to charities and NPOs include:

- risk assessment and management;
- clear strategic planning and performance monitoring;
- a clear and clearly communicated vision and mission and (for larger charities, at least) set of values;
- careful selection of the board of trustees and a clear understanding of duties, responsibilities and division of power on the board.

For directors from commercial backgrounds, moving into the not-for-profit sector can be something of a 'culture shock'. This, however, should not be allowed to overshadow the fact that they can make a real difference as well as benefit from the experience.

The National Health Service

Introduction

Governments have been keen to introduce private-sector discipline to public-sector organisations. Nonetheless, the challenges for directors working in these organisations remain great.

Interference from officials and politicians means decision-making can be painfully slow. Targets set by government may be contradictory or seem to fly in the face of commercial common sense. And, when things go wrong, the law of 'spin' means the board, rather than the minister and their aides, is the first to be blamed.

This may sound like a daunting (even alien) environment for company directors, but there is a real need for their expertise, patience and determination to be used for the benefit of the community. The principles for success are really quite straightforward and differ only in a small way from the principles required by a commercial organisation.

This chapter looks at the challenges of building an effective board in the National Health Service (NHS). Although NHS trust boards are nothing new, their importance has significantly increased since the introduction of Foundation Trusts. Established by the Health and Social Care (Community Health and Standards) Act 2003, these new organisational entities represent a major step in the process of decentralising the National Health Service, and there are now more than 120 of them in the UK. The thinking behind them is gradually to replace much of the previous 'command and control' role of central government, and thereby increase efficiency and accountability. In order to achieve this objective, Foundation Trusts are crucially dependent on the operation of effective boards.

NHS Foundation Trusts: the regulatory environment

Governance structure

The position of Foundation Trusts within the governance structure of the NHS in England is shown in Figure 11.1.

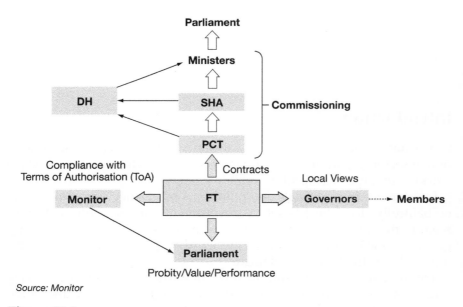

Source: Monitor

Figure 11.1

Their overall priorities are defined by the Department of Health (which is accountable to Parliament), and implemented through 10 Strategic Health Authorities (SHAs). Within each SHA, Primary Care Trusts (PCTs) commission healthcare services from a variety of providers. These include acute trusts and Foundation Trusts (FTs).

Foundation Trusts enjoy significant autonomy over financial and strategic decision-making. In contrast to acute trusts, they can make and retain surpluses, and any proceeds from asset sales. They are also able to borrow commercially, and could potentially be declared insolvent.

Foundation Trusts are often large and sophisticated organisations that employ several thousand people. A typical trust is likely to be responsible for annual expenditure of hundreds of millions of pounds. The governance structure of Foundation Trusts also includes a framework of local accountability through the involvement of local 'members' and a board of governors.

NHS Foundation Trusts have a dual board structure consisting of the board of governors and the board of directors. The board of governors is elected by the members of the trust (who are recruited from the local healthcare community). It is, in turn, responsible for appointing the chairman and non-executive directors of the board of directors. The chairman of the trust leads both boards.

A number of regulatory bodies oversee the activities of NHS Foundation Trusts. Monitor – the independent regulator of Foundation Trusts – is responsible for the initial authorisation of Foundation Trusts, and thereafter defines many of the principles that guide how they operate. From the perspective of healthcare standards, Foundation Trusts are regulated by the Care Quality Commission. Both of these regulators have significant powers over trust boards, including the ability to replace them and their individual members. Consequently, although the boards of Foundation Trusts enjoy greater autonomy than earlier generations of NHS trusts, they must still work within a framework of centrally directed regulation and monitoring.

Governance code

Developing the competencies of decision-makers within the new legal framework is a major challenge. New appointees may come from a variety of professional and sectoral backgrounds and will not, necessarily, have extensive experience on boards. New trusts must ensure their board of directors, board of governors and associated committees are able to function effectively within as short a time span as possible.

Monitor has developed a code of governance to guide the boards of Foundation Trusts. The purpose of the code (published in October 2006 and updated in April 2010) is to assist fledgling boards (or trusts aspiring to Foundation Trust status) by outlining best practice. It is an essential resource for the boards of Foundation Trusts.

The Monitor code is explicitly based on the private sector UK Corporate Governance Code and is applied by means of a similar 'comply or explain' principle. This principle presumes that the default position for each Foundation Trust is to 'comply' with the code provisions. However, trusts may deviate from individual provisions if they believe that an alternative approach is justifiable (which must be 'explained' in their annual reports).

Key issues for the boards of Foundation Trusts

Many of the challenges facing the boards of Foundation Trusts are similar to those facing the boards of private sector companies. However, based on the initial experience of Foundation Trusts over the past five years, a number of key boardroom issues are particularly worth stressing.

As in a private sector company, the central focus of decision-making at a Foundation Trust is the board of directors, which is collectively responsible for all aspects of the trust's activities. The directors' key objectives can be summarised as:

- to establish and maintain the trust's vision, mission and values;

- to decide its strategy and structure;

- to delegate authority to management, and to monitor and evaluate its implementation of policies, strategies and operational plans;

- to account to – and be responsible to – stakeholders.

Making decisions; managing conflicts

The job of the board is not to take management decisions: that's the role of the trust's chief executive and management team. Rather, it's to set the overarching policies that help determine decisions, and hold the management team accountable for the use of the decision-making powers it's been given.

Directors owe a duty of care to the trust. This means that board members must, wherever possible, act on the basis of accurate and adequate information. Directors should not hesitate to ask questions of management about proposals or analyses, and should seek second opinions, where required, before making a decision.

Directors also have a duty of loyalty to the trust. Where a director has a particular interest in a decision before the board, conflicts can arise. If, for example, they are a supplier or patient of the trust, or if they are related to someone who is being treated by or doing work for the trust, they might find it hard to be objective.

These kinds of problems can be addressed through disclosure to the rest of the board. When a conflict of interest is known, the chairman can take steps to isolate the director from the decision-making process.

Understanding strategy

It's essential for the specific objectives of the trust to be explicitly determined and approved by the board. In a private sector organisation, the objectives of an enterprise are relatively unambiguous. However, a trust may have a variety of social and community-specific objectives, and it's important that directors understand the basis on which the success or failure of the trust will be evaluated.

Strategy is always a fundamental board issue. For a Foundation Trust, it may encompass issues such as the specialisation of the trust in a particular area of healthcare provision, or the acquisition or disposal of major assets. The entire trust board should be involved in strategic development. Independent directors in particular can provide a perspective to the discussion based on their experience outside the healthcare sector.

Managers of the trust (led by the chief executive) are generally responsible for initial strategic development. They should present their primary and alternative strategies to the board along with their background material, rationale and reasoning. This material should be sent to the board in advance to allow directors time to digest and analyse it before meeting with management. The board should then thoroughly test management on its assumptions and the details of the strategy by asking questions.

The board may decide to listen to presentations by outside advisers – such as academic researchers and consultants – who can provide analyses of trends in healthcare and alternative strategic options.

Managing risks

The oversight of risk management is a key responsibility for the board of a Foundation Trust. The risks facing a trust may assume a variety of forms: potential categories include clinical risk, financial risk, operational risk, health and safety risk, and reputational risk. The board should understand the relative significance of each of these risk categories to the trust and satisfy itself that they are being appropriately managed.

Boards may get a better feel for the trust's risks by visiting the major clinical units and administrative departments. To ensure that an appropriate risk consciousness is embedded at all levels of the organisation, directors should discuss risk management issues with administrators, physicians and nursing staff. Directors may also request reports on the trust's safety and clinical outcomes record, and ask about the level of professional training among different categories of staff.

The board should have a crisis management plan. It should think separately about the kinds of crises the trust could encounter – for example, the death of the chief executive or a departmental head, a security incident, a fire, or a major outbreak of infection. As part of this plan, the board should identify who would be the trust's spokesperson and talk to the media, and who could take over the duties of the chief executive if required.

Developing an effective board

Division of responsibilities

The role of director of a NHS Foundation Trust is both challenging and rewarding. There's no doubt of the value that excellence at board level makes to the trust's performance. 'The Sharon Jones diaries' case study (see pages 199–203) is based on the diary of a newly appointed director of a large NHS Foundation Trust who, to preserve confidentiality, we've called 'Sharon Jones'. Her story provides a valuable insight into the definition of a good board.

As in a private sector enterprise, the chairman is absolutely central to the effective functioning of a Foundation Trust board. The chairman should ensure that board meetings are run efficiently and should consider developing board guidelines on meetings and agenda-setting. The chairman is required to walk a narrow line. They must be well informed, engaged and alert, and be prepared to intervene when required; but, at the same time, they must avoid becoming too involved in the day-to-day business of the trust (which is the responsibility of the chief executive).

It's sensible to clarify the board's role relative to the role of the chief executive in a formal statement of responsibilities. This document should define what matters are reserved for the board rather than management (see Box 1.2, Chapter 1) and should be reviewed annually.

An important organisational decision for the board is the delegation of responsibilities to committees. The three committees specified in the Monitor code – and those most commonly observed in private-sector companies – are the audit, nomination and remuneration committees. However, there may be a case for additional committees to tackle areas of the trust's activity. A health and safety committee, for example, could play a vital role in safeguarding the trust's reputation.

The contribution of the independent non-executive directors who will sit on such committees can be enhanced by providing access to certain key departmental managers, including the trust secretary and the internal audit department. Non-executives can also be helped by independent external advisers, paid for by the trust. Their over-riding requirement, however, is for accurate, clear and adequate information. If the board fails to provide this, non-executives will be unable to oversee the strategy effectively.

Best practice

The building blocks of best practice can be summarised as clarity and communication. Leadership is most likely to be effective if:

- Senior departmental managers and clinicians are invited to board meetings and, where appropriate, committee meetings, to make presentations and respond to directors' questions.

- Members of the board make the effort to talk to senior members of staff outside formal meetings.

- A trust secretary is appointed. (Reporting jointly to the chairman and chief executive, they will ensure the timely flow of information between management and the directors.)

- Board evaluations encourage honest discussion about what is going right and what is going wrong on the board, and cover issues such as the efficiency of the board's committee structure, and whether directors are asking the right questions.

The role of the board of governors

The challenges

The board of governors of an NHS Foundation Trust does not have a direct equivalent in the UK private sector. However, it can be broadly compared with the supervisory board, a distinctive feature of corporate life in countries such as Germany.

Supervisory boards face a number of governance challenges.

- Communicating with the management board is often difficult, and the flow of information poor, making it hard for them to play an effective role in decision-making.

- The diversity of their membership means they don't always work effectively as a unit, reducing their ability to form a common position towards the management board.

- Their large size can prevent effective operation and decision-making.

The governors of Foundation Trusts should take these potential problems into account when considering their mode of operation.

While specific governors may be nominated or elected by members of the local community, it's important for them to carry out their duties in a non-partisan way. The board of governors should not be viewed, or act, as a parliament of individual representatives for various constituencies. Governors should seek to act in the interests of the trust as a whole.

A collegiate attitude will increase the cohesiveness of the board of governors and this, in turn, will increase its effectiveness and credibility in the eyes of the board of directors. Creating a collegiate culture is a task for both the chair and the governors themselves.

Due to the wide-ranging backgrounds of governors, gatherings that are less formal than board meetings may be the best way to encourage free and frank discussion. The chairman could hold such events each month, between the quarterly meetings of the main board of governors.

Greater effectiveness may also be achieved through the appointment of a board of governors with fewer members. Although larger boards mean more diversity, smaller ones are likely to make communication and co-ordination of tasks easier, and to accelerate decision-making. When governors can respond promptly, they're often more effective in holding the board of directors to account.

Governors should think carefully about the type of information and input they require from the board of directors. Awareness of operational performance issues – albeit at a less detailed level – is central to their role in strategic oversight. Sometimes, a degree of training or induction may be needed to help them understand the information they receive.

The key principles

The following key points should be borne in mind.

■ The governors have the right and the ability to intervene on any major governance issue (such as remuneration and board nominations). However, there should be a reasonably high barrier to such intervention.

■ The board of governors should not set itself up as a duplication of the board of directors or seek to second-guess board decision-making. It should define in advance the types of decisions it's likely to be involved in; this should be done explicitly in the written statement of the role and responsibilities of the board of governors.

▨ As well as contributing to the internal development of the trust, individual governors should recognise their responsibility in representing the activities and strategy of the trust to the wider community. Their role is likely to be as much outward as inward looking.

The Sharon Jones diaries

Sharon Jones is a qualified chartered director and a chartered accountant.

Eighteen months ago, while in full-time employment in the business services sector, she decided to look for a position on a board. Realising that the first board appointment is the toughest to get and keen to help make a contribution to her community, she applied for an advertised post with a local Foundation Trust.

The ad made clear the search was for two new non-executives to replace retiring directors. The trust was looking for someone with financial experience to sit on the audit committee and for a second candidate with a strong strategic background. Sharon got a place on the shortlist, and an interview time was given to her.

On arrival at the administration offices, she was ushered into a room where the chairman and three non-executives sat at the other side of the table. It was daunting on entry. The chairman was a retired deputy leader of the local council, who, as the interview process made clear, had little experience of business.

Questions had been predetermined and were divided up among the members of the panel, who took it in turns to question Sharon. They seemed satisfied with her responses but, to her surprise and disappointment, made few attempts to follow-up initial questions or push her on key points. When it came to her turn to ask questions she focused on the range of experiences and expertise on the board. Once again, the responses were superficial.

Reflecting on this experience, Sharon wrote:

> If they want the most effective board why do they limit the candidates to those living in the trust's geographical area?
>
> Surely the priority should be to have people on the board with the right skills and experience rather than representatives from local government and other worthy bodies?
>
> I do wish they had asked me in detail about my accounting and numeracy skills and what I would expect to see in a well-led audit committee. I don't feel they understood the essence of me and how I could contribute.

About a week later, Sharon was advised that she had been successful and that a meeting with the CEO had been scheduled.

This session was lively and open. The CEO made it known that she believed the board to be ineffective and that she saw her biggest challenge as working around this to get things done. She was hopeful that, with new blood on the board, the situation could be improved. In addition to hiring the non-executives, the plan was to replace the chairman with a leader who could encourage the executive and bring about change. Buoyed by the meeting, Sharon decided to accept the appointment.

She wrote:

> If the board is there to add value and to provide the strategic direction and monitor the progress against predetermined objectives, how can a situation exist where the board is viewed negatively by the senior team? Check out the chairman's leadership and the competencies of the board.

Sharon asked for an induction programme before her first board meeting. This included one-to-ones with the chairman, the CEO, the finance director and the heads of departments. It also included a walking tour of the major patient care areas of the trust. Sharon wisely used this time to start building relationships with these key people and to ask them about their roles – their hopes and frustrations, their progress and failures.

She wrote:

> There is a lot of talent here but it does not seem to have been harnessed properly.
>
> There are so many targets and artificial ways to achieve them without really improving the patient experience.
>
> There is a lack of priority and direction, due not solely to the complexity of trying to meet the various, often conflicting targets but also to boardroom failures.
>
> Looking over the content of past agendas, there was a heavy emphasis on finance and targets and, indeed, on the trust's place in the NHS 'pecking order'.

The day arrived for the first board meeting, and the agenda, dominated by reports from the CEO, the finance director and progress against the dreaded targets, was received a good seven days in advance. At the meeting, most of the time was taken up by presentations from the executive and questions from the non-executives.

There were a couple of non-controversial capital items but very little else. Sharon had decided that at this first meeting she would remain largely on the sidelines, taking the role of interested observer and listening carefully to what was being said.

The approach taken by the board at the next meeting was similar, and here the budget was the central item. It was clear that there were greater claims than resources available. It seemed to Sharon that the priorities for allocation were not totally clear and that a generic target for reducing the overall number of claims would be too simplistic. She was determined to contribute more this time, searching out the key priorities and suggesting a root-and-branch review of the costs and benefits of different areas of the trust's work. This kind of interrogation, however, necessarily had a limited effect: the budget had to be finalised by the meeting's end.

Reporting to the board was through predetermined silos, and there was little evidence of interest in producing a balanced score-card that would give a better picture of the health of the trust. She felt that she should press for full understanding of the health of the business, and the CEO suggested the next practical step might be to look at the Dr Foster Quality Account for 2008–9. This covered questions such as:

■ What is the hospital's overall death rate?

■ What is the hospital's death rate for emergency admissions?

■ What is the death rate for stroke patients?

■ What is the death rate for heart attack patients?

■ What is the death rate for patients admitted with a broken hip?

■ What is the death rate for patients admitted for low-risk procedures?

■ Is the hospital fully compliant with national patient safety guidelines?

■ How consistently are patient safety incidents reported to the NRLS (National Reporting Learning System)?

■ How quickly are patient safety incidents reported?

- How many patient safety incidents were reported in the first half of last year?

- What is the ratio of hospital staff to beds?

- How well does the hospital control infection?

- How committed is the trust to patient safety?

Sharon wrote:

> There is a need for a comprehensive balanced report to the board that includes the Dr Foster Quality parameters.
>
> There is a need to agree that the patient experience is at the centre of all that is done and reported on at the trust.
>
> There is a need to have greater, more open learning at the coal face of patient care. This may include video recording the teams providing the care and identifying and reporting unsafe practices.
>
> Training for medical staff must include team dynamics and inter-personal skills and motivation.

The appointment of a new chairman proved a turning point for the board. Under the leadership of someone who combined experience in the commercial sector with genuine empathy for the trust's work, things improved significantly. There was less 'show and tell' from the executive, more discussion and more informed decision-making.

Over the subsequent weeks the board agreed some changes to the annual agenda. Included now were the following items:

- full-day strategic discussion and strategy review;

- the annual plan;

- succession planning and management development;

- risk identification and management;

- health and safety reviews at least twice a year;

- a board effectiveness review and individual director development plans, including discussion on board succession plans;

- ensuring clarity on the values of the trust and an annual review of how these values were reflected in the decision-making of both the board and the executive.

Twelve months later, Sharon wrote:

> What a difference a year makes! The role of chairman can transform an organisation; the balance-on-the-board argument applies to NHS Foundation Trusts as much as it does in the commercial sector.
>
> Having the right, 'rounded' information helps a non-executive to make a better contribution and to be challenging but empathetic to the executive.
>
> Looking at the annual agendas and how the board has historically spent its time is instructive. It is also fodder for improvement!
>
> Thank goodness we put in place the board appraisal programme. We have all learnt from this and improved as a result.
>
> Remember the importance of the patient at the centre of all we do.
>
> The culture in the organisation is an essential condition for change and effectiveness.

Summary

The growing role of decentralised boards in the NHS is a reflection of the difficulties of managing a massive healthcare organisation from the centre.

NHS boards have different objectives from those in the private sector, and must operate within a distinctive regulatory framework. In addition, Foundation Trusts have accountability to a board of governors and members of the local healthcare economy (rather than shareholders). However, successful boards in the NHS and the private sector are not dissimilar. Both depend on independently minded and well-informed board members – co-ordinated by an effective chairman.

Our case study shows that the culture of the trust and the leadership of the board are key factors in releasing the talent of the team to improve patient care.

Ethics

Introduction

Effective directors are, as we've seen, guided by strong and clear values. In all but the smallest organisations, these will be committed to writing and promulgated. Clearly communicated to and fully understood by all employees, they become embedded in the organisation. This chapter explores the complementary dimension of ethics – the moral principles that must govern business behaviour.

It's helpful to understand the interlocking nature of the different sources from which ethical dilemmas can arise (see Figure 12.1, from the Institute of Business Ethics). For me, the basic foundation is the personal values of the individual director.

The case for ethics

Principles and profits

The idea that principles hold a business back, that success is always linked to 'sharp practice', that business people must push moral boundaries if they are to make money for themselves and their shareholders is wrong. Increasing numbers of businesses are making values and ethics part of their USP. Cafédirect is the 'UK's largest Fairtrade hot drinks company'; Freeplay Energy is the 'leading global brand of clean, dependable energy products'; Innocent Drinks wants to 'leave things a little

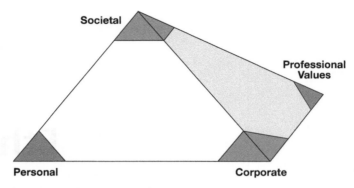

Reproduced with permission of IBE.

Figure 12.1

better' than it finds them, making products that are '100 per cent good for people' from ingredients that are 'procured ethically', minimising its carbon footprint and giving 10 per cent of its profits to charities in its suppliers' communities.

These relatively young companies are in tune with the zeitgeist but they shouldn't be seen purely as products of their own time. They're part of a tradition of principled business. Think Cadbury, think Rowntree, think John Spedan Lewis in the UK. All were philanthropists; all built profitable businesses.

The most precious asset any leader has is their good name. The same is true of their 'host' organisation – be it a business, a not-for-profit organisation or a charitable foundation. When reputations are lost so, too, is value. Sales and share prices fall. Nike, engulfed by a sweatshop scandal in the 1990s, is just one company to have discovered this. Good names are rarely built on bad behaviour.

Recruitment and retention

The difference between a top-performing organisation and an average one is the talent within it. Increasingly, individuals will look carefully at the ethical behaviour of an organisation before they decide to join it and will monitor it from their own observations once there. No one wants to work for a company they're ashamed of.

In a 2008 survey sponsored by the business services company Serco, the Institute of Business Ethics (IBE) found that, in the UK, full-time employees were generally less tolerant of unethical practices in the workplace than they were in 2005.

Law and regulation

In the UK, there have been successive attempts to crack down on malpractice and call more errant directors to account. The Corporate Manslaughter Act 2007, for example, is designed to make it easier to prosecute companies that fail in their duty of care to customers, employees and other stakeholders. Meanwhile, the legal regime for financial crime is getting tougher. In 2001, the civil offence of 'market abuse' was introduced as a further deterrent to insider dealing and market manipulation. It requires a lower standard of proof than the criminal offence of insider trading, and anyone caught is liable for a hefty fine. (See Chapter 5 of *The Director's Handbook* for full details.)

The rules on insider dealing and market abuse can apply not only to directors and senior managers but also to lowly employees who have access to inside information. To protect themselves, companies must:

■ have a clear policy on when directors and senior managers can and cannot trade shares;

■ follow Stock Exchange regulations on 'closed' periods;

■ make sure everyone who might have access to inside information understands that it must never be used for personal gain or be passed on to anyone outside the organisation, unless they are created insiders.

(Closed periods and insider trading are discussed further in this chapter under 'Fiduciary duties', page 216.)

Bribery and corruption have also come under scrutiny from legislators in recent years. The 'everybody's doing it' argument and the excuse that bribes are an accepted part of business life in many overseas countries simply will not wash. A stark reminder of this was provided by the scandal that engulfed BAE Systems in 2009. The new team at BAE now has to work hard to put the past behind it, making sure that good ethical standards are embedded in the organisation and that reputational risk is reduced.

The UK's Bribery Act 2010, which consolidates previously fragmented UK law, is intended to toughen up the rules. As well as making it an offence for individuals to offer or receive a bribe, the Bribery Act requires companies to have 'adequate procedures' to prevent bribery being committed on their behalf. The legislation will apply to all companies and individuals doing business in the United Kingdom, although the offence could relate to an act of bribery taking place anywhere in the world.

Before the new corporate offence comes into force (in early 2011), the government will publish guidance on what constitutes 'adequate procedures' to prevent bribery. It is expected that the standard required of companies will vary according to considerations such as the organisation's size, sector and the countries in which it operates.

So, there are strong practical, as well as moral, arguments for ethics in business. Ethical behaviour, it's clear, reduces legal and PR risks. I believe, however, that the moral imperative is the most powerful. Without a fundamental commitment to being a 'good' business or a 'good' organisation, the approach to ethics is likely to degenerate into box-ticking (see 'Honesty and integrity' on page 215).

What are ethics?

This brings us to the question of defining ethics.

Some writers spend a great deal of time explaining the difference between values and ethics. But most would probably agree that in one important respect at least they're the same: they're both essential elements of effective leadership.

If you qualify the word 'values' by the word 'moral', there's little to choose between them: moral values = ethics. If you qualify it by the word 'business', things get more complicated – but not that much. The IBE sets out common words that describe business values and ethical values. These are listed in Table 12.1. On the left we have a list of those things that will be important to a business – *what it values*. They are the cultural norms of the organisation. On the right are the qualities or behavioural standards important in observing/maintaining them. You can't, for example, have effective teamwork or customer service without integrity, respect, fairness and trust.

Table 12.1

Words to describe business values	Words to describe ethics
Customer service	Highest ethical standards
Efficiency	Integrity
Good governance	Honesty
Reliability	Responsibility
Profitability	Respect
Teamwork	Trust
Quality	Fairness
Value for money	Openness
Initiative	Transparency
Shareholder value	

(With kind persmission of IBE)

The challenges

The 2008 national Ethics at Work survey, referred to in 'Recruitment and retention' earlier, found that:

- employees felt less pressure to compromise ethical standards than they did in 2005;

- staff saw their organisations as more ethical than they were in 2005;

- there was evidence of higher standards of ethical behaviour in the workplace.

Sadly, however, these positive findings are not the full picture. There remains work to be done. Other results from the survey show:

- female employees are generally stricter on ethics than their male counterparts, and the young (those aged 16 to 34) are significantly more tolerant of unethical workplace practices;

- about a quarter of British employees are aware of misconduct but only 60 per cent of this quarter report it;

- attitudes of indifference and the belief that corrective action is unlikely to be taken deter employees from reporting misconduct to management;

- minor fiddling is seen as inevitable in modern organisations.

The 'If you can't beat 'em, join 'em attitude' implicit in the last finding will not have been helped in the UK by the MPs' expenses scandal. Employers determined to implement high ethical standards may now face increased employee cynicism.

Ethical business: the starting point

Most FTSE 350 companies have a statement of ethical behaviour. Some companies, for example, Balfour Beatty, have a detailed manual that sets out the standards expected of their staff in different scenarios.

Ethical statements reinforce the values of the organisation and set out the moral code for employees. In many businesses, they support and supplement the CSR (corporate social responsibility) agenda. A code is essential for any organisation with 50 or more employees, but it will be meaningless unless directors (or their equivalents) lead by example, and the standards are practised and enforced.

The 'nice words' of the statement must have a life beyond paper. An organisation must practise what it preaches. If it doesn't, the main effect of the statement will be to expose its leaders as hypocrites. This was amply demonstrated by the case of Enron and Kenneth Lay. Enron had a detailed and theoretically excellent code of ethics, which set out how the corporation was to be run. Lay, then chairman and chief executive officer, introduced it in 2000 with these words:

> We want to be proud of Enron and know that it enjoys a reputation for fairness and honesty and that it is respected. Gaining such respect is one aim of our advertising and public relations activities, but no matter how effective they may be, Enron's reputation finally depends on its people, on you and me. Let's keep that reputation high.

The very next year, Enron collapsed under a mountain of 'hidden' debts, and Lay and fellow director Jeff Skilling faced allegations of fraud. Exhortation is not enough. It must be fully supported by action.

What should a code include?

Bearing in mind the caveats above, it will be useful to examine the contents of an ethical code. This is best done by way of an example, and I include, in Table 12.2, the public Code of Ethics for the Australian company, RailCorp. This is a brief statement written for public understanding and will no doubt be supported with more detail for the directors and staff.

Table 12.2

What we expect of you	What you can expect from us
All suppliers of goods and services to RailCorp must:	We will:
<ul><li>comply with the conditions and requirements stated in documents supplied by RailCorp</li><li>comply with all codes of tendering and practice that apply</li><li>respect the obligation of RailCorp employees, contractors and suppliers to comply with government procurement policies and guidelines</li></ul>	<ul><li>comply with applicable RailCorp and government policies/procedures</li><li>show fairness in our treatment of all individuals or organisations that supply goods or services to RailCorp</li><li>encourage fair and open competition while seeking value for money</li></ul>

- disclose any situation that involves or could be perceived to involve a conflict of interest
- not act fraudulently or secretively
- prevent the unauthorised release of privileged or confidential information such as commercial-in-confidence information
- not discuss RailCorp dealings with the media without first obtaining RailCorp approval
- respond to reasonable requests for advice and information
- not offer RailCorp employees, contractors and consultants any financial inducements or any gifts or other benefits which may lead to, or be seen as leading to, an unfair advantage in dealings with RailCorp (refer to 'practical guidelines' section)
- ensure that all contractors they engage to perform work for RailCorp are aware of and are required to comply with the Statement of Business Ethics
- not engage in collusive practices

- try to minimise costs to suppliers participating in the procurement process
- protect commercial-in-confidence information
- deal honesty with suppliers
- be accountable and act in the public interest
- avoid situations where private interests conflict with public duty
- disclose any situation that involves or could be perceived to involve a conflict of interest
- not ask for or accept financial or other benefits from a potential, current or past supplier for performing official duties
- respond to reasonable requests for advice and information without delay

In Box 12.1 the much more detailed statement of Biocon, written both for employees and external stakeholders, is reproduced. Biocon is an Indian company, employing around 1,000 people, but I believe its code sets an example for any organisation that takes ethics seriously.

Box 12.1
Code of Ethics and Business Conduct, Biocon India

This code is applicable to all directors, officers and employees of Biocon Ltd and its subsidiaries.

Biocon Group is committed to conducting its business in accordance with the applicable laws, rules and regulations and with the highest standards of business ethics. This code is intended to provide guidance and help in recognising and dealing with ethical issues, provide mechanisms to report unethical conduct and help foster a culture of honesty and accountability. Each director, officer and employee is expected to comply with the letter and spirit of the code.

All employed in the company must not only comply with applicable laws, rules and regulations but should also promote honest and ethical conduct of the business. They must abide by the policies and procedures that govern the conduct of the company's business. Their responsibilities include helping to create and maintain a culture of high ethical standards and commitment to compliance, and to maintain a work environment that encourages stakeholders to raise concerns for the attention of management.

This code does not attempt to describe all potential problem areas that could develop, but some of the more common ones are described below.

Conflicts of interest

These can arise from:

- action or interests that may make it difficult for employees, officers and directors to perform their work pragmatically and effectively;

- the receipt of improper personal benefits as a result of one's position in the company (including benefits for family members);

- an outside business activity that detracts from an individual's ability to devote appropriate time and attention to their responsibilities in the company;

- the receipt of non-nominal gifts or excessive entertainment from any person or company with which Biocon has current or prospective business;

- any significant ownership interest in a supplier, customer, development partner or competitor of the company;

- any consulting or employment relationship with any supplier, customer, development partner or competitor.

All employed by the company should be scrupulous in avoiding conflicts of interest. Where there is likely to be a conflict of interest, the person concerned should make full disclosure of all facts and circumstances to the board of directors or to the committee or officer nominated for this purpose, and prior written approval should be obtained.

Honest and ethical conduct

The directors, officers and employees shall act in accordance with the highest standards of personal and professional integrity, not only on the company's premises but also at company-sponsored business, social events and elsewhere. They shall be free from fraud and deception. They shall always conform to the best standards of ethical conduct.

Corporate opportunities

All have a duty to the company to advance its legitimate interests when the opportunity arises. Directors, officers and employees are expressly prohibited from:

- taking for themselves personally opportunities that are discovered through the use of the company's property, information or position;

- competing directly with the current business of the company or its likely future business;

- using company property, information, or position for personal gain.

If the company has made a final decision not to pursue an opportunity, an individual may follow it up only after disclosing the same to the board of directors or to the nominated committee or individual.

Confidentiality

All shall respect confidential information on the company, any of its customers, suppliers or business associates. Disclosure of such information should only be made where authorised or required by law. The use of any confidential information for personal gain is strictly forbidden.

Fair dealing

All Biocon employees at all levels should deal fairly with those we do business with. No one should take unfair advantage of anyone through manipulation, concealment, abuse of confidential information, misrepresentation of facts or any other unfair dealing practices.

Employees

The company will not tolerate discrimination on any grounds whatsoever. All employees will be treated fairly and given the opportunity to grow and develop within the company. Promotion will be on merit. Bullying or harassment is regarded as a serious offence and will not be tolerated.

Protection and proper use of company's assets

Everyone has a duty to protect the company's assets and ensure their proper use. Theft, carelessness and waste of company assets damage profitability. These assets should only be used for legitimate business purposes.

Compliance with laws, rules and regulations

All employed by the company shall comply with all relevant laws, rules and regulations. All employees at all levels are expected to know how these laws and rules apply to their area of decision-making. In the event of any uncertainty, the employee concerned should consult the company legal department before taking action.

Compliance with the code

If any person suspects or knows of a violation of this code, they must immediately report the same to the board of directors or the designated person or committee. The company has a whistle-blowing policy that will protect their anonymity; details of this are on the intranet.

Violations of this code will result in disciplinary action and, in some cases, dismissal. Full details of the disciplinary procedures and the appeal processes are included on the company intranet.

Interpretation of this code

Interpretation of this code is reserved for the board.

The board may appoint a designated committee or designated person to act on its behalf in interpreting and clarifying this code.

Key principles of a code

Some of the main elements of and principles behind the Biocon code are looked at more closely below. They are the key components of business ethics.

Honesty and integrity

Chapter 6 on effective leadership emphasised the importance of integrity for directors. Without this quality, a person is unlikely to be sufficiently interested in or guided by an ethical code.

The director who has integrity will want the organisation's values to be compatible with their own. They won't want to work for or lead an organisation they feel uncomfortable with.

Standards of acceptable behaviour are both objective and subjective. While there are some moral absolutes in business, some things that are clearly wrong (stealing, cheating, misappropriation of money, making false or deliberately misleading statements to the stock market, exploitation of workers, etc) there are grey areas, too. When do tactics to beat the competition become dirty tricks? When does 'tough negotiation' become bullying or abuse of economic power? When do PR and 'spin' become deception and lies?

Individuals will decide where the boundaries are according to their *personal ethical code*. If there are others in the organisation who continually act outside these boundaries (with the blessing of the board), then the director with integrity has no choice but to leave.

It must also be emphasised that what's 'right' in good times for the company must also be right in bad. Moral values must not bend in the wind. Exploiting loopholes in the law to keep investors happy is wrong. Ernst & Young's agreement to the use of the Repo 105 accounting 'rule' to keep debts hidden from the balance sheet of Lehman Brothers had catastrophic consequences, leading, in 2008, to the biggest bankruptcy the world has ever seen. The key point is that it's not just a question of following the letter of the law, it's a question of acting in the *spirit* of honesty and fairness.

Fiduciary duties

Central to business ethics is the concept of fiduciary duty. Directors act on behalf of others – the many people who trust them to act honestly, capably and in the best interests of the organisation as a whole. The company's assets are held for the benefit of others; they do not *belong* to the directors. This is the legal principle that put newspaper tycoon Conrad Black in the dock.

The interests of the company must come before narrow self-interest. Directors must absent themselves from discussions and decisions on subjects in which they have a personal financial interest. This applies even in cases where the interest is limited or indirect, or lies with a family member. Any real or potential conflict of interest must be disclosed to the board. Chapter 2 of *The Director's Handbook* discusses in detail the circumstances in which a director may be in breach of their fiduciary duty, but 'when in doubt disclose' is a good dictum. The director's position as a fiduciary means it's unethical for them to use 'inside' information for direct or indirect personal gain.

Directors must not trade their shares during 'closed periods' – ie, times when information likely to influence the movement of the company's share price has not been made available to the investing public. Trading will be blocked between balance dates and the announcement of results and when market-sensitive information – such as news of a takeover bid or new contract – has not been released. Again, Chapter 2 of the *Handbook* includes much useful information on this.

Behaviours and culture

The IBE has identified five factors critical for an ethical culture:

1. Leaders support and 'model' ethical behaviour; they lead by example.

2. Consistent communications come from leaders.

3. Ethics are integrated into the organisation's goals, business processes and strategies.

4. Ethics are part of the performance management system.

5. Ethics are part of the recruitment process and selection criteria.

The key point is that the ethical code must be followed and practised at the highest levels of the organisation and clearly communicated to every employee.

Assurance

The boards of some larger companies have an ethics committee, made up of non-executives. Its primary purpose is to monitor the non-financial aspects of management activity – ethical conduct, social and environmental responsibility, health and safety, etc.

An ethics committee may be an imperative for high-risk sectors such as pharmaceuticals and oil and gas extraction, and where a company trades with countries that are economically and politically 'immature' and have different 'ethical norms'. For most others, it's probably unnecessary. A separate committee on ethics may:

- divert the issue from the main board;

- duplicate the work of the audit and risk committee;

- 'layer on' more process.

The main board should instead be able to provide assurance through an ethical health check. This can be carried out annually, or as the need arises. (An ad hoc review may be necessary when breaches of the ethical code are suspected.) Box 12.2 is a list of questions for a 'model' health check.

Box 12.2
Ethical health check for directors

- Is there a clear policy, approved and reviewed annually by the board?

- Has the board considered, understood and agreed the process by which its values are embedded in the business?

- Is the policy set out in clear terms, communicated well throughout the organisation and agreed to as a part of individual employment contracts?

- Do staff members see adherence to the policy as an important part of their employment or more as 'window dressing' for the company?

- Is the policy considered in appraisals and training and development?

■ Is there an effective whistle-blowing policy and a procedure that protects the whistle-blower?

■ Do ethical values inform the board's decision-making and choice of strategic initiatives?

■ Does the board have mechanisms that measure ethics pragmatically?

Monitoring systems

How do you measure the ethical performance of the business? How do you judge the extent to which you've succeeded in embedding ethical values? Absence of lawsuits does not prove that all is as it should be.

Systems for ethical assurance are still being developed, and it may be some time before best-practice guidelines are established. What's more, the complexity and importance of monitoring business and organisational ethics means that a 'one-size-fits-all' template is unlikely to work. In all cases, however, the first task must be to ensure that the code of ethics is relevant and up to date, and the next to ensure there is a system to pull together all the information needed to provide assurance to the board. (Often this will be found in many disparate places, nurtured in the safety of silos.)

Thereafter, objective monitoring can take several forms. It will be up to the individual board to decide what suits it best. The merits of three of the principal approaches are explained below.

1. An ethical survey, involving employees, suppliers and investors, can test the level of awareness of the code and the whistle-blowing policy. More than this, it can test the level of *confidence* in the code and the directors. Stakeholders will tell you whether the code is clear, concise and practised, and whether they'd fear the consequences of reporting a breach.

2. Recording the number and nature of complaints, the number and nature of calls to the 'ethical hotline', for example, will be a useful indication of the level of compliance. (Year-on-year comparisons of these records should, though, be used with caution. Decreases are not necessarily evidence of an improvement in performance; it may be that whistle-blowers have been reluctant to come forward/been frightened off.)

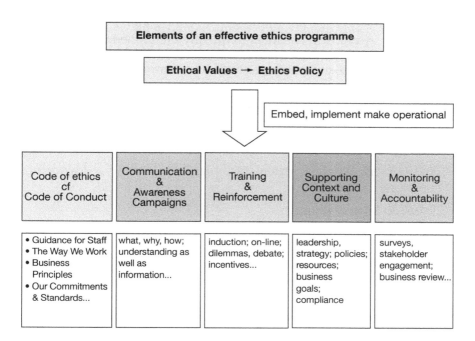

Figure 12.2

3. Asking the internal audit function to report specifically on ethics in the business is a sensible option for larger companies. It will provide assurance (or not) that the building blocks exist across the organisation (particularly important, perhaps, where the geographical spread is wide), that the ethical code is understood and that decisions are compatible with it.

In addition to monitoring its ethical performance, the 'ethically immature' organisation – ie, one where ethics have yet to be embedded – will want to track its progress. For this reason I include, in Figure 12.2, an IBE diagram showing the various stages and various components of an ethics programme.

Ethical reporting

Looking through a selection of annual reports and accounts recently published in the UK, it's clear that the quality of ethical reporting is quite variable. Many policies are discussed in very general terms and are unsupported by metrics. The most frequently mentioned topics are:

■ responsibility to and participation in the communities in which the company operates;

■ public health issues (particularly in the food and drink and pharmaceuticals sectors);

■ fair employment practices and non-discrimination;

■ environmental policy statements, plans to become a low-carbon company;

■ health and safety issues;

■ good citizenship – eg, good pay and conditions in developing countries.

Convincing readers (investors, stakeholders, campaigning groups, the public, etc) that these issues are taken seriously depends on a more rigorous approach to reporting.

If people are to believe values and codes of conduct are more than well-meaning fluff they'll need facts and figures. The good news is that an increasing number of companies now recognise this. There is a significant trend towards environmental reporting that includes performance metrics. This is seen especially in sectors exposed to high environmental risks – eg, the oil and gas, chemicals or extractive industries – where some companies commission independent environmental audits and include the report in the annual report and accounts. However, retailers and makers of consumer goods are also starting to include more meaningful information.

Ethics and the supply chain

A company must take reasonable care to ensure that its standards and ethical values are understood and adhered to by all its suppliers.

Furore followed War on Want revelations in December 2006 that Tesco, Primark and Asda, all members of the Ethical Trading Initiative, were using clothing factories in Bangladesh that paid less than the living wage and breached health and safety standards. In December 2009 Asda also faced criticism from environmentalists and British farmers when it chose to source turkeys from Brazil.

A requirement for ethics must be written into contracts with suppliers and business partners and it must be enforced (see the RailCorp code in Table 12.2). Mining company Rio Tinto has declared it's prepared to withdraw from business relationships if any partners do not live up to its values. Marks & Spencer asks suppliers to sign up to minimum standards and makes clear that failure to ensure they're observed can lead to loss of contract.

Microsoft announced at the end of March 2007 that it had dropped one of its suppliers in the UK because it failed to meet the company's standards on employee diversity. Dave Gartenberg, the UK director of human resources, was quoted as saying:

> Microsoft is committed to ensuring we have a diverse and inclusive workforce, and we want to work with companies that share these principles. Consequently, we are looking at how we can take a leadership position in driving positive change, while respecting local legislation.

This is a strong message to give to other companies.

Compliance with ethical codes and standards can be measured by a system of self-assessment (where the supplier reviews procedures and pay and conditions) and by spot checks and audits by the client/ outsourcing company.

Summary

Ethical codes set the moral standards for directors (or, in the case of a charity, trustees) and all those working with and for them, including suppliers and their employees. They mean nothing, however, without ethical behaviour. And that starts at the top. The board must act with integrity, with honesty and for the greater good of the company, its shareholders and stakeholders. Its members must not misuse the assets of the company or abuse their power. To provide effective leadership on ethics, directors must have a close personal affinity with corporate values and principles. Where there are significant conflicts, where codes diverge, a director must leave the organisation.

The demand for 'ethical intelligence' among business leaders – awareness of their wider responsibilities and an understanding of fair play – is probably at an all-time high. Ethics, like good governance, will build trust and confidence among shareholders, the public and stakeholders. They will strengthen an organisation's most valuable asset – its good name.

I have no doubt that good ethics make for good business.

Appendix: Current business ethics issues

- Bullying and harassment.

- Racial discrimination.

- Corruption (*in the widest sense of misuse of entrusted power*).

- Conflicts of interest.

- Dishonesty and fraud.

- Diversity in the workplace.

- Environmental impact.

- Executive pay.

- Human rights standards, including labour rights.

- Marketing (*Is the company making false claims? Is it targeting vulnerable groups?*)

- Money laundering.

- Payment terms for smaller firms.

- Whistle-blowing arrangements.

- The supply chain (*Do offshore centres meet the standards of the International Labour Organization?*)

- Tax avoidance (*Are companies overly aggressive in exploiting 'loopholes'? Are they putting back what they should?*)

- Work-life balance.

(Source: *Living Up to Our Values*, Nicole Dando and Walter Raven, Institute of Business Ethics, December 2006)

Corporate Governance in Turbulent Times

Introduction

The need for robust decision-making increases during times of difficulty and uncertainty. When the building blocks of good governance have not been laid, organisations will fail to respond to crises effectively. I believe this to have been amply demonstrated in the recent recession.

The case for good corporate governance has been examined in detail in Chapter 3, and I will not repeat it here. I want, instead, to look at why it's proven during turbulent times, using evidence from around the world.

The financial crisis

The so-called 'credit crunch' or worldwide recession that hit in 2008 has created problems for organisations in most countries. Many businesses have closed; others have faced serious threats to their viability.

An interesting question is to what extent businesses might, themselves, have contributed to the crises. A combination of factors lies behind companies' demise; only some of them will have been beyond their control. The causes of the downturn in economic activity and of commercial failures can be summarised as:

- A serious decline in the balance-sheet strength of banks and financial institutions as a result of a failure to manage risk.

- Knock-on or 'domino' effects on inter-bank lending, individual banks' ability to make loans and sources of commercial and personal credit.

- Heavy borrowing by businesses during the 'good' times – over the years that preceded the crisis, balance sheets had become more leveraged, companies less resilient. The leveraged buy-out, a popular mechanism for unlocking value, had left many businesses vulnerable.

- A 'relaxed' approach to cost management, on the assumption that the cycle of growth and profitability gains would continue.

To put it simply, some companies failed to fix the roof while the sun was shining.

The response in the UK

The speed at which UK businesses anticipated the problems was variable, but most in the very early stages of the new cycle continued with their historic business model, assuming that this would weather the storms. When it became clear that we were experiencing a serious reversal of the previous growth phase, there were differences in responses.

Those companies most at risk reviewed all of their costs and cash outgoings to see what, if any, could be deferred or indeed avoided altogether. The most targeted areas for cuts were advertising and marketing, management development initiatives, and research and development activities. In some cases, capital projects were delayed, even when they were aligned to the strategy and financially justified.

In others, especially, perhaps, those in the SME sector, the board applied the blunt instrument of reducing every department/manager's budget by a fixed percentage. Conditions in the economy were such that a number of enterprises took the opportunity to review their organisations, making roles redundant and trying to create a more 'fit-for-purpose', cost-effective structure in order to secure their long-term futures.

Meanwhile, some companies with stronger balance sheets and the capacity to ride out the storm took the opportunity to improve their competitive position through top-up acquisitions and the recruitment of top talent. They, too, had a fresh look at the business model to see whether it could withstand current conditions.

Keeping the faith

It's clear that, along with the stories of receivership and collapse, there's some good news, too. There's evidence, for example, that budgets for training and development have, in some organisations at least, held up. At the height of the recession, in July 2009, the IoD published the results of a survey. Of the 937 directors who participated:

■ 80 per cent said that their organisations had either maintained (51 per cent) or increased (29 per cent) investment in training over the past six months;

■ 20 per cent reported that their organisations had been forced to reduce investment in training over the same period. Of these, 45 per cent had cut training investment by 15 per cent or less;

■ 88 per cent of directors reported that their organisations were planning to maintain (56 per cent), or to increase (32 per cent), training investment over the next six months; 12 per cent were planning to reduce training spend.

Businesses have, then, maintained their commitment to skills. This contrasts with what's happened in the past. One director of a training organisation told us:

> In previous recessions, training has always been one of the first areas to be cut. In my opinion, this is because it has been seen by senior managers and finance managers as a cost rather than an investment. There is a definite difference this time.

The value created by good governance also seems to be being recognised. Asked whether, in the current conditions, there was any change to the approach taken to or the emphasis on governance, the majority (some 85 per cent of the sample of large, medium and small companies) said no: it was still seen as an important part of the control environment and an important way of ensuring shareholder confidence. The remainder said they had increased their focus on governance, as the company was more at risk and they would need a paper trail showing directors had acted in shareholders' best interests.

Set out on the following page is the approach of a small, AIM-listed company in the UK that's known to follow good standards of governance.

Case study: Windsor Research

Windsor Research (name changed by agreement), is an AIM-listed company with a market capitalisation of £20–£25 million. Its board consists of an independent chairman and senior non-executive director, two non-executive directors not deemed to be independent, and three executive directors.

The company funds early-stage research and develops commercial products with health-giving properties. As a small company, it does not have the muscle to take its products to market, so it sells them on to others. The buyers might be international food and drink businesses or ingredient providers able to make use of their contacts and distribution power.

Windsor has a track record of discovering technologies and developing them into products suitable for mass marketing. Given it has limited resources, in terms of both people and cash, time to market is critical for the company.

It has four streams of activity: Alpha is the most advanced product and is ready to be sold on to the distribution trade; Beta is about 18 months behind it; the other two are in the proving stage. The business that buys the rights to Alpha will need to invest heavily not only in initial marketing but also in the plant and equipment to produce the base ingredient according to the intellectually protected methodology.

Given the impact of the credit crunch, the majors in the distribution trade have deferred the launch plans for Alpha by 18 months. More risk-averse than they used to be, they are considering a trial in one country rather than a roll-out across Europe.

The Windsor board of directors responded to the changing environment in the ways listed below.

■ They 'stress tested' the strategy for the current climate. Was it robust enough? Did they need to change direction?

■ They reviewed the cash forecasts and made the technologies most likely to deliver value in the shorter term the R&D priorities, holding the other two on the back burner.

■ They held a fundamental review of business costs, switching to zero-based budgeting so that all expenditure had to be approved. In this way, costs could either be eliminated or postponed.

■ They held special meetings specifically to review the strategic alternatives and to ensure that the chosen option was best in the current environment. At the same time, they agreed to test the market for the company and to assess its potential value, in case a sale of specific technologies or the whole business proved necessary.

■ They consulted their professional advisers about their possible options and made sure the fact they'd done so was recorded in the minutes and the supporting documents.

■ They upgraded and re-examined the system for risk assessment and control, and the audit and risk committee undertook further work to ensure that the control environment remained robust. (They felt the time was not right for a full-blown board effectiveness review.)

■ They switched to a form of reporting more akin to the balanced scorecard, but with heavy emphasis on strategic milestones and the measurement of resources.

The company took a considered approach to the difficulties caused by the credit crunch, but one that included a real-time review of the strategy against the best possible alternative. The focus of the board's attention changed, and this was reflected in extra meetings and changing agendas. In addition, there were concerted efforts to improve risk assessment and control and to ensure minutes and documents would stand external scrutiny. Importantly, these were changes made to an established governance structure. The company was not starting from scratch or 'bolting on' processes to a framework that was inherently weak.

Risk in turbulent times: lessons from the Economist IU

Emphasis on risk assessment and control has increased in recent years. It now forms part of strategic discussions and is the core of audit work. Fewer people see it as a process to be 'ticked off': it's now integral to corporate governance.

Organisations understand not only that risks must be identified and managed but also that the management of risk must be led from the top and embedded in the business. Risk identification and management starts with the strategy and is part of the continuous management of the organisation.

Failures in the banking and financial sector made the management of risk more important in all sectors of business. The UK Corporate Governance Code has since highlighted it as a key board activity. A number of organisations, especially larger companies, have split risk assessment and control from the audit committee and set up a separate risk committee.

Companies have had to ask some very hard questions. Had the profit motive and the demand for increased profits and management bonuses blinded boards to the risks they were taking? Had the risks inherent in their chosen strategy been fully understood and appreciated? Had they assessed alternatives on the basis of associated risks? Did they simply rely on the experiences of the past and assume it would be business as usual?

Box 13.1
Ten lessons in risk control

Following research based on interviews in 2009, the Economist Intelligence Unit published 'Managing Risk in Perilous Times'. It drew out 10 lessons or principles for risk assessment and control. These are, in no particular order:

1. Risk management must be given greater authority.

2. Senior executives must lead risk management from the top.

3. Institutions need to review their risk expertise, particularly at the highest levels.

4. Institutions should pay more attention to the data that produce risk models, and combine this output with human judgment.

5. Stress testing and scenario planning can arm executives with an appropriate response to events.

6. Incentive systems must be constructed so that they reward long-term stability, not short-term profit.

7. Risk factors should be consolidated across all an institution's operations.

8. Institutions should ensure that they do not rely too heavily on data from external suppliers.

9. A careful balance must be struck between the centralisation and decentralisation of risk.

10. Risk management systems should be adaptive rather than static.

Examples from abroad

I am fortunate in having worked on board effectiveness and good governance outside the UK. How have companies responded to recent crises there? What can we learn from the international arena?

To give some insight into the different responses, I have chosen the specific examples of Du Pont in the United States, and Biocon, an Indian company with shareholders in the UK, mainland Europe and North America. I have also looked at the findings of general research on companies in Russia.

Du Pont in the US

Ellen Kullman, CEO of the US chemicals company Du Pont, says that since the financial crisis of October 2008, she and her team have followed four key leadership principles.

1. The first principle might be simplified as the law of 'low-hanging fruit'. Kullman believes that if you get staff to focus on the things they can do something about and encourage them to take the necessary action, they are less likely to be overwhelmed by the extent of the environmental change. (Allied to this principle is a commitment to staff training and support: when a company's short-term focus changes, as it often must in times of turmoil, long-established working practices might have to change with it.)

2. The second principle was to rethink the business model. Kullman says that people are willing to embrace change when markets are in disarray and when there's uncertainty about what will work in the future. The critical thing is to match the company's competency to market opportunities. For Du Pont, traditionally a 'make and sell' manufacturing company, this meant developing service-based models and finding new ways to engage with customers.

3. Third is the importance of staff communication. Kullman insisted that her leadership team 'got out in front of the troops' with a consistent message. She personally visited plants in Germany and Ohio where people were being laid off, answering tough questions about employees' relationship with the company. (The better the communication with the workforce, the more secure the 'psychological' contract.)

4. Last is the need to maintain the integrity of the company's mission. Employees must never feel that the company's core beliefs are being lost. 'They want direction linking their daily activities to a broader purpose,' Kullman says.

For me, the key lesson from Du Pont's experiences is that a company's mission (in this case 'sustainable growth') can survive periods of rapid and quite radical change. Yes, a company must be flexible; yes, it must respond effectively to changes in the wider environment – but not at the expense of its underlying principles.

Employees must know that change is being introduced under a governance framework that's consistent and sound. Communication is, as Kullman says, vital in times of crisis.

Russian companies

Background

For the past 15 years, Russian business has demonstrated significant progress in developing corporate governance. Based on the recommendations of the Russian Corporate Governance Code, developed under the Federal Securities Commission's guidance, stock exchanges introduced corporate governance requirements in the listing rules mandatory for publicly traded companies. What's more, the government has announced plans to replace state officials on the boards of the state-owned companies with independent directors.

Nonetheless, general corporate governance in Russia might still be described as immature. There are several reasons why.

■ Many companies are governed by a founder/dominant shareholder of the 'first generation' and this can lead to conflict on the board.

■ A shortage of domestic capital has led businesses to look for financing from abroad, forcing the adoption of international corporate governance principles. What others would see as adding value is, therefore, in some Russian companies at least, seen just as 'window dressing', a costly distraction. (The principle that independent directors act as an important check and balance for the board is not fully established.)

■ Under Russian legislation, investors owning 2 per cent or more of the shares can nominate candidates for the board. The board can only put forward candidates where shareholders do not submit their nominations. Having a nomination committee is not a common practice. The result is a board whose members represent not the common interest but the interests of the group that selected them.

What's more, the corporate sector in Russia has, over the past four years, seen renewed involvement and intervention from the federal government. This is manifested both in the expansion of the state's share in the capital of major companies and in the establishment of holding companies with a controlling state interest (in aeronautics, shipbuilding, atomic machinery and arms manufacturing).

The credit crunch and the global financial crisis have, of course, accelerated this trend. As in other countries, the state has had to step in to support the economy. In 2009, the government allocated the equivalent of around £65 billion to support 295 strategic companies, and pumped roughly the same again into the banking sector.

All this means Russian boards are living in 'interesting times'.

Research findings

Despite the above, an encouraging picture emerges from *Leading in Turbulent Times: Priorities for your board*, an Independent Directors Association study of 159 major Russian companies, 75 per cent of which are publicly traded. Of these companies:

- 85 per cent have board committees;

- 72 per cent reject the statement that 'corporate governance does not create value during a crisis';

- 50 per cent believe corporate governance is even more important in a crisis, but 27 per cent see it as an unnecessary cost when valuations crash and capital is unavailable.

(The last finding no doubt reflects the fact that companies have put governance in place to meet the requirements of the Western stock exchanges, for example, AIM. In other words, it's been a question of ticking boxes rather than embedding principles.)

The interviewed directors shared some interesting practical experience on how to deal with unforeseen emergency situations. The main suggestions are summarised below:

- Financial crisis rescue plans, supported with communication plans, and held on file in case of serious failures or breaches of important financial covenants, etc.

- Anti-crisis scorecards for those times when standard balanced scorecard reporting might not be sufficient. (It was felt that monthly one-page reports from management would be useful in tracking progress on anti-crisis measures and specific goals – free cash flow, debt position, cost cutting, capacity reduction, etc. It was also felt that the cash position and financial covenants should be monitored monthly and feature regularly on the board agenda.)

■ Board-level involvement in important operational decisions by management.

The idea of a special crisis committee was not supported by the majority of respondents.

How can Russian companies build on the foundations for good governance to see them through crises? Below are some suggestions. They will be useful for any organisation struggling in turbulent times.

General conclusions and suggestions

1. The board effectiveness review, not common practice in Russian companies, is a useful tool for improving performance. It will add value to the board and help ensure it's a strategic asset to the company. Crucially, it may help focus on the bigger picture and ensure a considered rather than a knee-jerk response to changing circumstances. (The reaction of the board needs to be prompt, not rash.) Once a proper template is established (see Box 1.4, Chapter 1, page 13), board evaluation exercises need not be costly or time-consuming.

2. Risk assessment and control, and management development and succession planning need the attention of the board. If they're neglected, a company is unlikely to be 'crisis-proof'.

3. Lines of communication, both external and internal, must be open and clear. Information supplied must be accurate and adequate. Failure to communicate in stressful times will damage the company: there will be rumours, nervousness and false assumptions.

4. The companies that responded most effectively to the credit crunch were those that ensured their board agendas changed with the changing environment. Sufficient time must be allowed for the big, strategic decisions. During periods of turmoil, board agendas should be regularly reviewed.

5. The directors must check they receive the right information, at the right time. During crises, the short-term and current needs of the business will need to be addressed. Cash control, current and projected borrowings and the company's ability to meet its financial covenants must be monitored weekly.

6. The board should make positive use of committees, rather than see them as 'token' structures set up to tick the governance box. Delegation of powers can leave executive directors freer to focus on the big issues.

7. A recurrent theme of *Leading the Board in Turbulent Times* is that boards lack the right balance of skills, are insufficiently diverse and are not subject to the 'control' or challenge of genuine independent directors. There is a case for rethinking the way directors are appointed, using the nomination committee as a sub-committee of the board (see 8, below).

8. The three main committees of the board, specified in corporate governance codes, can add value to the board and help it function more effectively. The key points to remember about each are given below.

   – The audit committee is a key committee of the board and must be appropriately staffed with the right balance of skills. At the foundation of an effective audit committee is risk assessment and control. In times of crisis, the committee should be a relatively simple model that relies on the minimum of process.

   – The remuneration committee should monitor the 'market' on executive remuneration and compensate managers fairly to motivate them to bring maximum value to the company. Talent is always a key asset for the business. Cancelling payment for independent directors will be counterproductive, send the wrong signal to the shareholders, lessen the motivation of the board members, and create problems in attracting professional directors in the future.

   – The appointment of directors through the active lead of a nomination committee can ensure a strong field of suitably qualified candidates (bearing in mind the existing skills set on the board) and ensure that recommendations are made to the board only after a rigorous selection process. A nomination committee can, among other things, increase the quality of the board members, shareholder confidence and the board's competitive advantage.

The response in India

Background

Indian corporate governance is regulated by the Securities and Exchange Board of India (SEBI) and has its statutory underpinning in the 1956 Companies Act. Clause 49 of the listing agreement lays down the fundamentals of corporate governance for public companies and takes the same 'comply or explain' approach as the UK Corporate Governance Code.

India's general record on corporate governance might best be described as mixed. As in Russia, the ownership structure of companies can sometimes be an impediment to best practice. In many companies, blocks of shares will be owned by the family that – often through several generations – has built up the business. In others, the promoter (under Indian law, the person who founds or organises an enterprise) may well have a controlling or significant shareholding and be dominant in the management of the company. Clearly, the risk for shareholders is that an individual may have what the UK Corporate Governance Code terms 'unfettered powers' in the decision-making process.

In some cases, non-executive directors will be chosen from a narrow band of compliant people known to be supportive of the promoter, and board meetings will be taken up largely by routine and administrative tasks. At the same time, there are companies in India that take corporate governance very seriously. While a percentage of these will focus mainly on compliance with Clause 49, others are thinking more of the spirit of good governance and how it can add value to an enterprise.

An objective review of board effectiveness in India was published in the first quarter of 2009 by Vivek Gambhir, Ashish Singh and Karan Singh of Bain & Company. This detailed study concluded that Indian boards needed to focus on strategy and improve governance to perform effectively. Importantly, it identified weaknesses in the management of risk and found there to be a lack of financial management and accounting expertise on many companies' audit committees.

The problems in the Indian 'system' crystallised in early 2009 when a long-running and large-scale fraud was uncovered at computer services group, Satyam. This giant, family-dominated outsourcing company had, for several years, been massively inflating its profits. The founder and chairman, Ramalinga Raju, wrote to the stock exchange to admit that the balance sheet was largely a work of fiction and that figures for cash ($1 billion) and other current assets were false. The fraud was complex, yet the accounts were audited each year by one of the big four international auditing firms.

Satyam's share price fell by 80 per cent on this announcement, and the Bombay Stock Exchange by 7.3 per cent as investors became concerned about standards of governance in India, particularly among promoter-led companies. 'This has put to question the entire corporate governance system in India,' said R K Gupta, managing director of Taurus Asset Management in New Delhi. 'In a bull market, people forgot about it [corporate governance],' said Singapore-based Ashish Goyal, chief investment officer at Prudential Asset Management.

The shock was made worse by the fact that Satyam had twice received the 'Golden Peacock' award for excellence in corporate governance. Was the idea of good management and business probity in India little more than corporate myth? It was clear that failures in governance needed to be addressed if global investors were to have confidence in Indian companies.

Lessons from the Satyam scandal

Recessions put additional pressure on boards to sustain profits and, therefore, increase the temptation to flout financial reporting norms. To counteract this, investors and analysts need to make sure they fully understand how a company's business model has delivered reported results, and directors need to make sure there is an effective mechanism for risk management and internal control.

Tightening up of regulatory codes (though perhaps an understandable response) will have limited effect. Increasing the number of boxes to tick further increases the likelihood of a compliance-driven, box-ticking approach by both companies and their investors. Companies need to make sure integrity and probity are part of their DNA – once they are, temptations will either not present themselves or be easier to resist. And investors need to look beyond the surface to the true level of governance in an organisation.

In the pharmaceuticals sector, biomarkers are used to evaluate the progress of a disease, whether it's early-stage or advanced. It might be helpful to look at corporate governance in the same way. In my view, there are five essential markers for value-added governance.

1. *Strong values embedded in the organisation*. There must be a statement of values that's consistently followed by the board. The way decisions are made can be a good indicator of the integrity of the company's values; employee feedback and staff surveys will show whether the values are part of the corporate DNA.

2. *Balance and independence on the board*. It's important to induct independent directors who can add value through experience and expertise. Many boards today still look to the familiar, well-known names that are seen to give credibility to the board. The preference should be for challenging, skilled, independent directors who have broad experience and time to devote to the business.

3. *Relevant and comprehensive agendas*. A review of annual documented agendas will provide a good picture of the information supplied to the board and of the attention paid to important items. A board that frequently assesses and monitors risk across the organisation is one committed to protecting shareholder interests.

4. *A robust audit committee*. Central to a good control environment is an audit committee chaired by a financially competent independent

director who knows the business but does not shy away from constructive challenge. (Independents should never 'go native'.) Good governance mandates that the auditor reports to the chairman of the audit committee and he or she provides a forum in which concerns or differences in judgments in the accounts can be vigorously debated. Any deviation from such a structure compromises governance standards.

5. *A structured board appraisal process.* The best boards know that they can always improve their own effectiveness through an annual review that also gives directors the opportunity to raise concerns with the chairman and identify those areas where the working of the board can be improved.

Board appraisal in India

A board appraisal exercise is not the usual practice in Indian companies but, in January 2009, Biocon, a large, leading, international biotechnology company based in Bangalore, asked me to undertake a full board effectiveness review.

The company, which operates in scientific research, drug discovery, and pharmaceutical manufacturing and marketing, is 60 per cent owned by its promoter, Kiran Mazumdar-Shaw, and her family. The company is internationally known and well respected for its ethical standards (see Chapter 12). The board has a majority of independent directors, one of whom is based in the UK and two of whom are very experienced directors based in the US. The other is a leading commercial lawyer in Bombay.

The board meets regularly, and the challenge and discussion is robust. The company is fully compliant with Clause 49 and would rank as a company with good governance by standards in the UK. The summary of its review is included in Box 13.2.

Box 13.2
Biocon board effectiveness study

Methodology

Directors were asked to fill in a questionnaire covering board leadership, composition, meetings and agendas, appointments to the board, information for directors, performance evaluation, including management development, and succession planning and internal control. They were then given the opportunity to express any general concerns they had.

To get a more rounded picture, discussions were also held with key executives just below board level and with the external and internal auditors. The board then discussed the findings and agreed a schedule for making improvements.

Findings

The following key areas were seen to be very satisfactory:

▨ The balance of skills on the board and the time given by the non-executive directors.

▨ The balance of power on the board: no one director has undue influence on the board or dominates proceedings; the level of challenge is robust.

▨ Communication and understanding: all directors have a good knowledge of the strategy and key objectives of the business.

▨ Succession planning for the top executive team.

▨ Performance evaluation for the senior executives.

▨ The composition of and skills on board committees and the level of assurance committees provide to the board.

▨ The control environment.

▨ Board agendas – the right amount of time is given to important and strategic matters while, at the same time, the governance environment is not ignored.

The following were identified as areas where improvements could be made:

▨ The coherence of the strategy process and external analysis of the operating environment.

▨ Updating and embedding the company values.

▨ The process of appointing independent directors – it was felt that formal letters and contractual dates would help with succession planning.

■ Information packs for the board and the timeliness of the flow of information to the board.

■ Directors' individual evaluations/appraisals.

The challenge for Biocon is how to communicate what is undoubtedly a superior level of governance among the Indian cohort. Say too much and it risks being accused of 'protesting too much'; say too little and it hides its light under a bushel. The company has chosen to make a low-key comment under governance in its annual report and to provide more information to analysts when presenting to them.

Summary

We need to recognise that we live in a world of constant and accelerating change. With this comes the need to deal with discontinuity; strategies will need to be stress-tested against a new, perhaps even hostile, environment.

Significant changes in the wider environment – whether they're political, economic, social or ideological (think, for example, of the effect of the green movement on business and the consumer) – call for significant changes in emphasis in the boardroom. Agendas must change to allow directors to reflect on what's happening and what steps should be taken.

Responses will vary from company to company and, as we've seen, from country to country, but some common governance themes will emerge. This was clear from the credit crunch and financial crisis that hit the world economies in 2008.

Evidence from companies in the UK, America, Russia and India shows that belief in the value of good governance has survived. In the UK, 85 per cent of a sample of large, medium and small businesses felt their governance structures were here to stay; in the comparatively immature market of Russia, 72 per cent rejected the idea of corporate governance as an optional extra or unnecessary cost. In India, meanwhile, the Satyam scandal has renewed interest in 'real' governance and the performance of the board.

In summary, the recent recession has taught us that:

■ The balance and skills sets on the board are of paramount importance to board effectiveness. Independence and the ability to challenge decisions with the benefit of wider experiences are invaluable.

■ The best boards are able to identify reversals of past trends early and react accordingly.

■ The responsive and 'nimble' board reviews its priorities through changing agendas, even providing additional information relevant to the new challenges.

■ Those that have undertaken a board effectiveness review have identified areas for improvement and better practice and then go on to implement changes.

■ Board committees can be important 'response units'. In particular, the work of the audit and risk committee and the remuneration committee has increased. Members of the audit and risk committee must have the knowledge, expertise and experience to carry out their duties effectively. Independent directors need to understand the businesses they represent more fully and be prepared to increase their hours during times of crisis.

■ Companies that are less risk-averse and more prudent in their balance sheet gearing are able to respond better to adverse change. Some can even work the downturn to their advantage, buying up businesses and luring new talent from struggling competitors.

■ The best boards adapt their strategies rather than destroy them. Recessions should force changes in emphasis, not in substance.

Practical Issues for Boards and Directors

Introduction

Directors are expected to be aware of the current issues and trends (for example, socio-economic and demographic change) that affect them and their shareholders and stakeholders. This applies whether the organisation is big or small, commercial or non-profit making.

This chapter focuses on three subjects that no board today can ignore: pensions, sustainability and risk.

Pensions

The problems

Pensions, discussed in detail in Chapter 8 of *The Director's Handbook*, directly affect the individuals on the board and the employees in the organisation. The first requirement is to understand how they work.

A pension plan is, of course, a way to save for retirement. There are three main types of pension: state, personal, and company (or 'occupational'), these days usually a money purchase or defined contribution scheme.

In theory, it's all very simple. During their working life, individuals build up a fund for their retirement. And, if they're really lucky and belong to a defined benefit scheme, their income in retirement will be based on their salary when they give up work.

In practice, however, it's much more complex. Those few remaining employers that have a defined benefit scheme bear all the risk associated with the volatility of investment returns and the increased life expectancy of scheme members. Those employees who have money purchase schemes or personal pension plans bear all the risk that the capital sum (accumulated over periods of falls and rises in the value of assets) may not be enough to provide them a pension for life.

The main problem is longevity. Since World War II, when the 'cradle-to-grave' welfare state was born, there's been a big increase in average life expectancy. A man retiring aged 65 was once reasonably expected to live until he was 77; now, the average is 84. Assuming mortality rates continue to improve, the average retirement could soon last between 22 and 28 years. The double whammy is that as people live longer they are likely to need more medical care, putting further claims on the state (or personal wealth if they have private healthcare provision).

Funding a 25-year retirement from a 40-year working life is a major challenge not currently being addressed. This applies to the state and especially to the local government and civil service pension schemes, which are unsustainable. Understanding these issues makes it easy to see why many employers have moved away from defined benefit schemes and closed these to new entrants, as well as making future accruals for those remaining less attractive. It is a risk reduction exercise.

Let me give you an example to demonstrate the point. An individual with a 40-year working life, with salary increasing in line with inflation, will need to have saved 17 times their salary at retirement to provide a pension of 65 per cent final salary with that pension increasing with inflation. This equates to a saving over the working life of 24.5 per cent. Of course, where an employer is contributing to the pension plan this contribution is included in the 24.5 per cent, leaving a smaller gap for the individual to fill. Nonetheless, the required level of saving is still significant – in excess of current levels. As 20 per cent of the population is aged 65 and older this is a big problem. Rises in retirement ages will help, but not fix the problem.

Tax in relation to pensions

The rules for tax relief on pensions are complex, and specialist advice will need to be sought. Generally speaking, an individual gets tax relief on pension contributions up to 100 per cent of salary and earned income, subject to a yearly maximum. The annual allowance for the year ended 5 April 2010 was £255,000, whether contributions were made by the individual, by the employer, or by a combination of both. If the allowance is exceeded, a tax charge of 40 per cent is payable.

In addition, there is a lifetime maximum allowance against which the benefits built up in the fund will be tested. The maximum lifetime allowance for the year ended 5 April 2010 was £1.8 million. The 2010 budget made clear that the lifetime and annual allowances will stay fixed until 2016. Benefits in excess of the maximum lifetime allowance are taxed at 25 per cent if taken as income; 55 per cent if taken as a lump sum. This makes managing the lifetime allowance extremely important.

The lifetime allowance test is made on the date when the pension is drawn or when compulsorily made to be drawn at 75 years of age. However, changes in the 2009 budget, confirmed in the 2010 budget, limited tax relief on pension contributions for people earning more than £130,000, whether those contributions are made by the employer or the individual. Again, specialist advice should be sought by individuals earning over this figure, or by employers with employees in this category.

Key priorities for directors

Given the growing importance of pensions to individuals, employers will need to ensure their schemes are valued and competitive. At the same time, however, they will need to understand the liabilities associated with defined benefit schemes. When these schemes fall short, the deficit is treated as debt on the balance sheet. In some cases, this debt can be so great as to bankrupt the business.

Decisions about pension benefits must take into account:

- the assumptions that are appropriate for mortality;

- the rate of discount for future liabilities;

- future increases in inflation and wages;

- the investment strategy – the risks, the potential rewards and how they might affect the net valuation of the fund.

New developments

Auto-enrolment, which is being phased in between 2012 and 2016, is another important consideration. It will mean that, eventually, all employers (including the smallest of companies) will have to make arrangements for staff between 22 years of age and the state retirement age to join an appropriate pension scheme, and that they will have to contribute at least 3 per cent themselves. (Employees can opt out of pension saving, but they must be re-enrolled every three years.)

Auto-enrolment applies both to full-time and part-time staff and to temporary or agency workers earning between £5,035 and £33,540. It will be costly for employers in terms of both funding and administration. Employees can be enrolled on to existing schemes, provided they meet certain quality requirements, which differ for money purchase schemes, contracted-out defined benefit schemes and contracted-in defined benefit schemes.

It's important to stress that there is no get-out for smaller companies, not even those that were exempt under the stakeholder pension rules and have never had a pension scheme. The National Employment Savings Trust (or NEST), previously known as the personal accounts scheme, is designed to extend occupational pension provision to everyone. Some of its key features are listed below.

- It will be a trust-based defined contribution scheme regulated by the Pensions Regulator.

- The minimum contribution will be 8 per cent, of which *the employer must pay at least 3 per cent*.

- It will be a registered pension scheme subject to the Finance Act 2004 tax regime.

- It will be simpler but less flexible than a current typical defined contribution scheme.

A 2009 survey by PricewaterhouseCoopers found that there was considerable concern about auto-enrolment:

- 68 per cent of respondents believed there would be confusion among the workforce;

- 68 per cent were concerned by the extra administrative workload;

- 67 per cent could see that there was a need to change existing arrangements;

- 65 per cent recognised that there would be increased employment costs.

Research by the Institute of Directors shows clearly that there has been little or no planning for the reforms, particularly among small companies. Companies need to get ready for implementation and they need to begin (and then many times repeat) the task of communicating with employees.

Pension fund trustees

As Chapter 8 of *The Director's Handbook* makes clear, those who fail in their duties as pension fund trustees can face serious consequences.

The trustee board effectiveness review is a valuable tool for appraising the current state of governance and delivering improvements. The principles are very similar to those laid out in Chapter 4 (see Box 4.2). The content of the template is different, however; Table 14.1 shows a standard review questionnaire.

Table 14.1

Scoring		
1 = do not agree, 2 partially agree, 3 = unsure, 4= agree, 5 = fully agree	**Mark**	**Comments**

A. Board leadership

1. The board has a good mix of skills and experience

2. The board is the right size

3. The board works well together with good chemistry

4. The board is well led

5. The board makes clear and timely decisions

6. The trustees understand their responsibilities

7. The board effectively sets and monitors strategy

8. The board gives clear instruction to the advisers

9. There are satisfactory procedures for reviewing advisers' performance

10. Succession planning is considered by the board

11. Documentation is up to date and in place

B. Board administration

1. The trustees receive well-documented agendas in good time

2. Minutes are concise and reflect discussion and decisions

3. The big agenda issues receive sufficient agenda time

4. There is sufficient time for each trustee to express their views

5. We have insufficient meetings in a year to deal with the business

6. We have too many meetings

7. The quality of agenda papers is uniformly high

8. Regular updates on funding are clear and sufficiently frequent

C. Committees of the board

C.1 The audit and risk committee

1. The committe has appropriate terms of reference

2. The committee has the right skills and experience

3. The committee is well led

4. Trustees have confidence that the control environment is robust

5. The risk management process is robust

6. Trustees are aware of high-level risks

7. High-level risks are appropriately managed

8. I have confidence in the auditor's skill and experience

9. The auditor really understands
   our scheme

C2. The investment committee

1. The committee has appropriate
   terms of reference

2. The committee has the right skills
   and experience

3. The committe is well led

4. Trustees understand and agree
   the investment strategy

5. The investment committee
   report to the board is clear

6. I have confidence that investment
   manager performance is monitored

7. The investment committee
   members keep us up to date

D. Trustees

1. New trustees receive a good
   induction

2. I have every opportunity to
   improve my skills through
   training

3. I have every opportunity to
   participate in the meetings

4. I have a very good understanding
   of my role

5. I feel I am making a worthwhile
   contribution

E. Advisers

1. In general, I feel they are value
   for money

2. The actual consulting is of a high
   standard

3. The investment advice is of a high
   standard

4. The administration is of a good
   standard

5. There is a good relationship with the trustee and company reps

6. I have confidence in their input and management

7. I am satisfied the adviser is independent of the employer

F. Communication

1. The relationship with the employer is good but robust

2. The information updates from the sponsor and guarantor are helpful

3. The trustee has the right channels for employer access when required

4. Communication with members is timely and excellent

5. Trustees are clear on conflicts they may have

6. The trustee has a clear, up-to-date conflicts policy

G. Governance

1. I am satisfied that we have good governance in place

2. Scheme rules are clear and up to date

3. There are clear responsibilities between committees and trustees

4. I am satisfied there are no serious breaches

5. The Statement of Investment Principles gives sufficient investment freedom

6. Trustees have clarity over terms of office

H. Other matters

1. I am confident that the employer will fully meet scheme obligations

2. I am concerned about the size of the deficit

*Please indicate the areas where the
trustee is most effective*

*Please indicate the areas where the
trustee is least effective*

*Are there any items that are of concern
to you that have not been highlighted
on the risk register?*

Sustainability

The moral argument

As Chapter 12 made clear, good businesses have not followed the profit motive to the exclusion of all else. They have recognised their wider responsibilities to the communities in which they operate. For multinationals, this has meant making sure their values cross geographical and cultural boundaries and working only with those suppliers and contractors who understand and uphold them.

Along with the focus on 'inclusion' has come a growing emphasis on sustainability. Businesses and other organisations have recognised that the needs of tomorrow have to be addressed today – in other words, that the needs of the current generation must not compromise those of future generations.

The Institute of Chartered Accountants in England and Wales (ICAEW) has undertaken a special study on sustainability. It observes that 'business people broadly accept that sustainability issues present a real danger of catastrophic destruction of business value. It's no longer just an aspect of risk management'.

Sustainability is, increasingly, behaviour, rather than a bolted-on part of the business agenda. Organisations seek strategies and ways of operating for the long term. This may mean reducing reliance on fossil fuels; it may mean moving to flexible working practices: the scope of sustainability is wide.

US software company Oracle has set up a Green Customer Strategy Council. The areas it's focusing on are:

- ■ carbon emissions management;

- ■ the green supply chain;

- ■ responsible sourcing;

- green product development;

- waste management;

- working conditions, human capital management;

- regulatory compliance and governance;

- facilities and energy management;

- sustainability reporting and management.

The business case

Sustainable businesses are able to reduce their costs by avoiding waste and to spot opportunities to find new products and customers. Just as important, they are able to safeguard their reputations.

In the UK, boards now have a legal duty to take social and environmental factors into account when making their decisions. Failures in this duty will not be forgiven. Proof of this was seen in 1995 when public pressure forced Shell to rethink its plans to decommission an oil storage installation in the mid-Atlantic.

The 1984 Union Carbide disaster in Bhopal, India, is still remembered as one of the worst days in business history. Closer to home, Corby Council in Northamptonshire has faced legal action over claims that its failure to decontaminate an old steel works site led to birth defects in the mid-1990s.

If a business wants the support of its stakeholders, it must be able to demonstrate that it is meeting their legitimate concerns. This means:

- making sure sustainability is a business objective;

- championing the cause of sustainability at board level and making sure it's reflected in decisions made throughout the organisation;

- reporting publicly on progress made.

For those companies that want to develop deeper insights into sustainability, ICAEW has developed an excellent e-learning programme (see www.icaew.com/index.cfm/route/159696/icaew_ga/en/Qualifications/Specialist_qualifications_and_programmes/Business_Sustainability). There are three distinct modules:

1. 'What are business sustainability and corporate responsibility?'

2. 'What is the business case for corporate responsibility?'

3. 'Corporate responsibility in action.'

Reporting

Companies should report on sustainability and corporate social responsibility both internally and externally. Managers will need to report progress on predetermined goals; and directors will need to communicate with shareholders and stakeholders. The concept of the 'triple bottom line' – economic, social and environmental reporting – is now well established.

Multinationals and those operating overseas will have to bear in mind the differing reporting requirements of different countries. A 'less is more approach' is unlikely to work, but reporting can be comprehensive without being excessively detailed. The Global Reporting Initiative (GRI) is a global NGO (with links to the UN) that has developed a global standard for environmental and social reporting. As of 2009, around 1,500 organisations worldwide published a sustainability report based on the GRI standard. Larger organisations may want to follow the Global Reporting Initiative's template. This includes the following information and subjects:

- direct economic impacts on customers, suppliers, employees, capital providers and the public sector;
- environmental impact, including energy and water use, emissions, effluent and waste;
- third-party providers of goods and services;
- compliance in general;
- labour practices, industrial relations, non-discrimination and workplace environment;
- training and education;
- diversity and opportunity, human rights strategy and management;
- health and safety;
- child labour, forced or compulsory labour;
- bribery and corruption;
- competitive practices and pricing;
- advertising;
- product responsibility, health and safety of customers;
- political donations.

More information can be found at http://www.globalreporting.org.

While some businesses see external reporting as a cost that needs to be reined in, and provide the minimum amount of information across the different geographical regions they operate in, others insist that the focus on sustainability adds value to the enterprise. The latter camp will use a variety of metrics to prove their point – from using profit and loss statements for new initiatives and sustainable products, to assessing the value that's been transferred to the community at large or to suppliers' customers and labour.

Risk and the role of the board

Background

During the credit crunch and the subsequent recession, risk was on everyone's mind. Excessive risk-taking by the banks had, it seemed, plunged the world into economic crisis. In the maelstrom that followed, it was easy to forget one of the long-held principles of economics: *risk is a driver of profit; boards that do not take risks stagnate*. Risk is not the enemy; recklessness is. One of the most important jobs of the entrepreneurial board is to distinguish calculated risk from blind chance.

The risk management process is important because it adds value to the formation and delivery of strategy, and to daily decision-making. As Chapter 3 made clear, evidence from surveys shows companies with good governance, of which risk identification and management is a key part, win higher ratings from investment analysts.

So how do you ensure the risk assessment and management process is robust? The first thing is to make sure the basic building blocks of an effective board are in place. The key points, as I see them, are listed below.

■ The board must be clear about the matters reserved for it. It must not be a rubber-stamping body or the servant of a group of shareholders. There must be an appropriate balance on the board of skills, experience and non-executive directors.

■ All directors must be capable of understanding the business and the critical issues, and be challenging and fearless in discussion. They must have the time to give to the organisation and should be paid appropriately.

■ The leadership of the chairman is a crucial factor; he or she needs to get the best from the individuals on the board and oversee the decision-making process effectively.

▓ Each year, there needs to be a process for evaluating the performance of the board and identifying areas where it might improve. The evaluation should include key processes such as risk assessment and management.

The process

As Figure 14.1 shows, risk management has evolved into an important part of the corporate governance assurance programme. This, however, does not mean it's become more complicated or more bureaucratic. In the best organisations, it's about progress not process.

Evolution of Risk Management

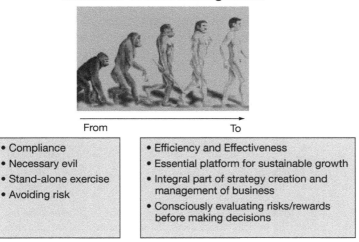

From	To
• Compliance • Necessary evil • Stand-alone exercise • Avoiding risk	• Efficiency and Effectiveness • Essential platform for sustainable growth • Integral part of strategy creation and management of business • Consciously evaluating risks/rewards before making decisions

• CG will never drive immediate value like sales, marketing or even operations can.
• But an absence of CG can definitely lead to massive losses of value.

Figure 14.1

There are some key points to bear in mind.

▓ The administrative part of the process will vary from organisation to organisation but it should be as light as possible: the focus should be delivering value and providing assurance. Risk management must be seen as a recognised competency rather than required compliance.

▓ It must be *simple and practical*.

▓ *People should be made accountable* – risk management should be part of what everyone does.

▓ Risk assessments should be relevant – the focus should be on value drivers and what really matters to the business.

▓ *Risk assessment* and review should be integrated into existing planning processes and personal development plans (PDPs).

So what, exactly, should the process (the methodology) include? The first step is usually to identify risks from each business group through analysis of the business strategy and financial risks and of wider, macro-economic and environmental (eg, market) trends. The 'bottom up' approach is married with the big picture 'top down' approach. Risks are then distilled through risk workshops and assessed for impact and likelihood so that a table of high and low risks is drawn up. High-level risks are then refined and discussed by the audit committee, the risk committee (where relevant) and the board. The analysis shown in Figure 14.2 would be fairly typical.

Typical Classification of Risks

		Remote <10%	Possible 10-50%	Likely >50%
IMPACT	Major >£m	Medium	High	Critical
	Significant £m-£m	Low	Medium	High
	Minor <£m	Low	Low	Medium
		LIKELIHOOD		

Figure 14.2

Non-executives and risk management

The non-executives who serve on the board and the remuneration audit and risk committees have a vital role in risk management. To fulfil it effectively, they need to:

▓ make sure there's a system to identify and rank the risks inherent in the organisation's strategy;

- understand the general appetite for risk on the board;

- make sure there is a mitigation process that identifies who is managing specific risks;

- see evidence that risk is routinely considered in the decisions of the executive.

Lessons from the financial crisis

The global crisis has provided an insight into how organisations have responded to risk. Although the lessons vary by country and by sector, some fairly generic observations apply.

- Many non-executives failed to understand the risks the business was facing and to stress-test the strategy or key products against potential risk. Their boards were unprepared for the crisis.

- Businesses had been seduced by the apparent wisdom of high leverage and easy money.

- Boards need a greater awareness of the 'risk culture' among management – is there a cultural sanctioning of excessive risk?

- Non-executive directors will need to devote more time to their companies, have fewer appointments and be far better paid.

- The reward system for money at risk needs to be better aligned to the longer-term interests of shareholders.

Non-executive directors may like to ask themselves some basic questions:

- Do I understand the risk profile of the company, and do members of the board agree on this?

- Do I understand the process as well as the high-level risks?

- Do I see risk assessment and management as a valuable exercise that I fully support and as one designed to deliver shareholder value?

Summary

The pensions crisis, the sustainability and CSR movements, and the credit crunch have all put additional (and different) demands on the board. The effective director makes sure they understand the implications of each and, wherever possible, looks for opportunities to add or unlock value.

Directors who are widely aware of trends in the economy and the community will be in a better position to 'future proof' their businesses. To be qualified to make judgments on current and emerging issues, they will need to keep up to date.

Responding effectively depends on the building blocks of good corporate governance and best boardroom practice, and open, clear and regular communication (including formal reporting) with managers, with shareholders and stakeholders.

In today's world, the maxim 'business as usual' does not always apply. Directors must be prepared constantly to adapt to changing circumstances; decisions must reflect the times we live in.

Bringing It All Together

Introduction

This chapter has two principal aims: to summarise the themes, ideas and purposes of the book in one 'place', and to guide readers to the areas most relevant for them.

Using this book

Good business books stimulate thought, discussion and a re-evaluation of personal views. They require readers to think about what the author is saying and to decide where it would add value to their work.

One of my aims in writing this book has been to follow this tradition. I've not wanted to 'hand out absolute truths' in the manner of Moses and the tablets of stone. I've wanted to *offer approaches* that are rooted in good theory and have been found to work well in practice; I've wanted to offer templates to draw from.

Read this book in the context of your own organisation.

The reach of this book

The Effective Board is written for a broad constituency. Both experienced directors and those preparing for the role will find it useful – whether they're in the public, private or not-for-profit sectors, whether they work for large or small organisations, whether they're based in the UK or overseas. (Material from the US, India and Russia adds an international dimension to the book.) *The Effective Board* complements the IoD's Chartered Director development programme but it is not for Chartered Director candidates exclusively.

Although its legal frame of reference is UK law, the book crosses national boundaries. Its central themes – good corporate governance and best practice – are important for organisations all over the world.

The scope of this book

The role of director requires good working knowledge of relevant rules, regulations and codes. Individuals must be clear about their legal responsibilities and potential liabilities and their fiduciary duties. They must know 'the facts'.

But this is the base position. The effective director has knowledge and experience far beyond this. Topics such as vision, mission and values, building personal effectiveness, leadership and the management of people are discussed in detail.

The book provides numerous insights into the processes and areas of focus important for the effective board. It's packed with practical tools for better performance such as checklists, tables and case studies. But it's also a guide to good theory.

The synopsis

Chapter 1 on the role of the board

Chapter 1 examines the key elements of boardroom governance. It includes lots of practical examples, and it's up to readers to assess how workable these are in their own environment.

Experience tells us some boards are capable of delivering greater value. The recent credit crunch and financial crisis exposed serious weaknesses in governance. Directors must make sure there's a robust system for the assessment and management of risk. If they don't, they will fail in their duties to shareholders and stakeholders.

The starting point for any organisation that wants to build a strong foundation for governance, however, is to agree those matters that only the board should decide. This achieves clarity – both for the board and those below board level. (Box 1.2 is a sample statement of reserved matters.) The next step is to 'secure' the supply of information to the board. For a clear and true picture of the health of the organisation, directors need the right information, at the right time.

The other key process is the board effectiveness review. It's clear from the 2009 Walker Report and the 2010 UK Corporate Governance Code that this is being given greater emphasis. (The Code recommends an external review of the board assessment process at FTSE 350 companies every three years.) An obvious tool for improving the performance of the board, the review should be thorough but not complex. If the exercise is protracted and too heavy on 'process', some of its value will be lost. Box 1.4 shows what a typical review might cover.

The chapter also makes clear that the relationship between chairman and chief executive is critical. The case study on Cosgrove Manufacturing shows what can happen when the appointment of a new chief executive fails and board processes are inadequate.

Chapter 2 on duties and liabilities

Chapter 2 explains some of the key legal principles governing companies and those leading them. It also looks at the pivotal relationships with shareholders (including private equity investors) and stakeholders. Box 2.1 is a practical summary of the seven duties of directors set out in sections 171–177 of the Companies Act 2006.

The chapter also looks at the position of directors when the business is in financial difficulties or insolvent – ie, when creditors take precedence over shareholders. The use of pre-packaged administration, more common since the recent recession, is discussed.

It's vital that directors understand their obligations, responsibilities and potential liabilities, but these should not be allowed to cast a shadow over their role. There is no expectation in the law of infallibility: the basic requirement is for the director to act responsibly, honestly and with reasonable care.

The key message of this chapter is that the role of director is not a burden: it's an opportunity. Do it well and you will make an invaluable contribution to an organisation and achieve your personal best. You will also derive great pleasure and personal satisfaction.

Chapter 3 on governance

The central idea of Chapter 3 is that governance is an opportunity to add value. Get it right and you will improve the organisation's reputation among shareholders and stakeholders. The key is to see good governance as something other than a compliance-driven activity. It's not about ticking boxes to demonstrate political correctness: it's about observing those elements of best practice that make decision-making more robust and give directors more effective *control*.

The chapter starts with a discussion of the concept of governance and why it's become important. The 'comply or explain' regime of the UK is contrasted with the approach taken in the US.

The main principles of governance embodied in the UK Corporate Governance Code are set out. As the Code makes clear, the system of internal control must be robust, so attention is drawn to the importance of the internal and external audit (particularly for larger companies) and of risk assessment and management.

Governance is not about lofty statements but the implementation of key principles based on the values of the company and the spirit of the Code. Communication of the way an organisation is being governed is critical but quite difficult to achieve in public statements alone. Box 3.1 is a template of the main items included in a corporate governance report.

The theme of good governance runs throughout the book, so this is the core chapter for all readers. It will, however, be of special relevance to private companies considering a listing on the Stock Exchange. Commitment to the standards of good governance, laid down in the UK Corporate Governance Code, will give assurance to advisers and to investors. The case study on Holden Services shows what a successful private company may have to do to get ready for flotation.

Organisations with good standards of governance will fulfil their purpose (their 'mission') and live up to their values.

Chapter 4 on the roles of the chairman and the non-executive director

Chapter 4 focuses on the roles of the chairman and the non-executive director, now more prominent in the UK Corporate Governance Code. More is expected of the chairman and the non-executive and independent directors: more time, more focus on the critical tasks of the board, more oversight of the executive's stewardship.

This chapter sets out the chairman's and the non-executives' formal duties and the structures under which they operate, but it also looks at the specific ways they can add value. The role of the chairman extends beyond the smooth and effective running of meetings to include mentoring the top team and leading the decision-making process, taking care to secure the involvement of the whole board.

Clear descriptions of the roles and tasks of chairman and chief executive will greatly assist their working relationship – as will a clear understanding of the kinds of issues that will normally be discussed between them. Regular contact is essential. Some chairmen and chief executives meet weekly; others less frequently. *Trust between chairman and chief executive is essential.* In my various roles as chairman, I've preferred to meet formally each month and have ad hoc meetings as necessary; and the chief executive has been free to contact me at any time, day or night.

Non-executive directors are a valuable asset for any organisation – provided they've been carefully chosen and encouraged to learn about the organisation and contribute fully to the board. Individual director appraisals that include feedback on performance of the chairman will improve the board's performance year by year.

Chapter 5 on key committees

The key committees of the board and their terms of reference are discussed in Chapter 5. The *remuneration committee* (remco) faces a delicate balancing act. Rewards for top executives must reflect their performance and they must be aligned with the interests of shareholders. At the same time, though, they must be sufficient to recruit, retain and motivate top talent.

Bonuses and other incentives for pay at risk have come under intense scrutiny – not only in the banking and financial sector but also in the commercial sector generally. Concerns have been raised about whether these payments are aligned with the best interests of the company. It seems clear that shareholders' preference will increasingly be for money at risk to be paid out over longer periods (perhaps up to five years) and to be conditional on the company's long-term performance. 'Rewards for failure' or one-way bets will not be tolerated – either by shareholders or the public.

The remuneration report will be examined closely by institutional investors and other shareholder groups. Clear explanation of the policy is essential. When the remuneration report is voted down at the annual general meeting bad publicity always follows.

The *nomination committee* meets much less frequently than the remco, but has the important role of managing the selection of directors. My preference is to see this committee led by the chairman of the company.

The Code states that the board should have formal and transparent arrangements for considering how it applies the corporate reporting and risk management and internal control principles. It needs to decide whether it will assign the assessment and management of risk to a special committee or include it within the authority of the audit committee. A discussion of the way risk is identified and managed and how risk management is *embedded* in an organisation is an important part of Chapter 5.

The *audit committee* plays a vital role in maintaining good controls and in supporting the board's determination to make governance add value.

Its role and ways to improve its performance are therefore examined in detail.

Chapter 6 on better performance

In this imperfect, fast-changing world, the demands on boards are great. All directors, and those who aspire to the role, will want to know how to improve their personal effectiveness. Chapter 6 identifies the building blocks for better performance. Since integrity is at the heart of a good organisation, integrity is at the heart of the chapter.

Directors create the culture of an organisation. If they fail to lead by example, to 'walk the talk', the enterprise suffers. Effective directors have an ethical code and live by it; their actions are consistent with their words; they have *personal* integrity.

Directors should be aware of the specific areas where they need to improve. The self-awareness checklist in Box 6.1 will help them identify these. They will also need to reflect on the general qualities needed for directors, and Box 6.2 lists the essential attributes. Finally, they will need to understand how to deal with stress. Without this ability, they will lack the emotional resilience for consistent performance.

Ways to deal with stress (increasingly, a fact of working life) are discussed in the last few sections of the chapter.

Chapter 7 on leadership

Leadership is the topic of Chapter 7. This chapter is short on definitions but long on practical observations about what makes leadership work.

The five dimensions of leadership given in Box 7.1 are a good starting framework. A great leader is very aware of their followers and their goals and aspirations. The 10 words most used by followers when describing a good leader are a useful insight. Think of these words and the behavioural characteristics and attributes given in Boxes 7.2 and 7.3 when considering your own leadership. The discussion on leadership is not just confined to the individual leader: a focus on leadership and the board provides useful insights for directors.

In recognition of the particular challenges they face and the adjustments they have to make, new directors are given a special section at the end of the chapter.

Chapter 8 on people

Chapter 8 explains how to get the most from the talent in the organisation.

The best organisations have the right strategy and the right plan of implementation, and the right people in the right places. And they make sure that they marry the two. There must be close alignment between the vision, mission and values of the organisation and personal objectives and milestones for individuals. This is why appraisals are so important a part of effective people management. People must be motivated and empowered to make decisions at the closest possible point of impact.

The board needs to make management development and succession planning an annual exercise. Potential future leaders need to be identified early and given the opportunity to develop on an accelerated path.

Chapter 9 on SMEs

Small and medium-sized and family companies are the focus of Chapter 9. For many of these, the challenge is how to observe best practice without layering on costly and unnecessary processes. To help, I look at the minimum requirements for good governance, providing, in Box 9.2, a governance checklist for SMEs.

Smaller companies can be vulnerable when they start to grow; standards of governance will need to keep pace. The case study on McTavish Ltd spells out some of the issues facing family companies that need new sources of capital and new skills to finance growth.

Owner-managers should remember the importance of good, independent advice. A non-executive director, a mentor, or a trusted adviser can make a big difference.

Chapter 10 on charities and NPOs

Chapter 10 is another special-topic chapter, dealing with charities and not-for-profit organisations.

Again, the approach is to guide directors and trustees towards the issues they need to be thinking about. Box 10.1 sets out the high-level areas of focus, but it is not a 'prescription'. It is more of a suggestion, a starting point, drawn from best practice.

Table 10.1 sets out a template for evaluating an NPO – a health check for trustees. The key message is that running a successful charity or an NPO has much in common with running a successful commercial enterprise.

Chapter 11 on the NHS

Given the increasing importance of the work of the NHS Foundation Trusts, a separate chapter on NHS governance has been included.

Chapter 11 starts with an explanation of the governance structure of Foundation Trusts, set out in Figure 11.1 in diagrammatic form. The chapter goes on to examine the relationship between the board of directors and the board of governors.

The key challenges for Foundation Trust directors are discussed. These include getting the right balance of skills on the board and making sure there's 'constructive challenge' from appropriately qualified non-executive directors. As in commercial enterprises, the role of the chairman is critical: without good leadership, the board flounders.

The chapter concludes with the diaries of a non-executive director newly appointed to an NHS Foundation Trust board.

Chapter 12 on ethics

Next is the discussion on ethics in Chapter 12.

The case for business ethics is not only moral but also pragmatic. Tougher laws on insider trading, money laundering and bribery have significantly increased the legal risks of unethical conduct. Ethics build reputations; and reputations are invaluable assets.

Ethical dilemmas may arise when an organisation's standards conflict with those of directors, or indeed with those of society at large. The ethical code of an organisation and the ethical codes of its directors must converge. Where there are material conflicts, organisations and boards fail each other.

There needs, too, to be the utmost consistency between ethics and behaviour. An ethical code will, like a statement of values, be meaningless unless followed in practice. Consistency is achieved by:

▪ leading by example;

▪ communicating clearly with employees;

▪ making ethics part of the management performance system;

▪ making ethics a factor in recruitment and the choice of suppliers.

Chapter 13 on turbulent times

Chapter 13 looks at corporate governance in turbulent times. What can we learn from the way organisations around the world have responded to the recent financial crisis?

The good news in the UK is that a 2009 IoD study shows that the majority of companies have resisted the 'knee-jerk' reaction of cutting investment in areas such as training and development. Many have, like Windsor Research, the subject of our case study in this chapter, focused harder on strategy and cash management to help them weather the storm.

Evidence from the diverse markets of the US, Russia and India also suggests that faith in good governance as the way to add value and insure your organisation against unforeseen risks has held firm.

The importance of risk assessment and management is again discussed, with lessons from a study by the Economist Intelligence Unit, 'Managing Risk in Perilous Times', included in Box 13.1.

Chapter 14 on practical issues

Last but not least, in Chapter 14 practical issues for boards and directors are discussed.

The pensions crisis features in the first part of the chapter. Its implications for individuals and the board are examined, and there's a template for a board effectiveness review for pension fund trustees in Table 14.1.

The chapter then goes on to focus on the way sustainability has become part of modern business life. Increasingly, organisations recognise that they have a role on the wider stage – and that if they take it seriously they will win customers, recruit, retain and motivate employees, and protect their reputations. The wide scope of sustainability is discussed – from environmentalism to corporate social responsibility.

No chapter on current issues could exclude risk assessment and management, brought into sharper focus by the 2008 credit crunch and subsequent recession. The final part of the chapter looks in some detail at the process of evaluating risk and embedding risk management in the organisation.

Coda

- The effective director has knowledge and skills but understands that the state of perfection is never reached, that professional development is continuous.

- The effective director is curious, searching out new and better ways of doing things.

- The effective director is focused on those things that add greater value, and is an excellent implementer of practical initiatives that are aligned with the organisation's strategy.

- The effective director understands the difference between risk-taking and recklessness.

- The effective director has the courage to stand up for what they believe in and the humility to invite and accept constructive challenge.

- The effective director thinks about their legacy and understands the importance of succession planning.

- The effective director says 'people are our greatest asset' and proves they mean it.

- The effective director is conscientious but understands the need for work-life balance.

Appendix: Summary of the UK Corporate Governance Code and the Turnbull Guidance on Internal Control

1. Introduction

The UK Corporate Governance Code incorporates recommendations made by committees led by Sir Adrian Cadbury (1992), Sir Richard Greenbury (1995), Sir Ronnie Hampel (1998), Sir Derek Higgs and Sir Robert Smith (2003) and, most recently, Sir David Walker (2009).

The Code was last revised in June 2010. The latest revisions include the renaming of the Code (from the Combined Code on Corporate Governance to the UK Corporate Governance Code) and the arrangement of its principles and provisions on the basis of new thematic headings (see the next page).

The UK Corporate Governance Code must be applied by companies with a Premium Listing on the London Stock Exchange on a 'comply or explain' basis. Such companies are expected to comply with the Code's provisions most of the time and to give a considered explanation to shareholders of any departures from its provisions.

The Turnbull Guidance on Internal Control was published in 1999 and last updated in 2005. Its purpose is to provide guidance to directors in their implementation of the Code provisions relating to internal control. The FRC has announced its intention to undertake a further review of the Turnbull Guidance by the end of 2010.

In practice, the UK Corporate Governance Code and the Turnbull guidance have relevance to nearly all companies and organisations. The following extracts should be of interest to directors of most companies and organisations, irrespective of size and whether or not the company is quoted.

2. The UK Corporate Governance Code

Main principles

Leadership

- Every company should be headed by an effective board which is collectively responsible for the long-term success of the company.

- There should be a clear division of responsibilities at the head of the company between the running of the board and the executive responsibility for the running of the company's business.

- No one individual should have unfettered powers of decision.

- The chairman is responsible for leadership of the board and ensuring its effectiveness in all aspects of its role.

- As part of their role as members of a unitary board, non-executive directors should constructively challenge and help develop proposals on strategy.

Effectiveness

- The board and its committees should consist of directors with the appropriate balance of skills, experience, independence and knowledge of the company to enable it to discharge its duties and responsibilities effectively.

- There should be a formal, rigorous and transparent procedure for the appointment of new directors to the board.

- All directors must be able to allocate sufficient time to the company to perform their responsibilities effectively.

- All directors should receive induction on joining the board and should regularly update and refresh their skills and knowledge.

- The board should be supplied in a timely manner with information in a form and of a quality appropriate to enable it to discharge its duties.

- The board should undertake a formal and rigorous annual evaluation of its own performance and that of its committees and individual directors.

- All directors should be submitted for re-election at regular intervals, subject to continued satisfactory performance.

Accountability

- The board should present a balanced and understandable assessment of the company's position and prospects.

- The board is responsible for determining the nature and extent of the significant risks it is willing to take in achieving its strategic objectives. The board should maintain sound risk management and internal control systems.

- The board should establish formal and transparent arrangements for considering how it should apply the corporate reporting, risk management and internal control principles and for maintaining an appropriate relationship with the company's auditors.

Remuneration

- Levels of remuneration should be sufficient to attract, retain and motivate directors of the quality required to run the company successfully, but a company should avoid paying more than is necessary for this purpose.

- A significant proportion of executive directors' remuneration should be structured so as to link rewards to corporate and individual performance.

■ There should be a formal and transparent procedure for developing policy on executive remuneration and for fixing the remuneration packages of individual directors.

■ No director should be involved in deciding his or her own remuneration.

Relations with shareholders

■ There should be a dialogue with shareholders based on the mutual understanding of objectives.

■ The board as a whole has responsibility for ensuring that a satisfactory dialogue with shareholders takes place.

■ The board should use the AGM to communicate with investors and to encourage their participation.

3. The Turnbull guidance on internal control

■ The Turnbull Guidance provides guidance on how the board can maintain a sound system of internal control to safeguard shareholders' investment and the company's assets, and how the board should review the effectiveness of the company's system of internal control.

■ Internal control includes financial, operational and compliance controls and risk management.

■ The purpose of internal control is to help manage and control risk appropriately, rather than to eliminate all risks, since profits are in part the reward for successful risk-taking in business.

■ The board should adopt a risk-based approach to establishing a sound system of internal control, involving an assessment of risks faced by the company, determining what control activities are required to avoid or reduce the impact of those risks and ensuring that appropriate and timely information is communicated to directors to enable them to monitor performance and respond rapidly where change is required.

■ The risks to be managed should depend on the business, but should encompass more than just financial risk.

■ The board should regularly receive and review reports on internal control and undertake an annual assessment.

- The adoption of a risk-based internal control system should be embedded in the company's business processes, linked to the business objectives and not be just a separate exercise undertaken to meet regulatory requirements. In order to ensure that the system is not just left to run on its own, managers are required to report on specific areas assigned to them.

- Procedures and the frequency of reporting required should be communicated and agreed so that major control weaknesses may be reported immediately.

Board responsibilities

- The board must set appropriate policies on internal control, seek regular assurance that the system is working satisfactorily, and ensure that the system is effective in managing risks.

- In setting its policy, the board should consider the following factors:

  - the nature and extent of the risks facing the company, which risks are acceptable and to what extent;

  - the likelihood of the risks materialising;

  - the company's ability to reduce the incidence and impact on the business of risks that do materialise;

  - the cost of operating particular controls relative to the benefits of managing the associated risks.

- The board is responsible for reviewing the effectiveness of the internal control system. The appendix to the guidance sets out key questions that a board may wish to consider when assessing the effectiveness of the company's internal control system.

IOD

CHARTERED DIRECTOR

Are you qualified to be a director?

"One of the best ways of improving leadership standards in the boardroom is through the Chartered Director award."
Investors in People

Contact us now to find out how to qualify:

+44 (0)20 7766 2601

References and further reading

Arnott, J (2003) *The ICSA Charity Trustee's Guide*, ICSA Publishing, London

Bain, N (1996) *Successful Management*, Macmillan, London

Bain, N (2008) *The Effective Director*, Institute of Directors, London

Bain, N and Band, D (1996) *Winning Ways through Corporate Governance*, Macmillan, London

Bain, N and Mabey, B (1999) *The People Advantage*, Macmillan, London

Barker, R M (2010) *Corporate Governance, Competition, and Political Parties: Explaining change in European corporate governance*, Oxford University Press, Oxford

Beehr, T A (1995) *Psychological Stress in the Workplace*, Routledge, London

Belbin, M R (1997) *Team Roles at Work*, Butterworth-Heinemann, Oxford

Bennis, W (1990) *On Becoming a Leader*, Hutchinson Business Books, London

Brountas, P P (2004) *Boardroom Excellence: A commonsense perspective on corporate governance*, Jossey Bass, San Francisco, CA

Cadbury, Sir Adrian (1990) *The Company Chairman*, Director Books, Simon and Schuster, London

Cadbury, Sir Adrian (2002) *Corporate Governance and Chairmanship: A personal view*, Oxford University Press, New York

Carter, C B (2004) *Back to the Drawing Board: Designing corporate boards for a complex world*, Harvard Business School Press, Boston, MA

Carver, J (1990) *Boards That Make a Difference*, Jossey Bass, San Francisco, CA

Charity Commission (2007) *The Essential Trustee: What you need to know*, Charity Commission, London

Charkham, J (2005) *Keeping Better Company: Corporate governance ten years on*, Oxford University Press, Oxford

Clarke, T (2007) *International Corporate Governance: A comparative approach*, Routledge, London

Cliffe, S (1998) Human resources: winning the war for talent, *Harvard Business Review*, September–October

Colley, J L, Doyle, J L, Logan, G W and Stettinius, W (2003) *Corporate Governance*, McGraw Hill, Maidenhead

Covey, S M R and Merrill, R R (2006) *The Speed of Trust: The one thing that changes everything*, Free Press, New York

Dale, R A (trans) (2002) *Tao Te Ching*, Lao Tzu, Watkins Publishing, London

Dando, N and Raven, W (2006) *Living Up to Our Values: Developing ethical assurance*, Institute of Business Ethics, London

Department for Trade and Industry (2003) *Number of Trade Unions and Membership in Great Britain*, 1975–2002, DTI, London

EcoDa (2010) *Corporate Governance Guidance and Principles for Unlisted Companies in Europe*, European Confederation of Directors' Associations, Brussels

Ernst & Young (2009) *Board Members on Risk: Leveraging Frameworks for the Future*, Ernst & Young, London

European Industrial Relations Observatory (2004) *Trade Union Membership 1993–2003*, Dublin

Foster Back, P (2005) *Setting the Tone: Ethical business leadership*, Institute of Business Ethics, London

Gambhir, V Singh, A and Singh, K (2009) *Board Effectiveness in India*, Bain & Company, Boston, MA

Gardner, H and Laskin, E (1996) *Leading Minds: An anatomy of leadership*, Harper Collins Business, London

Goleman, D (1996) *Emotional Intelligence*, Bloomsbury, London

Grant, G (2004) *A Director's Guide to Corporate Governance*, ch. 4, Institute of Directors, London

Grant Thornton (2007) *Corporate Governance Review 2006*, Grant Thornton, London

Handy, C (1997) *The Hungry Spirit*, Hutchinson, London

Harrison, D (2007) *It's Time to Talk: The urgent need for dialogue to strengthen governance of UK pension schemes*, Economist Intelligence Unit, London

Higgs, Sir Derek (2003) *Review of the Role and Effectiveness of Non-executive Directors*, Department of Trade and Industry, London

Huffington, C (1997) Stress at work, organisations and people, *Quarterly Journal of AMED*, August

Independent Directors Association (2009) *Leading in Turbulent Times: Priorities for your board*, IDA, Moscow

Institute of Directors (2006) *Standards for the Board*, IoD, London

Institute of Directors/Pinsent Masons (2010) *The Director's Handbook*, Kogan Page, London

Institute of Internal Auditors UK and Ireland (2006) *Gaining Assurance on Risks*, IIA, London

Katzenbach, J R and Smith, D K (2003) *The Wisdom of Teams*, Harper Paperbacks, London

Kouzes, J M and Posner, B Z (2002) *The Leadership Challenge*, Jossey Bass, San Francisco, CA

Leblanc, R and Gillies, J (2005) *Inside the Boardroom: How boards really work and the coming revolution in corporate governance*, Wiley, Chichester

Lipton, P (2003) *The demise of HIH: Corporate governance lessons, keeping good companies*, Chartered Secretaries Australia, June, Melbourne

Lofthouse, G (2005) *CEO Briefing: Corporate priorities for 2005*, Economist Intelligence Unit, London

Mace, M (1986) *Directors: Myth and reality*, Harvard University Press, Harvard, MA

McNulty, T J (2003) *Creating Accountability within the Board: The work of the effective non-executive director*, DTI, London

Monks, R A G and Minow, N (1995) *Corporate Governance*, Blackwell Business, Oxford

Monks, R A G and Minow, N (2008) *Corporate Governance* (4th edn), Wiley, Chichester

Nadler, D, Behan, B A and Nadler, M B (2006) *Building Better Boards: A blueprint for effective governance*, Jossey Bass, San Francisco, CA

Neilson, G L and Pasternack, B A (2005) *The Cat That Came Back*, Booz Allen Hamilton, New York

Neilson, G L, Pasternack, B A and Van Nuys, K E (2005) The passive-aggressive organisation, *Harvard Business Review*, October

Odgers, I (2007) *The Common Ingredients of Leadership*, Board Paper Series, Odgers Ray and Berndtson, London

Odgers Berndtson (2010) *Going Public: How to prepare your board for IPO*, March, Odgers Ray and Berndtson, London

Pascale, R T (1990) *Managing on the Edge*, Simon and Schuster, London

Pfeffer, J (1994) *Competitive Advantage through People: Unleashing the power of the workforce*, Harvard Business Press, Cambridge, MA

Pfeffer, J (1998) *The Human Equation: Building profits by putting people first*, Harvard Business Press, Cambridge, MA

Phillips, F (2009) *Managing Innovation, Technology and Entrepreneurship*, Maastricht School of Management Series, Meyer & Meyer Media, Maastricht

Prahalad, C K and Krishnan, M S (2008) *The New Age of Innovation: Driving co-created value through global networks*, McGraw Hill, Maidenhead

Prokesch, S E (1997) Unleashing the power of learning: An interview with British Petroleum's John Browne, *Harvard Business Review*, September–October

Roberto, M A (2009) *Know What You Don't Know*, Wharton School Publishing, University of Pennsylvania

Spira, L F (2002) *The Audit Committee: Performing corporate governance*, Kluwer, Amsterdam

Starr, R, Newfrock, J and Delurey, M (2006) *Enterprise Resilience: Managing risk in the networked economy*, Booz Allen Hamilton, New York

Steinberg, R M (2000) *Corporate Governance and the Board: What works best*, Institute of Internal Auditors Research Foundation, London

Thomas, C, Kidd, D and Fernandez-Aroaz, C (2007) Are you under-utilising your board?, *MIT Sloan Management Review*, Winter

Townsend, R C and Bennis, W (2007) *Up the Organisation*, Jossey Bass, San Francisco, CA

Tricker, B (2009) *Corporate Governance: Principles, policies and practices*, Oxford University Press, Oxford

Webley, S (2006) *Making Business Ethics Work: The foundations of effective embedding*, Institute of Business Ethics, London

Webley, S and Werner, A (2009) *Employee Views of Ethics at Work*, The 2008 National Survey, Institute of Business Ethics, April 2009

Willis, M and Fass, M (2004) *Faith in Governance: Renewing the role of the director*, Industrial Christian Fellowship, London

Index

NB page numbers in *italic* indicate figures or tables